Accounting and Financial Management in the Hotel and Catering Industry

Volume 2

Accounting and Financial Management in the Hotel and Catering Industry

Volume 2

Peter J. Harris, M.H.C.I.M.A., C.Dip.A.F.
Principal Lecturer, Department of Catering Management, Oxford Polytechnic

Peter A. Hazzard, M.Sc., F.C.M.A., A.M.B.I.M.
Principal Lecturer, School of Accountancy Slough College of Higher Education

Hutchinson

London Melbourne Sydney Auckland Johannesburg

Hutchinson & Co. (Publishers) Ltd

An imprint of the Hutchinson Publishing Group

17-21 Conway Street, London W1P 6JD

Hutchinson Publishing Group (Australia) Pty Ltd
16-22 Church Street, Hawthorn, Melbourne, Victoria 3122

Hutchinson Group (NZ) Ltd
32-34 View Road, PO Box 40-086, Glenfield, Auckland 10

Hutchinson Group (SA) (Pty) Ltd
PO Box 337, Bergvlei 2012, South Africa

First published by Northwood Publications Ltd 1972
Second edition 1977
Third edition 1980
First published by Hutchinson 1983
Reprinted 1985

© Peter J. Harris and Peter A. Hazzard 1972, 1977, 1980

Set in Times New Roman

Printed and bound in Great Britain by
Anchor Brendon Ltd, Tiptree, Essex

British Library Cataloguing in Publication Data

Harris, Peter
Accounting and financial management in the hotel and catering industry – 3rd ed.
Vol. 2
1 Hotels, taverns, etc. – Great Britain – Finance
2 Food service – Great Britain – Finance
3 Hotel management – Great Britain
4 Food service management
I Title II Hazzard, Peter
647′.9541′0681 TX911.3.F5

ISBN 0 09 154211 1

CONTENTS – VOLUME 2

PREFACE TO THE THIRD EDITION

As with many other disciplines accounting may be likened to the flesh on an animal's back, forever changing. In recognition of this the foregoing text has again been revised and updated in an endeavour to keep abreast of modern developments and their applications in the hotel, catering and institutional industry.

In line with previous editions the needs of students studying for hotel, catering and institutional qualifications, executives and management within the industry and the small hotelier have been carefully borne in mind throughout this work. Volume 1 provides for the book-keeping and accounting requirements of:

(*a*) the hotel reception certificates and diplomas; and

(*b*) the ordinary diplomas in hotel, catering and institutional operations, year one.

Volume 2 provides for the accounting requirements of:

(*a*) the HCIMA professional qualification Part B (major study) Financial Management I; and

(*b*) the ordinary diplomas in hotel, catering and institutional operations, year two.

The combined volumes provide for the accounting requirements of:

(*a*) the higher diplomas in hotel, catering and institutional management;

(*b*) the HCIMA professional qualification Part B (major and elective studies) Financial Management I & II; and

(*c*) the various degrees in hotel, catering and institutional administration.

Notable changes in this edition of Volume 2 are:

1. Three new chapters, namely, Chapters 1, 2 and 3 have been introduced. The objective of this is to provide an introduction and conceptual grounding in accounting for those students pursuing advanced courses.
2. Chapter 7, Budgetary Control has been extended to include the control of gross profit in cases where standard cost ascertainment is impractical.
3. Chapter 9, Price Determination has been entirely rewritten and now covers the subject in a more balanced and comprehensive manner.
4. Chapter 11, Measuring Financial Performance has been modified by improving the investment ratios section and including the estimation of working capital requirements.
5. Chapter 16, Published Accounts of Limited Companies, formerly Chapter 2, has been extended to include an introduction to the Standard Statements of Accounting Practice (SSAP), Added Value Statements and the principles and effects of Inflation Accounting on external reports.

6. Chapter 17, Consolidated Accounts of Limited Companies, formerly Chapter 3, has been transferred in order to retain the more advanced aspects of financial accounting together.
7. Inflation accounting aspects have been introduced into Chapters 6, 7 and 15, whilst the principles have been included in Chapter 16.
8. Many of the questions and problems have been revised and extended by the addition of recent examination and other questions.

A point worthy of separate mention concerns the three new chapters at the beginning of Volume 2. The intention behind the introduction of a conceptual approach is twofold. Firstly, students pursuing more advanced studies, such as the degrees and professional qualification, do not necessarily encounter the fundamental financial accounting aspects contained in Volume 1 and therefore may commence their studies with Volume 2. Secondly, those who have studied for an ordinary diploma or the old HCIMA intermediate qualification will not usually have gained a conceptual grounding in accounting. For these students the chapters provide a revision element together with the conceptual underpinning necessary to continue their studies. From this it will be apparent that where previously the two books were primarily interdependent they may now also be used independently.

Finally, we should like to thank those who have drawn to our attention errors in the earlier editions and made suggestions for inclusion in this edition. As always, users' comments are most welcome.

P.J.H.
P.A.H.

Certain questions at the end of chapters are reprinted by kind permission of:

Hotel, Catering and Institutional Management Association	(HCIMA)
Institute of Cost and Management Accountants	(ICMA)
Association of Certified Accountants	(ACCA)
Scottish Technical Education Council	(Scotec)

Chapter 16 (Volume 2) contains extracts from the *Standard Systems of Hotel and Catering Accounting* published by the Hotel and Catering Economic Development Committee to whom we are grateful for being allowed to reproduce material.

Chapter 9 (Volume 2) contains the Hubbart Formula adapted to conform to the Standard System of Hotel Accounting in Britain. We thank the American Hotel and Motel Association (AH & MA) for permission to produce the modified form.

We thank also the Centre for Hotel and Catering Comparisons at the University of Strathclyde for permission to reproduce the chart of ratios used in the scheme operated by them.

CHAPTER ONE

ACCOUNTING: A BACKGROUND

ACCOUNTING has for centuries been concerned with *recording, summarizing* and *reporting* in money terms the transactions of an organization, although the scope has gone beyond these three basic procedures in modern times.

An example of simple accounting familiar to all readers is the 'statement of account' you receive from the bank. This statement is a copy of the bank's account with you and contains a *record* of the bank's transactions with you showing as a debit each amount paid to you – which you have withdrawn – and as a credit each amount received from you and paid into your account. The balance, being the amount of your money held by the bank – a credit balance – is a form of *summary*, and the whole is *reported* to you, the holder of the account, for information. The main and more complex accounting procedures of the bank would be to summarize all accounts and compile a report to shareholders containing a statement of profit made in the period and a balance sheet of the bank's financial position at the end of the period. Your credit balance would be amongst those shown as a liability in the balance sheet because the bank is liable, or obliged, to pay you the balance on request.

Accounting for exchange of money and services rendered presents few problems. Accounting for individual hotels and restaurants is not generally complicated as the unit it relatively small, whereas accounting for the large catering group with its centralized food production and freezing facilities introduces complications of valuing food stocks, pricing inter group trading and other problems.

Financial, Cost and Management Accounting

Accounting is wide in its meaning although recording of transactions in monetary terms is its central feature. Three recognized branches of accounting are:

Financial accounting which is specially concerned with reporting the financial affairs of an organisation to interested outside parties.

Cost accounting which is concerned with the ascertainment of costs and the analysis of savings or excess costs compared with some standard.

Management accounting which deals with providing managers with reports about their organization.

All three branches are closely related to one another and operate under an overall framework of *financial management*.

Accounting and Accountants

How is the qualified accountant concerned with hotel accounting? Accountants may be classified in many ways but for the present purpose can be placed into two categories:

1. Those who are practising accountants; that is they are either partners or employees in practising firms acting as auditors of companies, preparing accounts for small organizations like independent hotels, or providing taxation services and other similar work.
2. Those employed by an industrial or commercial organization such as an hotel group who are concerned with recording the group's financial transactions and advising management on a wide range of money matters associated with the financial health of the organization.

The important difference between these categories is that whereas the first accountant audits the books of a number of client companies in the course of a year, the accountant employed by the commercial company is concerned entirely with his own company's operations and is part of the management team. The hotel accountant, for instance, identifies himself with the hotel operations exclusively. Whilst these two kinds of accountant are involved with the accounting functions of recording, summarizing and reporting, mention might be made of the financier who, not necessarily an accountant, manages the company's finances from his position on the board of directors. He is sometimes criticized for the power he wields though this is often not justified because the importance of maintaining the large company in good financial health vis-à-vis the stock market for instance, cannot be overstated. There would be understandable concern if a top financier flitted from company to company in different industries without really appreciating the managerial aspects peculiar to each industry. The majority of accountants and financiers in the hotel and catering industry are steeped in the industry to good effect.

Accounting and Hotel and Catering Managers

How is the hotel and catering manager concerned with accounting? The independent hotel whose owner also manages the unit will usually retain the services of a practising accountant who advises on day-to-day accounting records and produces annual accounts for legal purposes. Ideally more frequent accounts would be prepared for management control purposes. It is important for the proprietor to have a sound grasp of accounting and financial matters, for the accountant would be available to advise on only the more important decisions.

The manager of a medium sized hotel which is part of a group is immersed in financial activities from participation in preparing annual budgets to justifying the financial results of his operation. An understanding of accounting records and of the likely effect of alternative courses of action on hotel profit is also required.

The large hotel may have its own accountant, but being a large unit decisions are more onerous and the responsibility greater. Working with the accountant as a member of a team requires the manager to understand clearly the financial implications of decisions he takes. Whilst important decisions such as expansion of operations may be taken centrally he is closely involved in estimating the financial outcome of plans.

The hotel and catering manager, therefore, cannot avoid being involved one way or another in the financial side of his operation. A more positive attitude is currently evident as managers accept they are in business to contribute to the profitable operation of their organization.

Accounting: Development

Well before the fourteenth century in England, accounting systems recorded and reported financial transactions as a check that stewards and agents had carried out their tasks in connection with secular and religious estates. The steward's accounts were submitted to the owner and subject to audit by him. The stewardship function has to this day been an important influence on the information provided to owners concerning the manner in which their resources have been managed.

Whilst estate accounting was operating in England, accounting for merchants' activities took place in Venice and this involved a double-entry system described by Pacioli in 1494 which was to become the basis of modern accounting systems. This system of accounting was given official recognition in the 1856 Companies Act requiring that books of companies had to be kept on a double-entry basis. Earlier in 1844 a Joint Stock Companies Act required the regular balancing of books and a 'full and fair' annual balance sheet without however, giving guidance as to the basis of valuing assets or requiring a profit and loss account. Not until the Companies Acts of 1928 and 1929 was a profit and loss account required, assets divided between fixed and current and the basis of their valuation indicated.

Accounting has developed along two main streams, one of which was in response to the demand of owners and shareholders of companies for annual information on the financial state of the organization and protection against fraud. This stream, associated with the financial accounting and the stewardship function can be clearly identified with the professional or practising accountants and their audit work.

The other stream, associated with cost accounting and management accounting, has developed to meet the demands of management for relevant information in decision making, which in turn has been influenced by the economist. This accounting is supplementary to and often integrated with financial accounting. Development here has been on an industry basis because each trade or industry is unique in its market, cost structure and planning needs, giving rise to special information requirements. Mass production in the early 1900s with its constant repetition of operations lent itself to the introduction of labour and machine time standards and standard costing. Hotel and catering, like many other industries, can only avail itself of standard costing to a limited extent, yet with increasing emphasis on labour saving methods and centralized food production, the industry is benefiting from this technique. Economics is contributing a great deal to this stream of accounting as accounting becomes more of an inter-disciplinary activity. In comparison with such techniques as standard costing, the use of budgets in businesses since the early 1900s has spread into all industries, because budgeting is concerned with the making of economic plans and this is regarded as essential in any well organized business.

More recent developments have been in uniform or standard systems of accounting which are introduced within an industry to provide a structure for assembling management information in a common form which then facilitates comparisons between firms. A standard system of hotel accounting was published in 1969 followed by one for catering in 1971.

The Managerial Approach

It is easy to fall into the trap of equating an appreciation of accounting with a superficial study of accounting practices and procedures. It is nonetheless difficult to know where to draw the line between gaining a fundamental appreciation of accounting and becoming familiar with the fuller aspects of accounting required by accountants. The object of this work is to help hotel and catering managers and potential managers to understand and use to advantage aspects of accounting they will meet in the administration of their undertakings.

The approach used here is the balance sheet approach rather than the double-entry book-keeping approach. Broad concepts are initially presented rather than minute detail, for otherwise there is a real danger of being confused by a mass of accounts.

Managers, by constantly making decisions, aim to achieve planned results using limited resources. Whilst this is done through people, the measurement of results and the resources used is mainly in money terms. Accounting, as noted earlier, is concerned with recording, summarizing and reporting, and the latter in particular provides the manager with financial information on resources and the results of his decisions. It is important therefore, that the manager should know how resources are obtained and used in his business and how the results are measured. The same basic concepts involved in this measurement apply to the small restaurant and the large hotel group.

The most essential financial information about an organization is contained in balance sheet form which shows from whence resources have been obtained and how they are currently used to generate profit. Only with an understanding of the balance sheet and of profit is it advisable to consider the particular hotel and catering accounting applications which occupy much of this work.

Chapter 2 introduces the balance sheet and profit statement without attempting to raise important issues which affect their preparation and interpretation. These issues are taken up in Chapter 3 to give the reader a chance to understand the assumptions which underpin these statements, and to meet the problems which arise in assessing profit and the measurement of balance sheet values.

Further Reading

1. Sidebotham, R., *Introduction to the Theory and Context of Accounting*, Pergamon Press; chapters 1 and 2.
2. Solomons, D., The Historical Development of Costing, *Studies in Cost Analysis* (edited by Solomons, D). Sweet and Maxwell; pp 3–49.

CHAPTER TWO

ACCOUNTING: FUNDAMENTAL STATEMENTS

THE most prominent financial statement of a business is a 'balance sheet', which by definition shows the financial position at a particular point in time. It could indicate one business to be in a strong financial position and another to be in serious financial difficulties. By comparing balance sheets at different times it is possible to determine the profit made in the period, so long as the owner has not invested or withdrawn resources such as cash during the period.

Profit generation is nevertheless the foremost objective of a business and this requires the preparation of profit statements covering different parts of the business at relatively short time intervals.

By demonstrating the effect some typical transactions have on the financial position of a business, concentration is on the output of the accounting system. This has the advantage of avoiding involvement with processing transactions through numerous accounts. The main reason accounts are used in practice is to accumulate common items so that balance sheets may be produced as required, say quarterly, instead of after each transaction, an almost impossible and certainly unprofitable task.

Dual Aspect of the Balance Sheet

Resources, debts and owner's interests are known respectively as assets, liabilities and capital.

Assets are anything of value owned by a business including resources and future economic rights such as money owed by customers.

Liabilities are financial obligations to outside parties repayable at some future time, such as a loan received from the bank.

Capital is the sum invested in a businss by the owner, partners or in the case of a company, its shareholders. Capital represents the rights of owners to the assets after the prior claims of outside parties (liabilities) have been satisfied in the event of the business closing. It is variously called owner's equity, owner's worth or net assets.

The most acceptable form of accounting for these three elements is known as double entry accounting and this is best expressed as a simple equation:

$$\text{Assets} = \text{Liabilities} + \text{Capital}$$

For accounting records to remain in balance an increase in one asset must be accompanied by a corresponding decrease in another asset or an increase in liabilities and/or capital. The balance sheet is a financial statement which truly reflects this dual aspect.

Description of business activities during a quarter

The dual aspect of the balance sheet will be demonstrated by tracing the activities of a business for three months from its formation on January 1st. The formal statements reflecting the transactions are in Exhibit 2–1 which will be used to explain further accounting aspects later in this chapter.

Jan. 1 Business formed with £70,000 in cash.

2 Premises (£62,000) and equipment (£8,000) purchased for cash. Banqueting business started.

31 Banquets in the month made a profit of £2,000. Sales revenue and all expenses, mainly food, wages and hire charges were cash transactions.
Owner's worth and bank balance have both therefore, increased by £2,000.

Feb. 1 Food stocks purchased on credit to supply further business. These stocks (£4,000) are financed for the moment by the suppliers who are therefore creditors.

28 Banquets in the month have again made £2,000 profit. However, food was drawn from stock (£3,000) leaving £1,000 in stock.
Both revenue and expenses other than food were cash transactions.
Cash balance has risen by £5,000 in the month despite a profit at only £2,000 because no purchases of food were made.

Mar. 1 Creditors were paid the sum owing to them. Cash falls by £4,000.

31 The third month's banqueting has produced a profit similar to that of earlier months. Owner's worth has therefore risen by £2,000 to £76,000. Only 'other expenses' of £5,000 are on a cash basis this month, for clients have been allowed credit (£10,000) and food costing £3,000 was bought on credit to maintain food stocks at £1,000.

The sequence of events in Exhibit 2–1 (pages 18 and 19) illustrates four basic accounting principles:

1. *Owner's worth (equity) is what remains at any time when total liabilities are deducted from total assets.* On February 1st, for instance, £4,000 deducted from assets of £76,000 gives owner's equity of £72,000.
2. *Owner's worth (equity) compared at different times represents profit generated.* If the owner has introduced or withdrawn assets in the period in question then this must clearly be taken into account. January 2nd when trading started compared with March 31st shows a profit of £6,000 as detailed in the profit statement.

EXHIBIT 2—1

(a) Balance Sheets Covering Three Months

	January 1st	January 2nd	January 31st	February 1st	February 28th	March 1st	March 31st	March 31st minus January 2nd
CAPITAL	£	£	£	£	£	£	£	£
Capital	70,000	70,000	70,000	70,000	70,000	70,000	70,000	—
Profit	—	—	2,000	2,000	4,000	4,000	6,000	+ 6,000
Owner's equity	70,000	70,000	72,000	72,000	74,000	74,000	76,000	
LIABILITIES								
Creditors	—	—	—	4,000	4,000	—	3,000	+ 3,000
Overdraft	—	—	—	—	—	—	2,000	+ 2,000
Total	70,000	70,000	72,000	76,000	78,000	74,000	81,000	+11,000
ASSETS								
Premises	—	62,000	62,000	62,000	62,000	62,000	62,000	—
Equipment	—	8,000	8,000	8,000	8,000	8,000	8,000	—
Stock of Food	—	—	—	4,000	1,000	1,000	1,000	+ 1,000
Debtors	—	—	—	—	—	—	10,000	+10,000
Cash at Bank	70,000	—	2,000	2,000	7,000	3,000	—	—
Total	70,000	70,000	72,000	76,000	78,000	74,000	81,000	+11,000

(b) Profit Statements for Period

	January	February	March	Quarter Jan./March
	£	£	£	£
Sales Revenue	(cash) 10,000	(cash) 10,000	(credit) 10,000	30,000
Less Food Cost of Sales (an expense)	(cash) 3,000	(ex stock) 3,000	(credit) 3,000	9,000
GROSS PROFIT	7,000	7,000	7,000	21,000
Less Other Expenses (paid in cash)	5,000	5,000	5,000	15,000
NET PROFIT	2,000	2,000	2,000	6,000

(c) The Relationship between Profit and Cash

		Cash Rise	Cash Fall	
				£
Profit for the three months to March 31st				6,000
		£	£	
But not all sales revenue has been received in cash	(Debtors)		10,000	
On the other hand not all purchases have been paid for	(Creditors)	3,000		
More food has been purchased than used in generating sales and profit	(Stock)		1,000	
		3,000	11,000	less 8,000
Resulting in net cash fall since trading started on January 2nd, requiring overdraft facilities				2,000

3. *The generation of profit in a period does not rely upon business being conducted on a cash basis as in January*. Revenue and costs are accrued, that is to say they are recognized and recorded when they are earned and incurred, not as money is received or paid. In March £10,000 sales have been invoiced and are regarded as revenue although these sales are on credit.
4. *Profit represents sales less expenses incurred in generating those sales.* Firstly, sales revenue is determined for the period and then expenses are said to be 'matched' with the sales revenue. In February although £4,000 food was purchased, only £3,000 of purchases went into the sales and became an expense for the period, apart from £5,000 for other expenses.

Profit v Cash

It is difficult to divorce profit management from cash management although the larger the enterprise the more each becomes a specialist activity. A fall in cash from a nil balance on January 2nd to an overdraft of £2,000 on March 31st is explained by reference to the balance sheets; Exhibit 2–1 (*c*) lists the reasons. The main reason is that clients were allowed credit in March. If their accounts had been settled by March 31st for the full amount the cash balance would have been £8,000. However, if a reduction in the charge were made for prompt payment, say 1 % off the total bill, then profit would have been reduced by £100.

It is necessary to carry stocks of food and other goods and if £1,000 worth of stocks is constantly needed then this has to be financed. The usual alternatives are creditors, and bankers in the form of overdraft for seasonal requirements. It is common for the hotel and catering establishments to carry relatively little stock and for creditors to more than balance the value of stocks carried as on March 31st. This has a favourable effect on the cash position.

Balance Sheet Structure

Assets, liabilities and capital are subdivided in a balance sheet into five main groups located as follows:

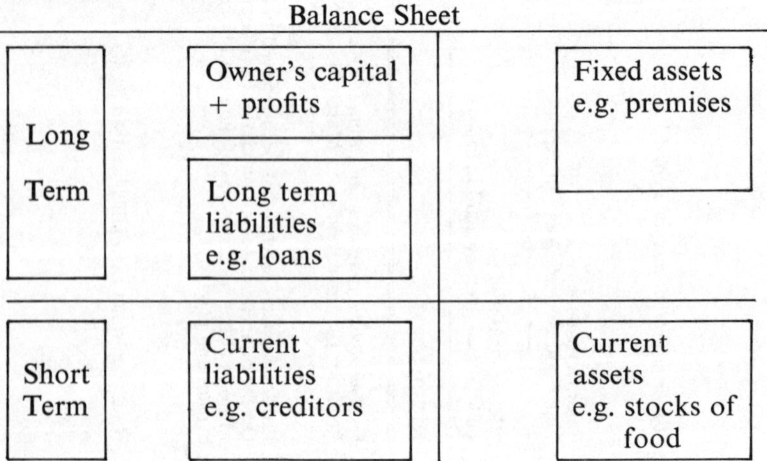

Groups are primarily established in relation to whether an item represents an asset or a claim on the business, and secondly in relation to time.

Long-term Items

Fixed assets are items owned by a business for use in the production of goods and services. They are expected to benefit the business over fairly long periods of time. The purchase cost of these items is called 'capital expenditure' compared with expenditure on assets purchased for consumption and on services which are called 'revenue expenditure'. Examples of fixed assets are land and buildings both freehold and leasehold, plant and equipment.

Long term liabilities normally take the form of loans which by definition are repayable at some future time.

Capital is of a more permanent nature and reflects the owner's investment in the business. Profits may be withdrawn or retained in the business.

Short-term Items

Current assets and current liabilities are of a less permanent nature. They comprise stocks, debtors, cash, creditors and overdraft which are needed to service the routine trading activities of buying, processing, serving and selling.

Current assets minus current liabilities is called net current assets or working capital. Components of working capital are constantly changing, forming some kind of cycle although there is generally no clear start or finish to the cycle. Purchases are made on credit which generate both creditors and stocks. Meals are sold, some on credit. Cash is received from customers and paid to suppliers. Surplus cash is still working capital but may be used to purchase assets or withdrawn from the business, both activities reduce working capital.

Balance Sheet Layout

Balance sheets originated as a list of balances remaining at the end of the year as shown in Exhibit 2–2. As presentation to interested parties became important, formats developed designed to help interpretation. Long and short term items were separated and a vertical form was introduced as in Exhibit 2–3 (overleaf). Current popular presentations emphasize that long term finance is used to supply both fixed assets and net current assets as in Exhibit 2–4 (overleaf).

Figures used in these presentations relate to March 31st in Exhibit 2–1.

Exhibit 2–2 *Balance sheet as a list of balances*

Capital & Liabilities		*Assets*	
	£		£
Owner's capital	70,000	Premises	62,000
Profit	6,000	Equipment	8,000
Loan capital	—	Stocks	1,000
Creditors	3,000	Debtors	10,000
Overdraft	2,000	Cash	—
	81,000		81,000

Exhibit 2–3

Balance sheet in vertical form

	£
Capital	
Owner's capital	70,000
Profit	6,000
	76,000
Loan capital	—
Current liabilities	
Creditors	3,000
Overdraft	2,000
	81,000

	£
Fixed Assets	
Premises	62,000
Equipment	8,000
	70,000
Current Assets	
Stocks	1,000
Debtors	10,000
Cash	—
	11,000
Total Assets	81,000

Exhibit 2–4

Balance sheet showing net current assets

	£	£
Capital Employed		
Owner's capital		70,000
Profit		6,000
		76,000
Loan capital		—
		76,000

REPRESENTED BY:

	£	£
Fixed Assets		
Premises	62,000	
Equipment	8,000	70,000
Current Assets		
Stocks	1,000	
Debtors	10,000	
Cash	—	
	11,000	
Current Liabilities		
Creditors	3,000	
Overdraft	2,000	
	5,000	
Net current Assets		6,000
		76,000

The Profit Statement

Revenue Recognition

Determining profit requires that revenue be identified in a period and the associated expenses deducted. Recognizing revenue is a relatively easy matter compared with the problems involved in working out the associated expenses.

Revenue is recognized as such and recorded when a sale has been agreed and the customer comes into possession of the goods. In a service industry such as hotel and catering, revenue is recognized when the service is rendered, such as:

1. When a guest books into an hotel.
2. When a customer is served with a meal in a restaurant or a drink in a bar.

Revenue and cash received

The relationship between revenue and cash received from sales is shown in three different situations:

1. The quick turnover restaurant often allows no credit. Customers pay cash. Revenue earned in a period is the cash in the till which should agree with all bills issued.
2. A banquet for a client company may be on a credit basis. The revenue is taken immediately to calculate profit but the balance sheet would show the amount owing as part of the debtors figure.
3. Advance booking deposits may be received by an hotel in an accounting period before the client books in. This is not revenue in the period but is shown grouped with creditors.

Cost and Expenses

The term *cost* refers to anything on which money is ultimately spent in running the business. This includes for instance weekly wages, equipment and food whether purchased for cash or on credit.

An *expense* is a cost which has benefited the firm in an accounting period. Food purchased for stock is a cost but becomes an expense in the period when used to prepare a dish for a customer.

Three expense categories are as follows:

1. Non-storable benefits. This is the most easily understood category and covers items which are not stored, such as wages, insurance and rent. The category is mainly associated with services.
2. Stocks. The cost of unused or unsold food and drink stocks will have been incurred in the expectation of future revenue. When this revenue is recorded such as meals or drink sold, the food and drink cost becomes an expense for the period.
3. Depreciation of fixed assets. Fixed assets are those assets which in the normal course of business will provide benefits over several years. The amounts by which the cost is periodically reduced and charged against revenue is known as depreciation, an expense.

Relating expenses to the correct period is often not a simple matter in practice. In order to explain accounting procedures necessary to the understanding of balance sheets and profit statements, three *timing* categories may be identified:

1. Costs which become expenses in the same accounting period.
2. Costs becoming expenses in a subsequent period.
3. Expenses which are not payable until a subsequent period.

These are now explained using figures from Exhibit 2–1.

1. Costs and expenses in the same period:
   (*a*) In Exhibit 2–1, other expenses were assumed to be wages, salaries, monthly hire payments and similar expenses which relate to the month stated. These kind of expenses are no problem as far as timing is concerned.
   (*b*) Food and other items normally stored which are used up and sold in the same period in which they were purchased are expenses in that period, as in January.
2. Costs becoming an expense in a subsequent period:
   (*a*) Stocks of food and other items used up and sold in a subsequent period are expenses in that period. Stocks are automatically charged as expenses to the correct period by either pricing issues of say food issued to the kitchen, or deriving the cost of food used by adding purchases in the period to opening stocks and deducting closing stocks.
   (*b*) Fixed assets such as purchased equipment, lose value with use and time requiring that the cost be allocated to accounting periods so as to charge a fair proportion to each period during the expected future life. This is *depreciation*, defined as a measure of the wearing out, consumption or other loss of value of a fixed asset whether arising from use, effluxion of time or obsolescence through technology and market changes. The equipment in Exhibit 2–1 might be expected to have a life of say 5 years. Equal amounts charged to each period, known as straight line method of depreciation, would require £1,600 per annum or £400 per quarter. This would have the effect of reducing profit for the quarter to £5,600 and the balance sheet value of equipment to £7,600 at March 31st.
   (*c*) Prepayments are amounts due to be paid in one period for services relating wholely or partly to subsequent periods. If an annual insurance premium of £400 is payable in advance, this would be included in January's other expenses. However, only £100 would be regarded as expenses for this first quarter, the other £300 relating to later periods would appear as 'prepayments' on the asset side of the balance sheet at March 31st.
3. Expenses payable in a subsequent period:
   Accrued expenses or accruals are expenses which have been incurred in an accounting period but are not due for payment until a later period. A quarterly gas bill covering January/March will not be received and consequently not paid until April. As an expense for the first quarter the amount, say £400, will be added to other expenses and shown as accrued expenses in the balance sheet at March 31st under current liabilities. It is similar to a creditor who is owed for goods supplied and is sometimes grouped with creditors in published accounts.

Expenses Matrix

To sum up, the matching of expenses with revenue requires that costs be classified as they are incurred into revenue and capital expenditure. Revenue expenditure is further separated into purchases for stock and all other expenses.

At the end of an accounting period the matching process requires adjustments so that the profit statement – the presentation form of the profit and loss account – contains only those expenses relating to the sales and to the period.

A summary of this procedure is presented in matrix form in Exhibit 2–5.

Exhibit 2–5

A CLASSIFICATION OF HOTEL AND CATERING EXPENSES RELATED TO PERIOD PROFIT

TIMING of EXPENSES	FORMS OF EXPENSES		
	Revenue Expenditure		Capital Expenditure
	Purchases which go into stock e.g. food and drink	Providing non-storable benefits e.g. wages, insurance, electricity	Depreciation of fixed assets
Costs and expenses in the same period	Stocks used up in becoming sales	Most expenses are in this position requiring no adjustment	
Costs becoming expenses in a subsequent period	Stocks are an asset in the balance sheet until used, becoming an expense when sold	Payment in advance e.g. for insurance. Cost carried forward to the next period is an asset in the balance sheet and grouped with debtors	Each period's depreciation expense is accumulated and deducted from cost of asset in the balance sheet
Expenses payable in a subsequent period		Accruals for services e.g. electricity. Similar to creditors in the balance sheet	
CRITERIA for charging expense to a period's profit and loss account	Related to sales in the period	Related to the period benefited by the expense	

Note to Exhibit 2–5:

1 This classification is presented to aid the understanding of financial accounting. Classification for management accounting purposes is covered in Chapter 5.

2 Where food has been processed and remains in stock, for example frozen made up dishes, then some depreciation and other expenses will be added to the food cost to arrive at the stock value.

The Profit Statement: Presentation

The significance of a balance sheet has been demonstrated because it is a vital part of accounting and at the same time is helpful to the understanding of accounting profit. However, deriving profit for a period by finding the increase in owner's worth is, in practice, inadequate for several reasons. One reason for supporting the balance sheet with a detailed profit statement is that it helps management to plan and control the business. Being aware of the detailed revenue and expenses making up the profit helps in the planning of the next period's results and the control of individual costs such as food.

Profit, although calculated in accordance with the matching principle, is presented in different ways to satisfy the different needs for instance of shareholders, the Inland Revenue and management. The profit and loss account compiled by double entry method is dealt with in Volume 1. The presentation of profit in the annual report and accounts of limited companies is shown in Chapter 16. For internal management purposes the presentation of profit, and in particular its constituent parts, is made in a 'profit statement' rather than the traditional profit and loss account. An account calls to mind the two sided account used in double entry book-keeping; a statement on the other hand, breaks away from the two sided account and seeks to show accounting information in a more meaningful manner for the non-accountant.

The simplest form of profit statement, in fact a summary, was shown in Exhibit 2–1(*c*) and is repeated here:

Profit statement for quarter to 31st March

	£
Sales	30,000
Less Cost of sales	9,000
Gross profit	21,000
Less Other expenses	15,000
Net profit	6,000

Attention is drawn again to the very important accounting concept that profit results from sales revenue less the cost of generating the sales, and not less the cost of purchases. The example drawn from Exhibit 2–1(*c*) could have been restated:

Profit statement for quarter to 31st March

	£	£
Sales		30,000
Cost of food used in sales:		
Opening stock	—	
Purchases	10,000	
	10,000	
Less Closing stock	1,000	
		9,000
Gross profit		21,000
Less Other expenses		15,000
Net profit		6,000

For management accounting purposes, the form of profit statement which gives one figure for cost of food instead of stating opening and closing stocks is usually adopted. For routine accounting purposes, stocks are valued at the lower of cost or net realizable value in accordance with the prudence concept considered in Chapter 3. A more detailed profit statement, including the three adjustments* noted on page 24 is as follows:

Profit statement for quarter to 31st March

	£	£
Sales revenue		29,800
Less Cost of sales		9,000
Gross profit		20,800
Plus Other revenue		200
		21,000
Less Other expenses:		
Wages and salaries	8,000	
Staff food and drink	1,250	
Administration	1,950	
Advertising	500	
Heat, light and power (including £400 gas*)	1,500	
Insurance * (£400 less £300)	100	
General expenses	300	
Repairs and maintenance	1,500	
Depreciation *	400	15,500
Net profit		5,500
Less Appropriations		3,000
Retained profit		2,500

Two additional items have been shown on page 27. 'Other revenue' refers to revenue other than from the main operating departments, for instance income received from advertising space in reception. 'Appropriations' item indicates the use of the profit that has been generated and could refer to cash drawn from the business by the owner. What is not appropriated for various purposes is retained in the business and increases owner's worth. However, in its present form the above profit statement is still of limited value operationally. Management require periodical profit statements which contain revenues and expenses expressed in terms of departmental responsibility and control.

A suitable format, and one similar in principle to those developed for the Industry's standard systems of hotel and catering accounting, contains an analysis of the main operating departments and identifies several intermediate profit levels. In general, the format contains the following information:

Sales revenue (Operating departments)
Less: Cost of sales
Departmental GROSS PROFIT
Less: Wages and staff expenses
Departmental NET MARGIN
Less: Allocated expenses
Departmental OPERATING PROFIT
Plus: Other revenue
Total OPERATING INCOME
Less: Other unallocated but controllabe expenses
Total OPERATING PROFIT
Less: Other unallocated but non-controllable expenses
Total NET PROFIT

A profit statement containing the information prescribed in the standard system of hotel accounting is illustrated below:

	Rooms £	Food £	Bevs. £	Total £
Sales				
Less: Cost of sales	——	——	——	——
Dept. GROSS PROFIT				
Less: Wages and staff expenses	——	——	——	——
Dept. NET MARGIN				
Less: Allocated expenses	——	——	——	——
Dept. OPERATING PROFIT	═══	═══	═══	
Plus: Other revenue				——

	Rooms £	Food £	Bevs. £	Total £
HOTEL OPERATING INCOME				
Less: Administration				
Advertising				
Heat, light and power				
General expenses			——	——
HOTEL OPERATING PROFIT				
Less: Repairs and maintenance				
Depreciation			——	——
HOTEL NET OPERATING PROFIT				
Less: Loan interest				——
NET PROFIT				====

The above profit statement seeks to highlight departmental profitability and various profit control levels.

Questions and Problems

2–1 What are assets, liabilities and capital?

2–2 Explain how the 'dual-aspect' concept and the 'accounting equation' are interrelated.

2–3 Give the relationship of assets, liabilities and owner's worth in three different equations (express each item as a function of the other two).

2–4 What is a balance sheet?

2–5 Distinguish between the following items:
(*a*) fixed assets and current assets
(*b*) long-term liabilities and current liabilities
(*c*) capital and long-term liabilities

2–6 What is a profit statement?

2–7 Distinguish between the terms 'cost' and 'expense'.

2–8 What do you understand by the term 'depreciation' in respect of fixed assets?

2–9 In what way is a profit statement connected with a balance sheet?

2–10 How may a profit statement, which is acceptable to owners and outside interested parties, be modified so as to provide relevant operational information?

2–11 Distinguish between the terms 'revenue' and 'receipt'.

2–12 Prepare two successive sets of balance sheets (i.e. a new balance sheet drawn up after each transaction), to show the effects of the following transactions, assuming that revenue is recognized:

(i) When cash is received; and
(ii) When goods are invoiced.

(*a*) Commence business with £100,000 cash
(*b*) Buy premises for £40,000 cash
(*c*) Buy stock on credit for £30,000
(*d*) Pay business expenses in cash for £3,000
(*e*) Sell stock which cost £16,000 on credit for £24,000
(*f*) Pay creditors amount due
(*g*) Collect cash £18,000 on account from the debtors.

Note: A suitable presentation for your answer to part (*b*) might be:

Trans-action/ Item	(a)	(b)	(c)	(d) etc.
Capital				
Profit				
Creditors				
Premises				
Stock				
etc.				

2–13 The following transactions relate to a new restaurant business which commenced on 1st May:

May 1 Business formed with £80,000 in capital and a £20,000 loan, both in cash.
2 Bought premises and equipment for cash £95,000.
31 During the month, transactions were:

		£
	Meal sales – cash	8,000
	Food expenses – cash	3,000
	Wages and other expenses – cash	2,000
June 1	Food purchased on credit from suppliers	5,500
30	During the month, transactions were:	
		£
	Meal sales – cash	9,000
	Food expenses – cash	1,000
	– from stock	3,000
	Wages, etc. – cash	2,000
July 1	Paid creditors amount outstanding and further food purchases made on credit to increase stocks to £8,000.	
31	During the month, transactions were:	
		£
	Meal sales – cash	2,000
	– credit	8,000
	Food expenses – cash	1,000
	– from stock	4,000
	Wages, etc. – cash	2,000

Prepare in respect of the quarter:

(*a*) balance sheets for each date;

(*b*) profit statements for each month and the quarter;

(*c*) a statement illustrating the relationship between profit and cash for the quarter.

2–14 The following information relates to a catering establishment for the year ended 31st December, 1979:

	£000's
Sales	300
Other expenses	42
Aggregate depreciation – fixed assets – 31st December, 1978	120
Current liabilities	12
Owner's capital	330
Cost of goods sold	120
Annual depreciation expense	6
Current assets	18
Wages	72
Long-term liabilities	210
Fixed assets at cost	720

Prepare, in vertical form, a profit statement for year ended 31st December, 1979, and a balance sheet as at that date.

Further Reading

1. Anthony, R. N., *Management Accounting Principles*, Richard D. Irwin, Inc., chapters 2 and 3.
2. Bull, F., *Accounting in Business*, Butterworths, chapters 1–5.
3. Glautier, M. W. E., and Underdown, B., *Accounting Theory and Practice*, Pitman Publishing.
4. Zeff, S. A., and Keller, T. F., *Financial Accounting Theory*, McGraw-Hill.

CHAPTER THREE

ACCOUNTING: THE CONCEPTUAL FRAMEWORK

ACCOUNTING is essentially a practical activity that has developed over the centuries. Of the concepts that have evolved some are enforceable by law whilst others are but recommended procedures. An understanding of accounting concepts is invaluable as they provide a guide to the purpose of the balance sheet and at the same time highlight the problems encountered in valuing business assets and the profit generated.

The term concept has a number of synonyms, one being principle, but no purpose would be served here attempting to compare them. Concepts are general ideas which have developed slowly through experience. Early accounting systems were intended to serve a limited range of purposes and had no need of the many concepts which are important today.

It is useful to place accounting concepts into two groups (Exhibit 3–1).

1. Accounting system design concepts.
2. Accounting operational concepts.

An attempt has been made to place the first group into a logical sequence relating to the setting up of an accounting system. Initially concepts are considered which deal with the inputs to the system in the form of recorded transactions and end with outputs associated with the summaries produced. There is little room to argue here, for recording and summarizing the end of period accounts should be in line with these concepts. The three operational concepts however, are open to different interpretations because of the subjective nature of the ideas.

Accounting Systems Design Concepts

Business Entity

The concept concerns the boundary around the area of economic activity or the business unit for which accounting reports are prepared. In starting a business a sole trader for convenience regards his business operations as a separate entity from his personal finances. All accounting records are maintained in relation to the business and not the owner. A limited company has a legal entity which is clearly defined and ensures accounting arrangements are separate from the owners who are shareholders.

It is implied in setting up a business entity that business will be conducted which will require financial measurement. This is the main object of the accounting system.

Exhibit 3–1

ACCOUNTING: SYSTEMS DESIGN CONCEPTS

Question	Concept
1. What is to be accounted for and reported upon?	1. Operations of a *business entity.*
2. Is it expected to have a long life?	2. Yes. A *going concern* is assumed.
3. What is to be recorded concerning the entity?	3. *Measurable business transactions.*
4. What unit of measurement is to be used?	4. *A monetary unit,* a relatively stable measure.
5. How are transaction amounts to be determined?	5. Using *objectivity,* i.e. unbiased and verifiable.
6. What is the essential structure of the main report?	6. A *dual aspect of assets and liabilities* forming a balance sheet.
7. How frequently are reports to be prepared?	7. At least annually, introducing a *time period.*
8. How are items to be related to time periods?	8. *Accruals or matching* concept.
9. What essential information is to be reported?	9. (*a*) The *worth of the entity* in the form of net assets. (*b*) *Profit* or *loss* made in the period measured in two complementary ways: (i) sales revenue less expenses; (ii) change in net assets over time, assuming no additional investment or distribution to the owner.

ACCOUNTING: OPERATIONAL CONCEPTS

Question	Concept
1. What is the criterion for deciding whether some item is classed as an asset or an expense?	1. *Materiality.*
2. Is the book value of an asset overstating its future worth to the business?	2. *Prudence* or *conservatism.*
3. Can figures be sensibly compared over several years?	3. *Consistency.*

Going Concern

A basic assumption is that in the absence of evidence to the contrary, a business will continue to operate into the foreseeable future. This affects the valuation of assets and liabilities for end of year reporting. Fixed assets for instance are used in the business to generate profit next year and should be valued in this light.

The going concern concept is therefore related to the accruals concept which requires a fixed asset cost to be allotted to the time periods benefiting from this item. A different and probably lower value would be placed on kitchen equipment for instance if it were valued on the basis of a forced sale because the business was about to close down.

Further concepts affect end of period values such as the prudence concept which takes into account inevitable future uncertainties. Nevertheless, the going concern is implicit in the valuation whatever further concept is superimposed on it.

Measurable Business Transactions

Relations between the business and parties outside the business are carried on by means of identifiable, separable and measurable transactions. Transactions are recorded in the books of account, summarized and presented to interested parties.

Monetary Unit

This concept states that only those business transactions which can be expressed in monetary terms are recorded in the accounts. The reason is, of course, that money provides the only common language into which diverse events may be translated. This concept is basic to all accounting records. Although a common language, money no longer provides a stable measurement and throughout this work reference will be made to the effects of inflation which need to be allowed for in many business situations.

Objectivity

This concept requires that recorded accounting data be free from bias in so far as there has been objective establishment of value determined by the market place. Objective evidence for the purchase of bar fittings will be in the form of an invoice which may be verified.

Historical costs of purchases are recorded and processed through the accounting system, laying a firm foundation for the initial valuation of assets at the end of a period. However, this value after allowing for depreciation, may be adjusted when assets are valued for balance sheet presentation purposes.

The Dual Aspect of Assets and Liabilities

This concept was illustrated in Chapter 2 where it was shown that;

$$\text{Capital} + \text{Liabilities} = \text{Assets}$$

To facilitate the preparation of a balance sheet a system of double entry is used by all but the smallest businesses. Indeed, the law requires that public companies maintain their accounts on the double entry principle, although small hotels and restaurants may use single entry when final accounts are prepared from so-called 'incomplete records'. (Volume 1 Chapter 10).

Time Period

Three major reasons require businesses to account for their profit at least annually. They are:

1. All businesses pay tax on profits and this requires an annual report of their financial affairs.
2. Legislation requires that company directors present annual accounts of their stewardship for the benefit of shareholders.
3. Managing a business effectively demands frequent knowledge of how operations are financially progressing so as to maintain control.

Although the Income Tax year ends on 5th April the twelve month accounting period of the business is determined by its owners or directors. Control of the business might require shorter accounting periods of quarters, months or weeks.

At the end of the accounting year, accounts including a balance sheet and profit and loss account are prepared, and they are called either end of year accounts or final accounts.

Accruals or Matching Concept

This concept, which is automatically complied with when annual accounts are prepared, was considered in the last chapter. Revenue and costs are accrued, that is recognized and recorded as they are earned and incurred, not as money is received or paid. The profit statement for a period shows the profit which is the value of sales less the matching expenses, and it is noted that cash movements *do not* affect profit directly.

Owner's Worth and Profit Concept

Concepts so far have concerned the inputs of the accounting system which, having been summarized, become the outputs of the system, providing the owner with financial information regarding the worth of his business and the profit generated.

The dual aspect of accounting being established, it has been seen that annual balancing is necessary in the life of a business. This gives rise to the concept of accruals or the matching concept which, in association with the dual aspect concept, determines the basis for finding at any time:

(*a*) The worth of the entity in the form of net assets.

(*b*) Profit or loss made in a period, measured in two ways
   (i) sales revenue less expenses incurred, and
   (ii) change in the value of net assets over time (assuming no additional investment or distributions to the owner).

This concept results from assembling the previous system design concepts into a structure and reflects the relationships associated with the balance sheet and profit and loss account.

Accounting Operational Concepts

Materiality

This concept recognizes that precision in reporting financial results is not always desirable because the cost to achieve it may far outweigh the benefits. At the end of the year a tin of spices in the kitchen store is conceptually an asset because it will be used to benefit sales in the next period. However, in practice, because of its low relative value it might for accounting purposes be regarded as an expense when purchased. The effect on profit therefore is one criterion of materiality, although there is no hard and fast rule to adopt.

Conservatism or Prudence

This concept states that it is better to understate asset values and consequently profit than to overstate them because understatement has fewer unpleasant effects than overstatement. Railway companies in the last century often did not depreciate locomotives and even appreciated their values by adding repair charges. This is clearly wrong, for profits were thereby overstated and excessive dividends paid, reducing the real net asset value of the companies.

The application of this concept is a reaction to the uncertainty of the future. Future profits should not be anticipated, but possible future losses should be provided for. An hotel shop with jewellery stock which cost £3,000 but now out of fashion might be expected to sell it for only £2,000 next year. Balance sheet value for this stock should therefore be only £2,000.

Consistency

Data cannot easily be compared unless they have been drawn up on a consistent basis. For accounting reports to be of material benefit to the user, the practices and procedures adopted to prepare them should be consistent from period to period. Modifications to practices, however, are sometimes necessary and such changes should be communicated to all interested parties.

Comments on Concepts

Accounting world-wide is experiencing rapid changes to both inputs and outputs of accounting systems. Input changes are associated with computer technology, although such changes have not affected the accounting system design concepts. Such concepts are so fundamental that they help to retain the balanced overview so necessary when systems change. They still are essential to the stewardship function.

Some changes to the outputs of accounting systems have been brought about by demands for more valuable financial information. Whilst some of these changes have been adjustments to final accounts, others have meant the preparation of additional statements and the disclosure of information not previously made available to those outside the company. Disclosure of additional information has not been restricted to financial information.

Although the concepts of money measurement and objectivity remain firm as essential to the recording of transactions, money measurement using historical cost has become unsatisfactory from the presentation point of view because of rapid inflation in the mid 1970s. The concept of consistency has been adhered to by recording historical cost but inflation has distorted values over the years, making supplementary statements to final accounts desirable. A method to overcome this problem is likely to be introduced in 1980 and this is described in Chapter 16.

Accounting information is used for a wide range of purposes, many of them economic, and concepts need to be used which are relevant to the purpose. Whilst the objectivity concept recognizes an asset's original cost which is relevant for taxation purposes, other concepts such as prudence admit other values which reflect its worth to the business.

Concepts considered in this chapter concern the preparation and presentation of annual accounts. Much of this work deals with the financial aspects of the planning and control of business operations which the annual accounts measure in total. These matters require the use of further concepts which are covered in Chapter 5.

Questions and Problems

3–1 What do you understand by the term 'business entity'?

3–2 In accounting only those business transactions which can be expressed in monetary terms are recorded. Why?

3–3 In what sense is the term 'objectivity' used in accounting?

3–4 Explain, using simple arithmetical examples, the 'accruals' or 'matching' concept.

3–5 How is the 'going concern' concept and the 'accruals' concept related?

3–6 Distinguish between 'accounting system design concepts' and 'accounting operational concepts'.

3–7 Do you consider an understanding of the conceptual framework to be important when dealing with practical matters of accounting? Why? Give examples.

Further Reading

1. Sidebotham, R., *Introduction to the Theory and Context of Accounting*, Pergamon Press; chapter 3.
2. As per chapter 2 reading list.

CHAPTER FOUR

INTRODUCTION TO FINANCIAL PLANNING AND CONTROL

PROFIT is achieved by the effective management of all available resources, which are basically people and finance, and an important aim of the accounting function is to supply information that will aid management in the effective use of such resources. A management accounting system, accordingly, provides information on which managers can better manage, and because it measures profit and decisions affecting profit, should embrace all matters stated in monetary terms.

Planning Aspects

Much management accounting work involves the preparation of routine statements to show whether the business is running as planned, an important function, but one which is rendered relatively ineffective if the plan itself is poor. A frequent business failing is the inability to be adaptive at management level although first-class routine control information is provided at the operating level. The result is effective performance of bad plans.

This situation may be illustrated by comparing the results of Restaurants A and B for a 12-month period (year 2) shown in Exhibit 4–1 (overleaf).

Restaurant 'A's' management planned to improve profit from £3,500 in year 1 to £5,000 in year 2, but in the event, turnover fell short of budget and food costs increased to 52% of sales, resulting in a profit of £4,200.

Restaurant 'B's' management pursued a policy of no change, concentrating its efforts on repeating year 1 results. Although food costs were controlled to 50% of sales, turnover increased and profit was £200 above year 1.

Which restaurant would you say was better managed?

To give a sensible answer requires a study of facts not present in this simple profit statement, although it might be said that if all other financial factors, such as working capital and property values, were identical, then Restaurant 'A's' management did the better job in increasing profit by £700 in the year compared with 'B's' increase of only £200.

Factors to be taken into account in assessing the results of A and B would include:

1. If A's profit has been achieved without additional investment, e.g. by better service or a pricing policy change, then existing resources have been more effectively managed and A's management is probably better than B's.

2. If A spent £20,000 on additional facilities in the year, the extra return of £700 (3½%) might be regarded as a disappointment. However, the payoff may be expected in year 3 and A's management may therefore be reasonably satisfied with year 2 results.
3. How are future profits likely to be affected by decisions taken in the year? A decision not to redecorate might adversely affect year 3 turnover and therefore profit.
4. Is the business in a position to settle its suppliers' bills as they fall due? A might not, even though an improved profit has been recorded. Sight of the balance sheet might help with this answer.
5. From what sources have finances been obtained? One restaurant may be paying more for its capital than the other because of poor management.
6. Has the increase in food costs of A been the result of a policy change, increased food prices, or increased wastage? If wastage is the cause then management has been at fault.
7. What has been the rate of inflation in the year? If 6% occurred in year 2 B might be worse off than in year 1 because £210 extra profit would be required to offset the fall in the value of money.

Exhibit 4–1

PROFIT STATEMENT

	Year 1 Actual		*Year 2 Budget*		*Year 2 Actual*	
Restaurant A	£	%	£	%	£	%
Revenue	17,000	100	20,000	100	19,000	100
Food costs	8,500	50	10,000	50	9,800	52
GROSS MARGIN	8,500	50	10,000	50	9,200	48
Other costs	5,000	29	5,000	25	5,000	26
PROFIT	3,500	21	5,000	25	4,200	
Restaurant B						
Revenue	17,000	100	17,000	100	17,400	100
Food costs	8,500	50	8,500	50	8,700	50
GROSS MARGIN	8,500	50	8,500	50	8,700	50
Other costs	5,000	29	5,000	29	5,000	29
PROFIT	3,50021		3,500	21	3,700	21

Most of these questions and many more can be answered by means of a good management accounting system which helps to quantify the effect of management plans and results.

It might be argued that management of restaurant B has failed to be adaptive in not benefiting sufficiently from an expanding market, partly through too much attention to the control side. In the 1960s, Trust Houses suffered on the one hand because there was no forward plan for the group as a whole, and on the other hand, the detailed control over hotel managers was so tight that it destroyed initiative.

It is clear in modern management where competition is keen, that the successful management is flexible in outlook, plans with care yet takes calculated risks, trying to anticipate its customers' requirements, the labour market and availability of finance.

How then can an understanding of the financial side of the business help the manager to plan more effectively? Basically in two ways:

(*a*) Participating in routine annual budgeting will highlight important relationships existing between management functions, co-ordination of which help in smooth running of operations and optimization of profit.

(*b*) Participating in the preparation of statements showing the effect on overall business profit of alternative courses of action, will give the manager confidence in seeking profitable opportunities.

The extent to which (*a*) and (*b*) above are formalized depends upon the size of the business, for the smaller undertaking will require a simple system; yet these two parts of the planning operation, routine budgeting and ad hoc profit studies, are relevant to even the smallest business.

It will be seen that at any time a business opportunity may be discovered which, when evaluated in terms of return on investment, is either rejected or accepted as falling in line with laid down policy and built into the next budget.

Planning for profit involves not only seeing that there is a surplus of revenue over costs, but also that sufficient cash and stock is available when needed, and that finance is obtained from the right source, i.e. that expansion involving purchase of accommodation and other long-term assets is not paid for by short-term credit, but from long-term sources such as the issue of shares, debentures and retained profit. The oldest financial mistake in the world is borrowing short-term and investing long-term.

Control Considerations

Whilst the importance of a good plan is stressed, *control* of costs, revenue, stocks, and cash is essential in order to avoid unnecessary loss and wastage leading to falling profit. Hotel and catering businesses are generally alive to the needs of good control routines, especially when concerned with the day to day control of food, sales and cash where underages and overages can be quickly identified and speedy action taken to bring the position back into control if at all possible. Such control procedures are largely to avoid fraudulent use of the assets involved, but are only a part, although an important part, of the overall control system of the business which aims to help supervisors and managers achieve planned results. Results need to be quantified for comparison with planned performance and may be, for example, number of portions for day to day control. Somewhere along the line the measurement must be in value as it flows through the management accounting system so that management can see the overall picture of departmental and company performance.

This overall picture is achieved by means of an operating statement which shows actual and budgeted departmental revenues and costs and other hotel income and costs; in other words it is a profit and loss statement used for control purposes. An attempt is made to use budgets to help those responsible to control revenue and costs at departmental and hotel levels. Exhibit 4–2 shows a pro forma operating statement with control levels recommended in N.E.D.O.s *A Standard System of Hotel Accounting*. Since any change in revenue or cost directly affects planned profit, investigation of the significant variances is most important to enable management to rectify the position if results are adverse or to exploit the position if results become favourable. A significant adverse food cost caused by a national price rise might call for selling price revision whereas a favourable turnover compared with budget, after investigation may lead to the discovery of an untapped source of customers.

Control of assets such as cash and stocks is aided only to a limited extent

Exhibit 4–2

FORM OF OPERATING STATEMENT WITH CONTROL LEVELS

Item	*Person initially responsible*	*Control period*	*Method of control*
Departmental net sales *Less:* cost of sales	Room, Food & Beverage Managers	Daily	Cash and credit sales records. Weekly/monthly summary Food & beverage control
Departmental gross profit *Less:* wages and staff costs	Room, Food & Beverage Managers	Monthly	Operated departmental comparison of budget with actual expenses
Departmental net margin *Less:* direct departmental expenses	Room, Food & Beverage Managers	Monthly	Operated departmental comparison of budget with actual expenses
Departmental operating profit *Less:* service & general apportioned expenses	Service Department Managers	Monthly	Comparison of service departmental budgets with actual expenses
Hotel operating profit *Less:* provision of plant and accommodation	Hotel Manager	Quarterly Annually	Expenditure fixed in nature and controlled largely by policy decision
Hotel net operating profit	Hotel Manager		

by comparison between actual and budget figures, since this only indicates whether policy in relation to levels of cash and stock holding is being achieved. More important, as mentioned earlier, is the stewardship function in maintaining accurate records of purchases and sales and ensuring that adequate physical control is exercised to avoid fraud.

Monthly and cumulative operating statements showing value and percentages help to indicate how the business is performing against budget, and may be said to be an internal control mechanism.

In recent years control has been aided by comparison with other hotels of percentages and ratios designed to indicate one's position relative to other similar establishments. This external control facility illustrates the continuing communication between the planning and control functions, for the greatest benefit is the guide management receives in setting better targets in areas where the business is producing a relatively poor performance.

Questions and Problems

4–1 Explain why a good financial plan is important to any business regardless of size of the undertaking.

4–2 A profit plan needs to ensure not only that sufficient profit will result, but also that there will be enough stock and cash available. Is a lack of cash more critical than making a loss? Explain.

4–3 Using assumed figures, explain why a business which has fallen short of a planned profit may be in a more satisfactory position than another business which has successfully repeated last year's results.

4–4 Should the current year's profit be the sole criterion of a successful management? Explain.

4–5 In a large hotel, which managers can influence the level of the following costs – food, kitchen wages, local rates, replacement of glass and china, maintenance of kitchen equipment?

CHAPTER FIVE

COST CHARACTERISTICS

THE object of this chapter is to explain basic cost characteristics and to give some idea of the uses of cost information. All levels of management are concerned with costs either in a dynamic situation making decisions, or in a more mundane manner keeping costs under control. In any event an understanding of costs, and especially their behaviour in relation to quantity of output, goes a long way towards using costs correctly to further the aims of the enterprise. The word 'cost' can rarely stand alone and should be qualified to ensure its meaning is faithfully communicated. It is the amount of expenditure incurred for some specific purpose.

Classification of Costs

There are several ways of classifying cost, depending upon the object of the exercise. For the present purpose only three need be demonstrated as shown in Exhibit 5–1.

Basic Elements of Cost

This is the simplest form of classification and is a convenient means of assembling costs to offset revenue in a Profit and Loss account.

Direct and Indirect Costs

Here begins a classification used for management purposes. The cost of direct materials, e.g. food, taken away from food sales gives the all important gross profit percentage. Direct wages taken away from gross profit shows departmental net margin. These residual figures are important checks on departmental profitability. Expenses are mainly indirect which together with indirect material and indirect labour are sometimes called overhead or burden (U.S.A. term). Direct costs are those which can be directly related to a product, saleable service or department.

Fixed and Variable Costs

This classification is immensely important and much attention will be paid to it elsewhere. Initially definitions will provide a basic knowledge of this classification.

THREE COST CLASSIFICATIONS **Exhibit 5–1**

Form	Basic cost elements	Direct and indirect	Fixed and variable
Purpose	Basic records for simple profit statement	Relating costs to departments for cost and profit control	Showing response to activity changes for various planning and control purposes
Total cost	Materials used Wages Expenses	DIRECT Materials used Direct wages Direct expenses INDIRECT Materials Wages Expenses	Variable costs Semi-variable costs Fixed costs

Variable cost: a cost which in total tends to vary in direct proportion to changes in volume of activity in a period. Activity refers to some productive activity such as dishes prepared, meals served, rooms occupied. An undisputed variable cost is the cost of food.

Fixed cost: a cost which accrues in relation to the passage of time and which tends to be unaffected by fluctuations in volume of activity in a period. Such costs as local rates, rent, manager's basic salary are clearly fixed costs.

Semi-variable cost: a cost containing both fixed and variable elements which is therefore partly affected by fluctuations in volume of activity in a period. A large number of costs fall into this category such as wages, electricity and laundry.

This classification does not usually feature in the routine accounting system largely because of the highly subjective nature of the split between fixed and variable categories. The few firms in other industries who do have this classification in their system would refer to it as a Marginal Costing System.

Cost Behaviour – Volume

For the purpose of illustrating various cost behaviour patterns relating to volume it is usual to measure the monetary value of cost on the vertical (y) axis and volume along the horizontal or (x) axis. Timescale is not usually depicted but a 12-month period is often assumed. Some examples of costs on cost/volume charts are shown below.

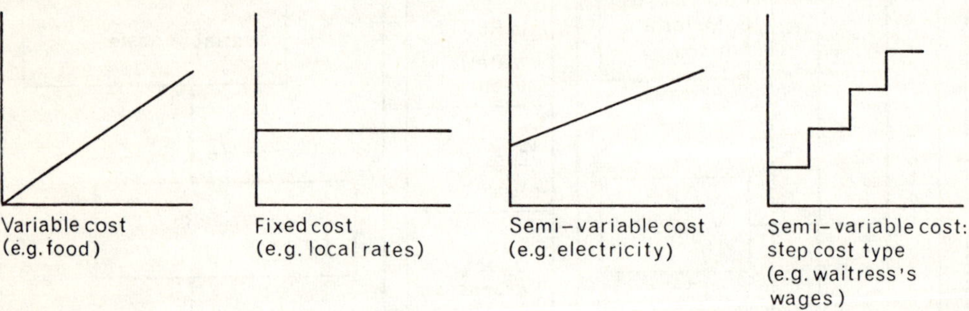

Many types of semi-variable cost patterns result from changes in volume of activity. One such is the step cost where another waitress has to be engaged who will serve a small range of extra covers, all for her extra wage – the rise in the 'step'. For practical purposes, the width of the 'step' will determine whether the cost may be regarded as variable or fixed. For example, in the case of the waitresses' wages the underlying behaviour pattern would be regarded as variable. These patterns show cost changes resulting from changes in volume of activity so that inflation, for instance, has to be considered separately.

Cost Behaviour – Semi-Variable Cost

The benefits from having the first two categories, fixed and variable, are numerous and are considered in Chapter 8, but the problem arises of placing all costs into these two categories. The semi-variable category has to be eliminated and there are several methods of apportioning these costs to the fixed and variable categories. In each case care is needed to ensure that costs taken from different points in time have had inflation effects removed.

(*a*) Technical assessment

Often the person closely involved with the cost item can give a fair estimate of the cost behaviour such as the chef estimating the variability in usage of some indirect foods.

(*b*) High and low points method
By taking the highest and lowest costs of a series of periods, it is assumed that the difference represents the variable costs related to the change in volume of activity. A cost related to meals prepared has records to show that over 12 periods the highest and lowest period costs were £642 and £603 with corresponding number of meals being 3,157 and 2,878 respectively. The variable cost calculation is as follows:

		Total costs	No. meals	
		£		
Highest cost – period 10		642	3,157	
Lowest cost – period 2		603	2,878	
	Difference	£39	279	
Variable cost per unit	=	£39	÷ 279	= £0·14

Fixed cost can be calculated:		£
Total cost period 10		642
Variable cost = 3,157 × £0·14	=	442
Fixed cost	=	200

Clearly a cost/volume chart could be drawn, using a suitable scale, to depict this by inserting one point for each period and joining the two points, extending them also to the (y) axis. The chart would appear:

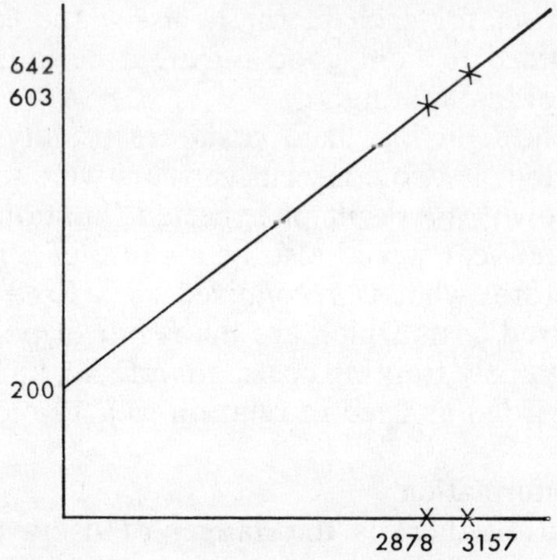

(*c*) Scattergraph or chart
This tends to be more accurate than the high and low method in that here all the 12 points available from a series of recordings are plotted instead of just

two. A straight line (line of best fit) is drawn through the points in such a manner that it passes roughly midway between them. Again, on meeting the (y) axis, the fixed cost component is determined.

(*d*) Method of least squares:
This is a statistical calculation that results in a technically accurate line of best fit or a regression line.

It will be noted, the three methods using past records assume that a straight line represents the cost changes, and this may not necessarily be true.

Fixed costs are fairly easy to identify, and apart from food, liquor and other direct sales, there are few truly variable costs, which simplifies their determination. The separation of semi-variable into fixed and variable categories is admittedly a rather imperfect exercise. It is nevertheless true that the accuracy obtained has been sufficient for many successful cost analyses used in decision making.

Cost Behaviour – Other Influences

(*a*) Variable costs: Among the more important factors, which influence total cost in a period of an item like food are:

1. Volume and mix of dishes served
2. Price paid for food including seasonal variations and inflation
3. Quality of food
4. Quantity lost between delivering and serving
5. Quantity of food in each dish

It can be seen that in the rather extreme case of food cost, a large number of assumptions are made when a straight line is shown to represent the way a variable cost rises in response to volume changes. On the other hand standards may and generally are set for each factor to assist the control of food costs and these can be assumed to hold good during a period, leaving volume the one factor to account for in planning.

(*b*) Fixed costs: Charts depicting fixed costs are usually for 12 months, the common planning period. If two consecutive years were to be depicted, then a step cost would be shown, the result of expected inflation in the second year. Expansion in the second year would also be a cause of a rise in fixed costs. In the longer term therefore, what is recognized as a fixed cost would become semi-variable. Some fixed costs which are the result of policy decisions can be varied almost at will, namely training costs, advertising and research. However, they would still be regarded as fixed in relation to a 12-month policy.

Correct Use of Cost Information

In using cost information there is the danger of using the wrong cost in a management decision and of not seeing the wood for the trees. Generally, the simple approach is best by taking account of the relevant information and ignoring all irrelevant information. For instance, the use of incremental or differential costs and revenue – those which would change if a decision were taken – avoids having to bother about many other costs and revenue which would not change. The following shows how costs may be used in decision making.

Irrelevance of Historical Costs
Decisions cannot alter the past and are entirely concerned with the future. The monetary information relevant to a decision are expected future costs and revenues, and where appropriate, future capital spending. Historical costs and book values of fixed assets are not relevant. Past figures may be used as a guide to future costs and revenues, but as a guide only. Past costs should not be used in a calculation to help in a decision.

Irrelevance of Some Future Costs
This sounds strange, but in the right context can avoid clouding an issue. A decision involving a comparison of alternative future costs may be hindered by the inclusion of those costs, mainly fixed costs, which in total are not going to be affected by the decision. There is the classic case of the hotel group closing an hotel because it was reckoned to be unprofitable. However, included in its costs was a charge for central administration services which pushed the hotel into the red. The result was that after the closure the group profit fell instead of rising because the central services expenses remained unchanged, and the group lost the surplus of the hotel's income over its own costs. The future expenses of the central services were irrelevant to the decision because in total they were not expected to change.

Decisions Should Improve Group Profit
Although this sounds trite it is easy to overlook. A decision which increases hotel profit may be made at the expense of group profit and similarly an increased department gross profit may reduce hotel profit. It is particularly appropriate to take care when there is inter-company trading requiring internal transfer prices to be set.

Selling Below Cost
A common fallacy is never to sell below cost. It will be seen that long-term prices must be set above cost, but short term, not to be repeated, prices like summer sales in fashion houses may be below cost. Original cost is irrelevant here where stock needs to be moved. Opportunity cost, or the market price becomes the operative cost.

Interest as a Cost
Decisions which involve significant capital spending and change the pattern of future cost and revenues beyond say two years demand that interest on capital be taken into account. A technique known as Discounted Cash Flow (DCF) is now accepted by many as the most appropriate way of dealing with interest in making investment decisions.

Unquantifiable Costs and Benefits

It should always be borne in mind that not all factors bearing on a decision can be quantified. Other factors may be judged to override calculated financial advantages. For example, although it may be shown that hotels receiving convenience food from a subsidiary rather than outside the group involves the group in a loss, this may be acceptable on the grounds that it widens the market for the food and is a form of advertising. The benefits are not quantifiable. Other factors may be convenience, certainty of supplies, helping to keep together a work force.

Value of Accounting Information

The value of information to an organization should exceed the cost of obtaining it. This is undoubtedly a rule which is very difficult to support with figures, because of the subjective nature of 'value' and the difficulty of costing information. Yet consciously or otherwise those in business tend to use this rule, and it is particularly true in management accounting which is essentially concerned with obtaining and presenting economic information to management. The effect of this rule is to constrain the urge in some quarters to amass more and more data, for it does not become information until it is communicated and often too much data means less really gets through as information.

An hotel group which expanded rapidly would be unwise not to introduce a standard system of accounting in which budgets were uniformly prepared and compared with actual results. The value of the improved financial control resulting would be likely to outweigh the cost of operating the system. Lack of financial control information has been the downfall of a number of expanding companies. An instance, however, where the cost exceeds the value is in the area of cost behaviour. An hotel group might spend £100,000 annually in order to set up and operate a system which predicted more accurately than before how each cost would change during the coming year. Its value would be very real in having a more accurate profit plan and cost control data, but the value would be incapable of accurate numerical assessment. This kind of system does not operate in the industry today because it would be regarded as uneconomic. Just to recover the extra annual cost, cost savings of £100,000 per annum would be needed from elsewhere in the group or extra turnover of say £300,000 per annum would be needed as a direct result of the better information provided.

Inevitably cost information in terms of behaviour is a compromise, and judgement is needed to assess the level of accuracy acceptable.

Management Accounting Reports

There are basically two kinds of management accounting report which reflect the different work involved.

Periodic Reports

These are systematically compiled and presented at regular intervals as part of the Budgetary Control System.

Occasional Reports

These are prepared when the occasion demands and usually relate to either 'What would happen to profit if we did this?' kind of question, or reasons for results not conforming to plan, e.g. how has inflation affected budgeted profit?

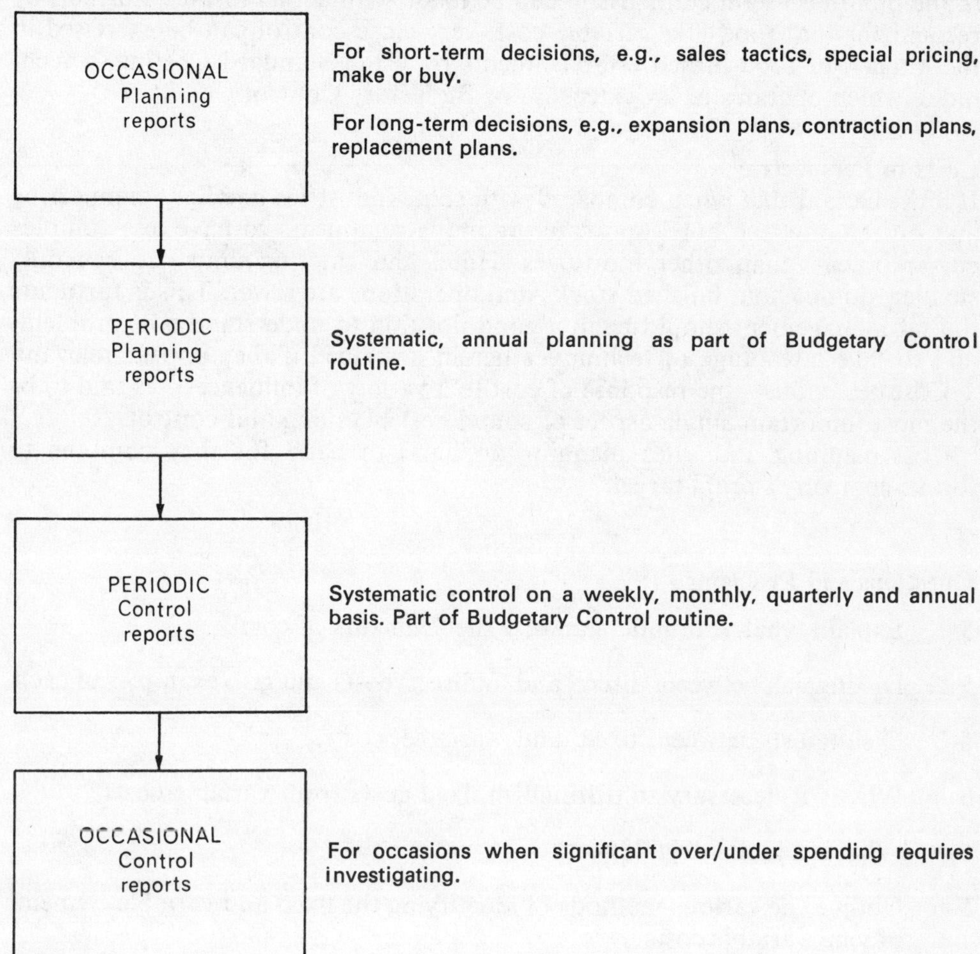

Budgetary Control

(*a*) Planning

It will be seen later than an enterprise needs to plan its operations, revenues and costs for a 12-month period at least, to enable a realistic profit target to be set and acted upon. Knowing the cost behaviour pattern of each cost enables a forecast of costs for each department and for the company to be prepared at different levels of activity. These can then be adjusted to forecast inflation. A monthly operating plan is in this way prepared to cover a 12-month period. A detailed study of this is in Chapter 6.

(*b*) Control

The benefits of a plan do not end with planning. At the end of each month an overall check is required to determine whether costs have matched expectations and by adjusting the planned costs to take account of the actual activity achieved in the month a useful comparison can be made with actual results. Further, by recognizing that food is a variable cost, very close control can be exercised in the kitchen of food-biased establishments by using Standard Costing, a technique which operates as an extension of Budgetary Control.

Costs in Perspective

It must be said that when compared with some industries like light engineering and oil refining, the hotel and catering industry appears to have less complex cost problems than other industries. Hotel and catering units are generally smaller, do not hold finished stocks and operations are fewer. This is fortunate in that management should be in a good position to understand cost problems and to take advantage of techniques herein described if they appear relevant.

Cost behaviour – the response of cost to a variety of influences – is said to be the most important single aspect of sound cost planning and control.

Cost planning and sales planning go hand in hand for they combine to form a company's profit target.

Questions and Problems

5–1 Explain what you understand by the 'elements of cost'.

5–2 Distinguish between 'direct' and 'indirect' costs and give examples of each.

5–3 Distinguish between 'fixed' and 'variable' costs.

5–4 Why is it necessary to distinguish fixed costs from variable costs?

5–5 What is a semi-variable cost?

5–6 Outline the various methods of identifying the fixed and variable elements of semi-variable costs.

5–7 'In the long term all costs are variable'. Explain.

5–8 A prospective client visited a banqueting suite to acquire a suitable menu quotation for his firm's annual dinner. For a single menu he was given the following quotations:

		selling price per head £
Menu 'D'	100 covers	3·00
Menu 'D'	150 covers	2·80
Menu 'D'	200 covers	2·65

Portion size and quality of the food and service being the same in all cases. Explain how it is possible for a banqueting suite to reduce the selling price per head simply because of an increase in the number of covers, and yet maintain the same net profit-to-sales ratio.

5–9 Sketch a graph from which could be read the *cost per unit* at various levels of activity in respect of:

(*a*) variable cost
(*b*) fixed cost
(*c*) total cost

Draw the three cost lines and label each one.

5–10 Below are details of a number of costs:

1. Spirits used up at a constant cost per measure.
2. Electricity charge consisting of a flat basic charge plus a variable charge after a minimum number of units have been used.
3. Depreciation of equipment where the charge is calculated by the straight line method.
4. Salaries of maintenance staff where 1 member of staff is required for 150 bedrooms or less, 2 members of staff for 151–300 bedrooms, 3 members of staff for 301–450 bedrooms and so on.
5. Cost of wine in bulk, where the cost per litre decreases with each litre until a minimum cost per litre is reached.
6. Laundry costs in an hotel which changes all its bedroom linen after each bednight.

You are to match each cost with its relevant graph.

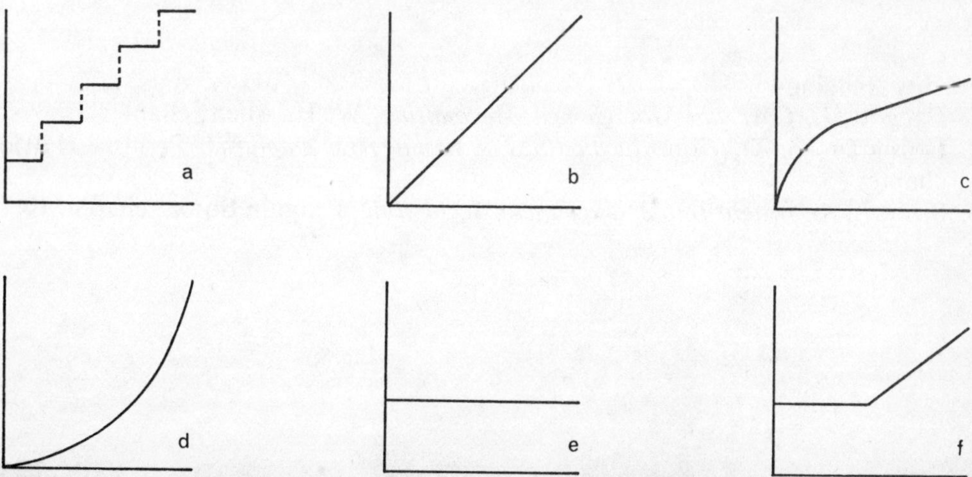

Note: The vertical (y) axis represents total cost and the horizontal (x) axis represents total activity.

5–11 Below are details of a number of costs:

1. Local rates.
2. Gas charge which consists of a standing charge for the service itself plus a variable charge per unit, for all units used.
3. Food used up in the preparation of meals at a constant cost per kilo.
4. Wages of banqueting waiters where 1 waiter is required for every 10 covers or less, 2 waiters for 11–20 covers, 3 waiters for 21–30 covers etc.
5. Rental of taped music equipment.

Sketch five graphs (not necessarily to scale) to match each of the five costs.

5–12 The following table shows the production quantities and related total costs of a company manufacturing a single product

Period	*Production Units*	*Total Cost*
1	1,500	£2,600
2	1,800	£3,256
3	2,500	£4,560
4	3,200	£5,800

Using the index 100 to represent cost levels in Period 1, the following indices apply to succeeding periods

Period 2	110
3	120
4	125

On the basis of the foregoing you are required to calculate the total costs to be expected in Period 5 during which production of 4,000 units is planned and the cost level index is expected to be 135.

Further Reading

1. Baggott, J., *Cost and Management Accounting*, W. H. Allen; chapter 3.
2. Horngren, C. T., *Cost Accounting: A managerial emphasis*, Prentice-Hall; chapter 25.
3. Sizer, J., *An Insight Into Management Accounting*, Penguin Books, chapter 10.

CHAPTER SIX

BUDGETARY PLANNING

Budgetary Control

One accepted definition of budgetary control is:

(*a*) the establishment of budgets relating the responsibility of executives to the requirement of a policy, and

(*b*) the continuous comparison of actual and budgeted results,

(*c*) either to secure by individual action the objective of that policy,

(*d*) or to provide a basis for its (the budget) revision.

Any definition contains the same essential ingredients,

PLANNING
COMPARING } CONTROL
ACTION }

The following chart (Exhibit 6–1) illustrates this definition and shows that

Exhibit 6–1

OUTLINE BUDGETARY CONTROL CHART

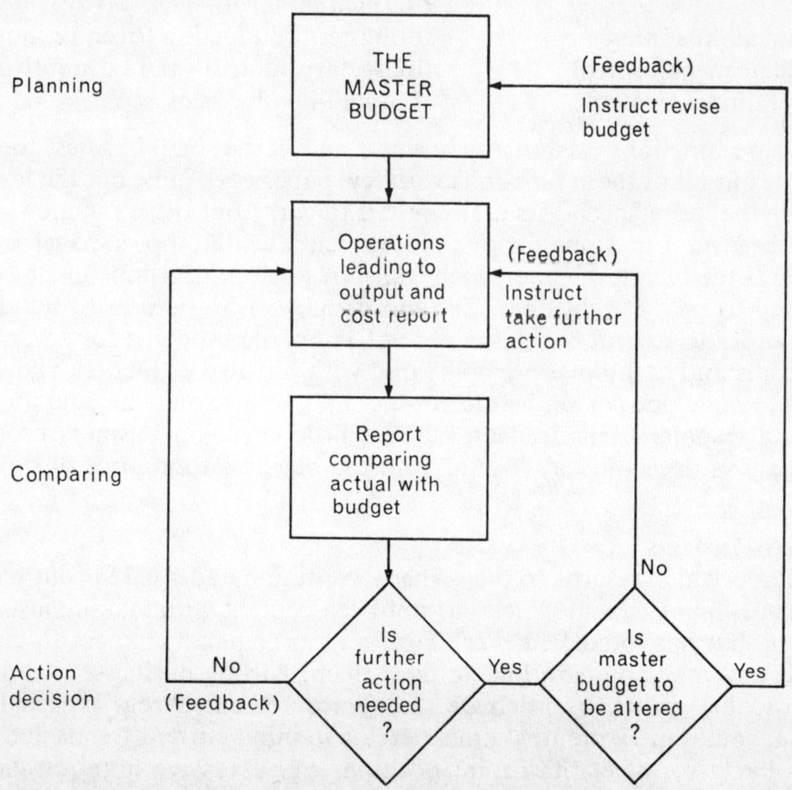

feedback is designed to trigger off action by advising the planners to change the budget or the operating personnel to take remedial action.

The approach made in considering budgetary control is to explain the planning side in this chapter and control aspects in the following chapter.

Planning Levels

Three planning levels are operated in the successful business, viz:

Strategic planning which is concerned with the objectives of the enterprise and the long-range plans required to achieve such objectives. Top management takes strategic planning decisions.

Management control which concerns middle management obtaining and employing resources effectively within the framework of strategic planning decisions.

Operational planning and control which is concerned with planning day-to-day work capable of fairly close control.

These levels concern general management and are introduced here to put budgetary control in perspective. The following is an attempt to equate these levels with Financial Management and Management Accounting work and it will be seen that only the lowest level is outside our terms of reference.

		Accounting involvement
Strategic planning	—	Long-term budgeting (over 12 months)
Management control	—	Budgetary control – the 12-month cycle
Operational control	—	Limited involvement

The above functions exist in any business and in the small business the owner may carry out all of these functions with few paperwork aids, but the larger the enterprise the more specialists are required to carry out these functions.

It has been said that one factor that differentiates the top manager from the operative is the length of time which transpires before decisions made by them are proved to be the right ones. The top manager who decides to build a new hotel in order to extend business does not know the outcome for several years when profits and cash flows are compared with his own estimates. The waiter's decision to serve one person before another may be a wrong one, and there is an immediate response. His decision has but little effect on business profit. The top manager's decision may lose or gain the business thousands of pounds.

Long-Term Budgets

The business which returns to the owner a continuing adequate profit will most likely have a management which has not been content with making just day-to-day plans, but has looked further ahead and anticipated changes in customer demands and made preparations to meet them. Airline businesses would go to the wall if they failed to anticipate the number of passengers expected to use particular routes in 12 months' time, bearing in mind current trends and known changes likely to affect the future position, e.g. extensive hotel development where passengers disembark. Besides, new aircraft have to be ordered years in advance of delivery making it essential that plans are laid in good time.

We see here the basis of two important forecasts, that of sales and of aircraft (capital equipment), required in the airline industry. Yet a business with relatively static sales, such as a biscuit manufacturer needs to forecast sales and indeed to influence sales, so that the most profitable sales mix is achieved. New lines may have to be introduced requiring experiment and the purchase of capital equipment. Unless profitable opportunities are taken by a business, competitors will take advantage of them.

The significance of the long-term planning function depends upon the industry and size of business within the industry. The huge airline corporations rely on expensively produced long- and short-term plans, whereas the smaller charter aircraft business may flourish with less sophisticated planning. So with the hotel and catering industry, the large hotel group requires relatively more and elaborate planning than the small restaurant.

Several forecasts, each covering sales, capital expenditure, finance and profit would be provided by the planners for a period of say five years, but based on different assumptions as to sales levels and gross margins, possible hotel sites, and methods of financing the expansion. The board of directors will satisfy themselves that one of the forecasts is likely to best carry forward their strategic plan and they would make this forecast the basis of their policy for the next five years. The forecast has become a budget because it is now the company's policy to carry out the plans contained in the forecast. This long-term budget will inevitably be only approximate and will be altered from year to year, but it is a target that the top management will constantly have in their sights, confident that when it was made it was the best available, and certainly a feasible one.

The foregoing applies to the larger enterprise, although the management of the smaller business will still consider possible changes in the next few years, but their sales, profit and capital expenditure projections may not be formalized as budgets, only recorded as memoranda to be considered when appropriate.

The first year of the five-year budget will be used to guide the planners in preparing the short-term 12-month budget which is the start of detailed budgetary control procedures.

Limiting Factors

The top manager's decision is part of a long-term plan which usually involves changes in the company's interest in fixed assets whereby a forecast demand for rooms in a district is satisfied by the building and operation of an hotel. Here we see a forecast of sales and a forecast of capital expenditure, which would demand a forecast of finance to ensure cash was available.

The planning function of the hotel group will consider factors likely to affect the industry generally in the coming few years, such as accelerated economic growth of the country; upward movement in family income groups leading to more discretionary spending power; increase in number of married women workers; increased mobility of population and increase in numbers of tourists.

The planners would then consider how these factors would affect the hotel group's turnover and profit. They would quickly discover one or more limiting factors, this is to say factors the extent of whose influence must be first assessed in order to ensure that other parts of the plan are reasonably capable of fulfilment. A sudden boom in trade would result in accommodation being the limiting factor, a situation which arose in London in 1969 when several million more visitors arrived than were expected. This limiting factor was partially overcome following requests by the B.T.A. for people outside the industry to put up those failing to find accommodation in hotels. Relating this to the business it can be seen that it is an important function of management to anticipate a limiting factor and to eliminate it, although inevitably another one takes its place.

In the long term, sales will be the limiting factor so that sales will be the first forecast, followed by the capital expenditure which will provide the facilities required to achieve the forecast sales. At the same time finance will be forecast to provide for the purchase or lease of the facilities. Besides sales other limiting factors may be space for accommodation or seating, labour of the right kind, finance for expansion, or even management itself may be a limiting factor in that it has not the capacity to meet the demands of the business.

Short-Term Budgets

The immediate few months ahead are of vital interest to all management and detailed plans would be prepared covering such matters as staff recruitment, equipment replacement, maintenance, advertising, food and accommodation pricing, stock levels, banking arrangements to name some of the items to be considered. One proven method of seeing that these arrangements are co-ordinated and comprehensive is to express them in monetary form; in other words a budget is produced. This we have seen is a plan to assist in the direction of resources and trading activities of a business in order to achieve a given objective and can be used to assist in the control of resources and activities.

A convenient period for a budget is 12 months since this covers a full cycle of activities; is a short enough period to plan in detail; and coincides with the period for which annual accounts must be presented to shareholders.

The greatest benefit is derived from budgeting when:

1. It embraces the whole of the enterprise so that the management plan is stated in the form of a budgeted profit and loss statement, balance sheet, and funds statement.
2. It is used to assist managers in the control of business operations by showing them periodically – say monthly – the variances of actual from budgeted results for which they are responsible.

In circumstances when these two points apply, budgetary control may be said to operate. This implies that there is a formal routine laid down, possibly in a budget manual, to ensure that budgets are properly prepared in correct sequence; at the right time; in the proper form; whenever possible in quantity before being converted into monetary form; and are formally approved by the chief executive. After approval the budgeted profit and loss statement, balance sheet and funds statement may be termed the master budget.

Cash Budgeting

An important point to appreciate is that no plan of operations is complete unless sufficient cash is on hand at all times to meet obligations resulting from the plan. A proper balance between available and required cash is one of the most important requirements for sound financial management, indicating a clear need for a cash budget or forecast in some form. Only when all other budgets have been prepared is it feasible to produce a cash budget except in those very small concerns which operate only on a cash basis and therefore have no integrated budget system.

A quick method of budgeting cash at the end of a budget period is to budget all items in the balance sheet except cash, and the balancing figure will represent cash, a matter of deduction. However, this result should be supplemented by a month-by-month cash budget based on the receipts and payments dictated by the requirements of the other budgets of a business. A convenient layout is used on pages 77 and 78 in which an 'operating cash budget', showing a surplus or deficit of cash arising from current operations involving revenue rather than capital items is followed up by a 'financial budget', comprising all other receipts and payments, such as rent receivable, capital expenditure, taxation, etc.

A further method of budgeting for cash is to use the funds flow method demonstrated in Chapter 14.

A cash budget is seen to be a very important part of the budgetary planning procedure, for a shortage of cash might threaten the business with liquidation and on the other hand too much cash for any length of time is wasteful.

Comprehensive Example

The following example shows how in the budgetary control process one starts with the present financial position as shown by the balance sheet and by applying planned changes, can derive budgeted end-of-year statements.

Question

The Golden Hotel Co. Ltd. plan to enlarge a restaurant at a cost of £8,000 for kitchen plant and furnishings in order to make use of rooms not at present utilized. This money, to be funded from cash generated by the company, will be required to be paid out on 31st March, 1979, and a full year's depreciation (£800) will be charged in the year. Arrangements have been made with their bankers for the present overdraft facilities of up to £1,000 to be extended to £8,000 for twelve months from 1st April, 1979, after which time the maximum will revert to £1,000.

Budgetary control is operated by management and from the following details they require:

(*a*) Budgeted profit and loss statement for year 31st December, 1979
(*b*) Budgeted balance sheet as at 31st December, 1979
(*c*) Cash budget for months of January, February and March, 1979

Budget details:

Budgeted Sales	*Jan. 79*	*Feb. 79*	*Mar. 79*	*Full year 1979*
	£	£	£	£
Accommodation	3,600	3,600	4,000	50,000
Food	2,500	2,600	2,800	40,000
Liquor	4,500	4,700	5,000	60,000
Other sales	250	250	250	3,000
Budgeted other income	—	—	100	300

Note 1. 25% of accommodation sales are on credit and one month is the average period of credit.
2. Total accommodation sales in December 1978 was £4,000.
3. No credit is allowed for food, liquor and other sales.

Budgeted Credit Purchases (one month average)
Food cost is 38% of sales revenue
Liquor cost is 50% of sales revenue
Other sales cost is 40% of sales revenue.

	Jan. 79	*Feb. 79*	*Mar. 79*	*Full Year 1979*
Budgeted Cash Costs	£	£	£	£
Wages and staff expenses	3,500	3,500	3,600	43,000
Departmental expenses	1,000	1,000	1,100	15,000
Heat, light and power	1,800	—	—	6,000
Administration	500	500	500	6,000
Advertising	2,000	2,000	1,000	5,000
Operational expenses	100	80	80	1,000
Rates and insurance		—	400	1,600
Repairs and maintenance	200	200	200	2,000
Other expenses	—	—	200	400

Balance Sheet Items
Land and buildings valuation, stocks and debtors are budgeted to be the same figures at 31st December, 1979, as 1st January, 1979. Plant, furniture and equipment to be depreciated 10%. Creditors are to be allowed to increase by 10% in the year.

Staff Accommodation Expenses
Wages and staff expenses shown under Budgeted Cash costs do not include staff accommodation expenses, budgeted at £1,000 for the year.

Balance Sheet as at 31st December, 1978

Employment of Capital	Cost £	Cumulative Depreciation £	£
Fixed Assets			
Freehold land and buildings at valuation 1.12.66	80,000		80,000
Plant, furniture and equipment	22,000	9,000	13,000
	102,000	9,000	93,000
Current Assets			
Stocks at cost	3,500		
Debtors	1,000		
Cash at bank and in hand	12,000		
		16,500	
Current Liabilities			
Corporation Tax payable 1.1.79	7,000		
Creditors	4,200		
Proposed final dividends – gross	3,500		
		14,700	1,800
			94,800
Capital Employed			
Share Capital – 70,000 ordinary shares of £1 each authorized, issued and fully paid			70,000
Revenue Reserve			14,800
Corporation tax payable 1.1.80			10,000
			94,800

Solution

Budgeted Profit & Loss Statement for year ended 31st December, 1979

	Sales £	Cost of Sales £	Gross Profit £
Rooms	50,000	—	50,000
Food	40,000	15,200	24,800
Liquor	60,000	30,000	30,000
Other sales	3,000	1,200	1,800
	153,000	46,400	106,600

Deduct: Operating Expenses		
Wages and staff expenses	44,000	
Departmental expenses	15,000	
Heat, light and power	6,000	
Administration	6,000	
Advertising	5,000	
Operational expenses	1,000	
		77,000
HOTEL OPERATING PROFIT		29,600
Deduct: Property Expenses		
Rates and insurances	1,600	
Repairs and maintenance	2,000	
Depreciation	3,000	
		6,600
		23,000
Add: Staff accommodation adjustment		1,000
HOTEL NET OPERATING PROFIT		24,000
Deduct: Other Expenses/Income		
Expenses	400	
Income	300	
		100
NET PROFIT		23,900
Provision for Corporation Tax		10,800
		13,100
Ordinary Dividends 10%		7,000
Retained profit for the year		6,100

Budgeted Balance Sheet as at 31st December, 1979

Employment of Capital	*Cost*	*Accumulated Depreciation*	
Fixed Assets	£	£	£
Freehold land and buildings at valuation 1.12.72	80,000	—	80,000
Plant, furniture and equipment	30,000	12,000	18,000
	110,000	12,000	98,000
Current Assets			
Stocks at cost		3,500	
Debtors		1,000	
Cash at bank and in hand (balancing figure)		17,110	
		21,610	
Current Liabilities			
Corporation tax payable 1.1.80	10,000		
Creditors	4,410		
Proposed final dividend – gross	3,500		
		17,910	3,700
			101,700
Capital Employed			
Share Capital – 70,000 ordinary shares of £1 each authorized, issued and fully paid			70,000
Revenue reserve balance 1.1.79		14,800	
Profit for the year retained		6,100	
			20,900
Corporation tax payable 1.1.81			10,800
			101,700

Cash Budget – three months to 31*st March*, 1979

	January	*February*	*March*
	£	£	£
Receipts			
Sales: Rooms – credit	1,000	900	900
– cash	2,700	2,700	3,000
Food	2,500	2,600	2,800
Liquor	4,500	4,700	5,000
Other sales	250	250	250
Non-operating income	—	—	100
	10,950	11,150	12,050

Payments			
Food and liquor	4,200	3,300	3,440
Wages and staff expenses	3,500	3,500	3,600
Departmental expenses	1,000	1,000	1,100
Heat, light and power	1,800	—	—
Administration	500	500	500
Advertising	2,000	2,000	1,000
Operational expenses	100	80	80
Rates and insurance	—	—	400
Repairs and maintenance	200	200	200
Taxation	7,000	—	—
Ordinary dividend	3,500	—	—
Capital expenditure	—	—	8,000
Other non-operating expenses	—	—	200
	23,800	10,580	18,520
Monthly surplus/(deficit)	(12,850)	570	(6,470)
Opening cash surplus/(deficit)	12,000	(850)	(280)
Closing cash surplus/(deficit)	(850)	(280)	(6,750)

Notes: 1. The monthly cash budget indicates that a cash deficit of nearly £7,000 is expected in early April. If the second quarter's figures were available a cash surplus would probably appear as turnover went up in the spring and summer. The annual payment of taxation would not recur until 1980.

2. The relatively high cash balance at the end of each year has been planned in anticipation of early payment of taxation and dividends.

3. The cash budget may be separated into two sections. One section may cover operations, showing an operating cash surplus or deficit and the other taking account of the total cumulative position by including taxation and other non-operating cash payments and receipts. This would highlight the expectation of an operating cash surplus for March of £1,630 but a deterioration in the cash balance of £6,470 in the month caused mainly by capital spending.

Budgeting Principles

The amount of recorded detail involved will depend upon the size of the undertaking and generally speaking the larger business will require the more detailed, formal plans to aid communication and co-ordination between personnel. As with profit-motivated work of all kinds, the cost of producing desired results should be related to the value to the undertaking of the results obtained, whether the results be meals or figures to aid management. It is likely that detailed budgeting is not economic for the very small establishment, however an understanding of what budgets and budgetary control mean will enable the manager of the smaller unit to adapt the principles to his needs.

A basic principle of budgeting which should be carried out wherever feasible is that one should first establish physical quantity of work required to be done before calculating the revenue and cost. This is obviously necessary when starting a business and should be considered at annual budgeting time. This principle might be applied to sales turnover, cost of food, staff gearing for functions, maintenance and other work contracted out.

Another budgeting principle is that responsibility which is delegated to personnel should include responsibility for sales revenue and controllable costs, where this is appropriate, and that personnel should participate in preparing the budget of the functions or activity for which they accept responsibility.

The more complex the budgeting, the more it costs to run the system. As one wants value for money, each size of business will require a budgetary control system tailor-made to its own needs.

Budgetary Planning Procedures

The exhibits which follow are designed to illustrate budgetary planning procedures and in particular how budgets tie in with one another. With modifications the procedure could be applied to any size of hotel, but it must be borne in mind that a prerequisite is a well-classified and possibly coded set of accounts, which will provide current figures in the right form to assist in the preparation of budgets.

Sales revenue budget

This important budget sets the pattern for all other budgets and is influenced by planned work to be done, e.g. catering for numbers of customers, and the pricing policy of management. Sales revenue forecasts for food, liquor and other sales which precede the budget, are of only limited value until they are related to cost of goods sold and the resulting gross profit. With the same floor space available as the previous year, it is management's job to attract more customers to fill any surplus capacity and/or to alter the balance of space usage so that turnover, which attracts the greatest gross margin, is increased at the expense of lower gross margin work. The relative combination of the quantities of a variety of products that make up total sales is known as 'sales mix'. The alternative is to increase facilities, although care is needed to see that the extra demand does in fact exist, or is capable of being created by sales promotion.

Experience is all important in forecasting sales, although statistical method involving trend analysis may be found useful.

Food and liquor cost budget

Cost of food, liquor and other sales being variable costs are determined by multiplying turnover by the expected percentage of cost to turnover. For instance, if one plans for a food turnover of £40,000 and an expected food cost of 40% of turnover, then budgeted food cost will be £16,000 and gross margin £24,000 or 60% of turnover.

Wages and staff expenses budget

This cost budget is very important since it may amount to 30% of the value of sales turnover and is largely a controllable cost. For each budget centre there will be prepared a detailed budget, as Exhibit 6–2, and summarized to give total wages and staff expenses for the business, as Exhibit 6–3. Comparisons with the estimated actual costs for the current year will highlight any significant planned increases or decreases in costs.

Where variable costs are budgeted the level of activity to which they relate should be stated to assist in the control of such costs in the budget period.

The wages and staff expenses budgets illustrated provide for details which help towards more accurate estimating, but which may be omitted to save preparation time, so long as accuracy is not significantly affected.

Departmental expenses budget

Departmental expenses should be budgeted for budget centres with reference to the previous year's expenses, and more important in relation to the expectations of the budget period. For example, in Exhibit 6–4 there may have been £50 spent on protective clothing for the maintenance personnel late in the previous year and knowing that this clothing is almost new, only £20 may be budgeted for replacements in the budget year.

The budgeted departmental expenses may then be summarized as Exhibit 6–6, in preparation for inclusion in the budgeted profit and loss statement.

Budget centre budgets

The preparation of budgets for sales revenue, food and liquor costs, wages and staff expenses and departmental expenses coincides with the preparation of departmental or budget centre budgets. Budget centres are used for budgeting and may conveniently relate to departments, the essential point being that a person is responsible for the activities and financial results of a budget centre.

A cost centre is defined on page 140 and in many cases it may be regarded as a budget centre. In large establishments food and liquor budget centres will be further broken down into banqueting rooms and bars budgets. Chapter 10 deals with the classification of departments for accounting purposes.

Each budget centre budget (e.g. Exhibit 6–4) consists of any wages, staff expenses and departmental expenses which are capable of being directly related to the centre. Additionally, operated (revenue earning) centres will have budgeted revenue included and therefore budgeted profit. At this stage in the budget preparation there will be a profit (or loss) known variously as Hotel Operating Profit (Exhibit 10–2) or Responsibility Profit (Exhibit 6–7), revenue and costs so far being largely controllable.

Simply prepared budgets will be required for such remaining expenses as rates, insurance, depreciation, 'other expenses and income' and for capital expenditure.

Exhibit 6–2

GOLDEN HOTELS LTD.—WAGES AND STAFF EXPENSES BUDGET FOR 1980
BANQUETING MANAGER

Personnel	Fixed or Variable Cost	Rate	No. Persons	TOTAL	Salaries and Wages	O/time	Nat. Ins.	Staff Foods	Staff Acc.	Misc. Staff Expenses
				£	£	£	£	£	£	£
Manager	F									
Head waiter	F									
Head wine waiter	F									
Waiters (casual)	V									
Wine waiters (casual)	V									
Porters	F									
1980 BUDGET				10,000*						
1979 Estimated Actual										

REMARKS	Variable costs are based on Sales of £ for the year

Prepared by	Date	Approved by	Date

* Transferred to Banqueting Budget (not illustrated) also Wages and Staff Expenses Summary Budget.

Exhibit 6–3

GOLDEN HOTELS LTD.

WAGES AND STAFF EXPENSES SUMMARY BUDGET FOR 1980

1979 Estimated Actual No. Persons	1979 Estimated Actual TOTAL	BUDGET CENTRE	No. Persons	TOTAL	Salaries and Wages	O/time	Nat. Ins.	Staff Food	Staff Acc.	Misc. Staff Expenses
	£			£	£	£	£	£	£	£
		Accommodation								
		General								
		Reception								
		Porterage								
		Linen room								
		Housekeeping								
		Food, Liquor & Tobacco								
		Kitchen								
		Restaurant								
		Banqueting rooms		10,000*						
		Bars								
		Cellars								
		Other Hotel Sales								
		Telephone								
		Cloaks								
		Administration								
		Gen. manager's office								
		Book-keeping								
		Operational expenses								
		Heat, light & power								
		Marketing								
		Repairs & maintenance		2,900†						
		TOTALS		60,000‡						

REMARKS

Prepared by	*Date*	*Approved by*	*Date*

* From Banqueting Budget † From Repairs and Maintenance Budget ‡ To Budgeted Profit & Loss Statement

Exhibit 6–4

REPAIRS AND MAINTENANCE BUDGET FOR 1980

1979 Estimated Actual £			1980 Budget £
	WAGES AND STAFF EXPENSES (Detailed on right)		2,900*
	Departmental Expenses		
	Hire charges	50	
	Laundry	30	
50	Protective clothing	20	
	Building repairs (outside work	200	
		—	300†
			3,200

REMARKS

Prepared by	*Date*	*Approved by*	*Date*

* To Wages & Staff Expenses Summary Budget
† To Departmental Summary Budget.

Exhibit 6–5

DETAILED WAGES AND STAFF EXPENSES BUDGET

WAGES & STAFF EXPENSES ANALYSIS	*Rate*	*No. Persons*	TOTAL	*S. & W.*	*N.I.*	*Staff Food*	*Staff Acc.*
			£	£	£	£	£
Manager Assistant							
1980 BUDGET			2,900				
1979 ESTIMATED ACTUAL							

REMARKS

Exhibit 6–6

DEPARTMENTAL EXPENSES SUMMARY BUDGET FOR 1980

1979 Estimated Actual	(Sample items only)	TOTAL	Accom-modation	Food	Liquor and Tobacco	Other Hotel Sales	Heat Light & Power	Adminis-tration	Marketing	Operational	Repairs and Maintenance
£		£	£	£	£	£	£	£	£	£	£
	Banqueting expenses	x		x	x						
	Bar equipment replacement	x			x						
	Bar supplies	x			x						
	Building repairs (outside work)	x									200
	Contract cleaning	x	x	x	x						
	China & crockery replacement	x	x	x							
	Directories	x				x					
	Dry cleaning	x	x	x	x						
	Guest supplies	x	x	x	x						
	Hire charges	x	x	x	x						50
	Kitchen equipment replacement	x		x							
	Laundry	x	x	x	x						30
	Linen replacement	x	x	x	x						
	Menus & wine lists	x		x	x						
	Rental of T.V., etc.	x	x								
	Silverware replacement	x		x	x						
	Uniforms & protective clothing	x	x	x	x	x	x	x	x	x	20
	Vending machine expenses	x			x	x					
	1980 BUDGET	20,000*									300†
	1979 ESTIMATED ACTUAL										

* To Budgeted Profit & Loss Statement.

† From Repairs and Maintenance Budget. To Budgeted Profit & Loss Statement.

GOLDEN HOTELS—BUDGETED PROFIT AND LOSS STATEMENT FOR 1980

	1980								ESTIMATED 1979				
	Sales	*Cost of Sales*	*G.P.*	*Wages and Staff Expenses*	*Wages/ Sales*	*Departmental Expenses*	*Profit (Loss)*	*% of Sales*	*Sales*	*G.P.*	*Wages*	*Profit*	
	£	£	%	£	%	£	£		£	%	%	%	£
OPERATED DEPARTMENTS													
Accommodation	x			x	x	x	x	x	x		x	x	x
Food	x	x	x	x	x	x	x	x	x	x	x	x	x
Liquor	x	x	x	x	x	x	x	x	x	x	x	x	x
Other sales	x	x	x	x	x	x	x	x	x	x	x	x	x
TOTAL	x	x	x	x	x	x	x	x	x	x	x	x	x
Operating Income	x						x	x	x			x	x
OPERATING PROFIT							x	x				x	x
Heat, light & power						x							
Administration				x	x	x					x		
Marketing						x							
Operational expenses						x					x		
Repairs & maintenance				2,900*	x	300*							
				x	x	20,000†					x	x	x
RESPONSIBILITY PROFIT							x	x				x	x
Rent, rates & insurance						x						x	x
Depreciation						x						x	x
						x	x	x					
	x	x	x	60,000‡	x	x	x	x				x	x
Add: Staff accommodation							x	x				x	x
Other Expenses and Income						(−) or (+)	x	x				x	x
NET PROFIT							x	x				x	x

* From Repairs & Maintenance Budget. † From Departmental Summary Budget. ‡ From Wages & Staff Expenses Budget.

Profit and loss budget

The revenue and expenses budgets need now to be amalgamated to form the profit and loss budget as Exhibit 6–7. Adjustments have to be made for staff accommodation expenses and other expenses and income before the budgeted net profit is arrived at.

It has been stated that forecasts precede budgets, and practice varies as to how many adjustments are made to a forecast profit and loss statement before the management is satisfied that the net profit is the right target for the next year. Forms such as those illustrated may be used for forecasting and are especially useful for budgets if they contain the previous year's estimated actual figures.

It must be appreciated that as the budgeting takes place before the end of that year an estimation of the expenses for the last month or two must be made and added to the latest actual figures available.

Budgeted balance sheet and cash budget

These two budgets complete the budgetary planning operation. However, a balance sheet needs to be prepared to show the expected position at the beginning of the budget period and, as explained, this would include estimated actual figures only. Further information to produce the budgeted balance sheet required, apart from budgets already mentioned, will be end of year stocks, debtors, creditors and any changes on capital account or on loan account.

The cash budget, as earlier explained, may be produced in a number of ways, depending upon whether or not a monthly figure is required.

Budgeting Inflation

Rapid inflation in the early 1970s encouraged some organizations to alter their budgeting procedures to take into account inflation as a separate factor. Large companies have specialists at head office who predict price level changes of specific cost items. Other cost items subject to local variation such as local authority rates, are forecast at local unit level. This means that budgets may be prepared initially assuming no price changes, and conversion factors may then be used to allow for predicted inflation.

If wages and staff costs for 1979 had been £43,000 and no staffing changes were expected in 1980, a forecast average increase for inflation of 10% would set the budget at £47,300 (£43,000 × 1·10). If the rise in local rates were expected to be no more than 5%, then a 1979 actual cost of £800 would become a 1980 budget of £840 (£800 × 1·05). This would be done for significant items only to avoid too much clerical effort.

Although such price rises are largely outside the control of management, the exercise does serve the purpose of helping to budget the financial outcome of the coming year. In addition, from the control viewpoint, variance calculations in the next chapter show the advantage in isolating the cost of actual compared with forecast changes in food prices.

A general benefit stems from the exercise of budgeting inflation. The manager is constantly encouraged to have his eyes on the future and to try to anticipate changes in customer demand and other changes. Anticipating price changes is one part of this forward looking attitude about which management accounting is so much concerned. Anticipating events allows a better chance to take evasive action when adverse conditions are expected, and to take advantage of favourable conditions that are expected. Examples are negotiating a bank overdraft when cash is forecast to be short, and finding an alternative supplier when a commodity is expected to be in short supply or unacceptably expensive.

Summary

Any commercial organization has a plan of operations and should have a profit target. Budgeting translates operating plans into accounting language and relates them to financial objectives. The operating plans originate in such areas as marketing, food production, personnel, accommodation, which constitute the non-financial aspects of management. These plans are then translated into revenues, costs, assets, and liabilities, which are summarized in the form of financial statements. A reasonable return on investment may be regarded as the overall financial goal and the evaluated plan must be seen to achieve this end. Budgeting and, in particular, budgetary control is potentially management's most useful and necessary tool.

The paper work involved in budgeting is to quantify and to integrate plans, an exercise which requires co-ordination of all personnel in any supervisory capacity. Discussing and eventually agreeing plans leads to a smoother working relationship at the manager/supervisor level.

Continuous or Rolling Budget

Preparation of budgets once a year covering a 12-month period has been a natural development of financial accounting practice. It makes sense to plan operations for a financial year and to alter plans at the 6-monthly stage if necessary. However, towards the end of the financial year the next annual budget is being prepared and at this stage only about 2 months of plans remain. Recognizing the disadvantages of discreet 12-month plans, some enterprises now prepare continuous or rolling budgets to ensure that at the end of each month or quarter there is a full 12-month budget in front of their management. This is done by replacing the month or quarter just elapsed with a budget for a similar period added to what remains of the present budget.

Dynamic Forecasting

Dramatic and sudden changes in the economic scene caused by inflation and material shortages need quicker responses by business to such environmental factors. To meet these situations some companies now revise the whole of their 12-month forecast, every month, after taking into account events of the month just elapsed. They therefore have two forecasts going at the same time and naturally the revised one is the more accurate. The advantage is that marketing management are motivated into constantly looking into the future and finding ways of getting back on target as represented by their original forecast. Although the original forecast would have been linked with the budget, the revised forecast would not relate to the budget. Should the revised forecast become so different from the original one it would then be used to revise the 12-month budget.

Questions and Problems

6–1 Explain the terms 'budgeting' and 'budgetary control'.

6–2 What is a continuous budget?

6–3 'Too many department heads think that budgets represent a penny-pinching, negative brand of managerial pressure'. Cost Accounting, a managerial emphasis by Charles T. Horngren. Discuss this statement.

6–4 Why is the sales budget considered to be such an important element in budgetary planning?

6–5 Explain how an hotel housekeeping budget may be prepared and how it fits into the overall budgetary control plan.

6–6 Your catering organization has decided to introduce a comprehensive system of budgetary control. As a first step it has been agreed to form a budget committee, and you have been requested to prepare a report for your managing director on the functions of such a committee and who should serve on it.

6–7 You have recently been appointed manager of a medium sized hotel. The firm operates a very simple system of budgetary control, in that at the beginning of each quarter the managing director, without consultation, sets financial targets in respect of revenue and of expenditure for all departments of the hotel. In order to stimulate the director's interest in management techniques and aids, you have been passing over to him your copies of *The Caterer's Journal* each month. In one edition there appeared the flow chart opposite depicting part of the budgeting process. The managing director has asked you to prepare a memorandum commenting on each of the stages on the flow chart. Your comments should indicate whether you think each stage is necessary, and in so far as they appear to differ from the present system, what benefits could be expected to accrue if those stages with which you agree were introduced into the hotel.

6–8 Describe the organization and operation of a system of budgetary control, emphasizing the importance of human factors in enabling the system to be effective.

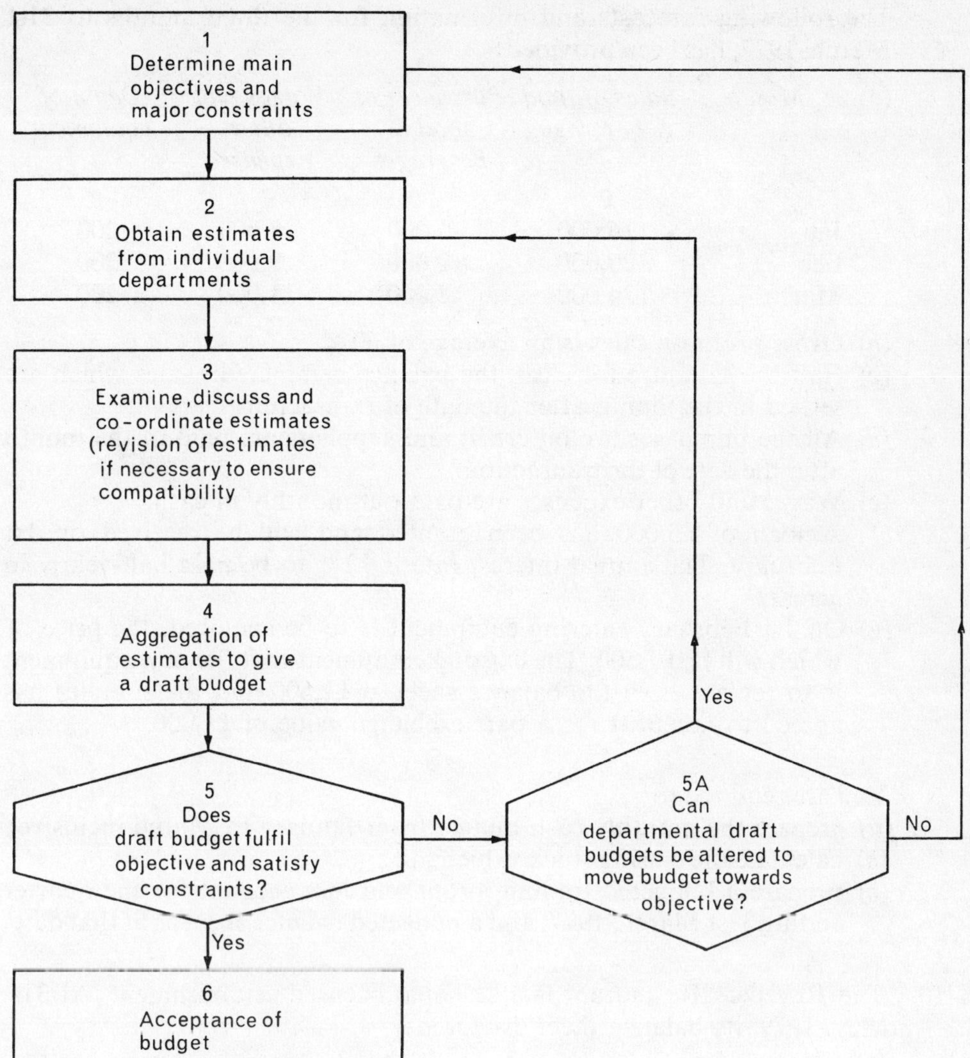

6–9 The Beach Restaurant is a seasonal licensed establishment. On 31st December, 1976, its balance sheet disclosed:

	£		£
Capital	50,000	Freehold property	30,000
Trade creditors	4,600	Equipment	12,500
		Stocks	9,200
		Debtors	2,000
		Cash at bank	900
	54,600		54,600

The following forecasts and information for the three months to 31st March, 1977, has been provided:

(*a*)

Month	*Sales of food & beverages*	*Purchases of food & beverages*	*Wages and other expenses*	*Dep'n of equipment*
	£	£	£	£
Jan	16,000	9,000	8,000	200
Feb	20,000	10,000	9,000	200
Mar	24,000	8,000	11,000	200

(*b*) Gross profit on sales is an average of 60%.

(*c*) Half the sales are for cash, the balance being credit sales which are settled in the month after the date of transaction.

(*d*) All the purchases are on credit and suppliers are paid in the month after the date of the transaction.

(*e*) Wages and other expenses are paid out monthly in cash.

(*f*) A loan of £5,000 has been granted and will be received on 1st February. The annual interest rate is 12% to be paid half-yearly in arrears.

(*g*) On 1st February catering equipment is to be acquired, the price of which will be £7,500. The existing equipment that the new equipment is to replace is in the balance sheet at £1,500 and the supplier has agreed to accept it for a part exchange value of £1,000.

You are required to:

(*a*) prepare the monthly cash budget from January to March inclusive;

(*b*) calculate the closing stock value; and

(*c*) prepare a budgeted trading, profit and loss account for the quarter ending 31st March, 1977, and a budgeted balance sheet as at that date.

6–10 The Revellers Restaurant is a seasonal licensed establishment. At 31st May, 1979, its balance sheet disclosed:

	£		£	£
Capital	40,000	Freehold property		26,200
Trade creditors	5,200	Plant, fixtures, etc.		12,000
Rent received in advance	500		£	
		Stock – Food	800	
		Beverages	4,000	
				4,800
		Debtors		2,000
		Cash at bank		700
	45,700			45,700

The budget committee has provided the following forecasts and information for the three months to 31st August, 1979:

Month	Sales		Stock Purchases of		Wages and Other Expenses	Depreciation of Plant
	Food	Beverages	Food	Beverages		
	£	£	£	£	£	£
June	12,000	4,400	6,500	2,000	8,000	100
July	15,000	5,000	7,000	2,200	9,250	100
August	18,000	5,600	8,500	2,500	10,750	100

Additional information:

(*a*) The gross profit on (i) food sales is 50%;
(ii) beverage sales is $66\frac{2}{3}$%.

(*b*) Three-quarters of the sales of food and beverages are for cash; the balance represents credit sales which are settled in the month after the date of the transaction.

(*c*) All stock purchases are on credit; the suppliers are paid in the month after the date of the transaction.

(*d*) Rent is received from shopkeeper tenants who pay at quarterly intervals in advance, on 1st August, 1st November, 1st February, and 1st May each year.

(*e*) Wages and other expenses are all cash, except the insurance premiums of £600 per annum which are paid in advance on 1st June each year.

(*f*) On 1st July, a loan of £2,400 is to be received from Finance Co. Ltd. The annual rate of interest payable is 10%, paid half-yearly in arrear.

(*g*) On 1st July kitchen plant is to be acquired at a cost of £3,400. The kitchen plant which it is to replace is in the balance sheet at a book value of £1,000. The supplier agreed to accept this kitchen equipment for a part exchange value of £750.

(N.B. Items (*f*) and (*g*) are not included in the forecast of the budget committee.)

You are required to prepare:

(i) the monthly cash budget for the period from June to August inclusive;

(ii) the calculation of the value of the closing stock of food and beverages;

(iii) a budgeted departmental trading, profit and loss account for the three months ending 31st August, 1979, and the budgeted balance sheet as at that date. (HCIMA)

6–11 Draw up a monthly projected cash statement for the six months September 1975 to February 1976 from the information given overleaf:

			£		£
Payments:	Purchases	Sept.	14,000	Dec.	18,000
		Oct.	16,000	Jan.	22,000
		Nov.	18,000	Feb.	18,000
	Wages	Sept.	13,000	Dec.	15,000
		Oct.	13,500	Jan.	16,000
		Nov.	15,000	Feb.	13,500
	Expenses	Sept.	13,000	Dec.	15,000
		Oct.	14,000	Jan.	15,500
		Nov.	14,500	Feb.	14,000
Income from Sales:		Sept.	53,000	Dec.	61,000
		Oct.	34,000	Jan.	65,000
		Nov.	32,000	Feb.	70,000
Other items:	Expenditure on Capital equipment			Sept.	10,000
				Nov.	10,000
				Jan.	15,000
	Sale of equipment			Dec.	5,000
	Sale of land			Jan.	10,000
	Dividend from subsidiary companies			Dec.	3,000
				Feb.	5,000
	Tax payment due			Feb.	6,000

The projected cash balance at the beginning of September is £3,000. It is planned to pay out a dividend of £26,000 in January.

Make brief comments on the position disclosed.

6–12 D. Server Ltd. intends to commence business as a caterer on the 1st January, 1977. Initial requirements are expected to be fittings and equipment £500, and stocks £4,500. Meals are expected to be sold at $33\frac{1}{3}\%$ above cost. Expected sales are £3,000 per month for the first two months and £4,000 per month for the remaining ten months. Three months' credit will be allowed on sales, and one month's credit is expected from suppliers of food and beverages and equipment. Monthly expenses paid out in cash will be £800. This does not include exceptional expense items of £100 which will be paid in February and August. Food and beverage stock will be replaced in full the month after they are used. You are required to:

(*a*) estimate the capital requirements of D. Server Ltd. with the aid of a cash budget for 1977. (Assume that an initial amount of £9,000 can be raised in the form of ordinary share capital, and any additional funds can be obtained in the form of a bank overdraft.)

(*b*) prepare a projected profit statement and balance sheet for 1977. (Fittings and equipment depreciation is to be calculated at 20% per annum, and taxation at 50% of net profit.)

(c) comment on the projected results for 1977. (The managing director of D. Server Ltd. considers that a satisfactory return on a capital is 18% before interest and taxation.)

Further Reading

1. Cox, B. and Hewgill, J. C. R., *Management Accounting in Inflationary Conditions*, I.C.M.A.
2. Boardman, R. D., *Hotel and Catering, Costing and Budgets*, Heinemann; chapters 16 & 17.
3. Bishop, E. B., Mackay, A. D., Chambers, A., Sizer, J., *Aspects of Corporate Planning*, I.C.M.A.
4. Horngren, C. T., *Cost Accounting, A Managerial Emphasis*, Prentice-Hall; chapter 5.
5. Clarkson, G. P. and Elliot, B. J., *Managing Money and Finance*, Gower Press; chapter 3.

CHAPTER SEVEN

BUDGETARY CONTROL

HAVING set a budget for a twelve month period, management take steps to monitor progress of actual operations and the resulting revenues and costs. The publications *A Standard System of Hotel Accounting* and *A Standard System of Catering Accounting* give excellent assistance to those looking for basic accounting systems to help in the control of revenues and costs. The intention here is to explain proved control mechanisms, some included in the standard systems others going beyond yet contained within the framework laid down. The approach here is to show how gross profit can be monitored from simple budget and actual comparisons to detailed standard costing variance control. Wages and other expenses are dealt with on a simple budget and actual comparison and then the flexible budget introduced for closer control.

Control Defined

Control may be said to be the guidance of the internal operations of the business towards producing the most satisfactory net profit at the lowest cost, and should be based on sound planning. Profit is influenced by volume, selling price and cost and is controlled by marketing management who generate revenue and by the entire management team who incur and control costs.

Control of physical assets such as equipment and food, the procedure of billing, the collection and payment of cheques, and the safe storage of cash are routines outside the scope of this work.

Profit Control

The business budget includes a budgeted profit statement and a budgeted balance sheet. Routine financial transactions that are recorded and summarized, supply information not only for statutory accounting purposes but also for helping to monitor actual profit compared with budgeted profit. Budgetary control of profit is a continuous activity consisting of budgeting, comparing budgets with actual results, reporting variances and taking corrective action on them if thought desirable. This is outlined in Exhibit 6–1 (page 55).

Interactions between sales and costs, budget, actual and variances are continuous. Nevertheless some isolation of financial information which affects profit is necessary in order to control sections of the overall system. Variances are isolated for this purpose but when they are interpreted they should be viewed together taking account of influences one variance has on another.

Exhibit 7–1

SUMMARY OF ALTERNATIVE PROFIT CONTROL SYSTEMS

GROSS PROFIT CONTROL

Control information presented	*Comments*
Percentages Control	
Budget *v* Actual with percentages	As recommended in the Standard System. (Exhibits 7–2, 10–4)
Variance Control	
Budget *v* Actual with simple variances	(Exhibit 7–3)
Budget *v* Actual with detailed variances	Applicable where standards are not set for ingredient price, usage and dish price. (Exhibit 7–4)
Standard costing with detailed variances	Applicable only where standard dishes are served and where standards are set for ingredient price, usage and dish price. (Exhibits 7–5, 7–6)

WAGES AND EXPENSES CONTROL

Control information presented	*Comments*
Percentages Control	
Budget *v* Actual with percentages	As recommended in the Standard System. (Exhibit 10–4)
Variance Control	
Flexible budget control statement where costs are fixed and variable only Volume and expenditure variances shown	This example is in summary form. (Exhibit 7–9)
Flexible budget control statement where costs are semi-variable as well as fixed and variable Volume and expenditure variances shown	This is a detailed statement showing each expense heading. (Exhibit 7–10)

Note: Standard costing would not generally extend to wages and expenses control.

Because of the different control systems available it is convenient to separate profit (net) control into gross profit control and wages and expenses control. Exhibit 7–1 summarizes the variations considered here.

Gross Profit Control

This control is vital for food and beverage operations and covers both sales control and cost control.

Budget v Actual

The simplest of control statements is Exhibit 7–2.

Exhibit 7–2

Standard Restaurant
Simple Control Statement

	Budget		Actual	
	£	%	£	%
Sales	6,400	100	6,600	100
Food cost	3,200	50	3,740	57
Gross profit	3,200	50	2,860	43

It can be seen that planned gross profit has fallen £340 and that food costs have risen more than the revenue. Although the food cost difference is £540, it could be inferred that food cost has risen only £440 because it should remain at 50% of sales. However this will be seen to be inaccurate when further information shows the sales mix to have changed. More information is needed to provide more meaningful control figures.

How far a business is prepared to systematically analyse the difference between budget and actual depends very much on the size and characteristics of the operation. A small restaurateur may be content with a simple control statement which acts as a check on what he expected the results to be, based on his close personal supervision. However, the manager of a large restaurant with many times the turnover would certainly require more detail to help him pinpoint factors causing an adverse position.

The simple control statement then is the minimum overall financial control acceptable, and the Standard System gives an example showing budget and actual for 'this period' and 'year to date' – Exhibit 10–4 (page 163).

Variance Accounting

Budget and actual results can be compared in absolute or relative terms. In a very basic control system such as the Standard System, actual revenues and costs are compared with budget with the help of percentages, i.e. in relative terms. An extension to this is the start of a variance accounting system in which absolute differences are shown in a third money column as in Exhibit 7–3. The term variance accounting refers to any accounting control system where variances are reported and is an umbrella term covering Budgetary Control and Standard Costing Systems where variances are used.

Exhibit 7–3

Standard Restaurant
Control Statement with Variances

	Budget		Actual		Variances*
	£	%	£	%	£
Sales	6,400	100	6,600	100	200
Food cost	3,200	50	3,740	57	(540)
Gross profit	3,200	50	2,860	43	(340)

* Variances which reflect an increase in profit compared with budget are called favourable variances and those which lower profit are called adverse variances. Adverse variances may be shown in brackets or in red figures.

Budget v Actual with Detailed Variances
A restaurant which offers a menu with a wide variety of dishes would not be likely to introduce standard food prices and dish costs for detailed control purposes. Whilst useful for planning, the high running cost of operating such a control system would be uneconomical. If however, it is practical to analyse food costs between menu divisions but no further analysis of food cost is thought worthwhile, the following system is appropriate. This gross profit control system is based on average gross profit percentages but variances are calculated as well.

The control statement in this form – Exhibit 7–4 – is constructed as follows:

1. Original budget. This would be budgeted before the start of the budget period.
2. At the end of the period,
   (i) Total recorded sales for the period, £120,000 is used to adjust budgeted gross profit for each menu division and in total:

   $$\frac{£120,000}{£100,000} \times £63,400 = \underline{\underline{£76,080}}$$

   This is the gross profit expected if actual sales mix had been as budgeted.

   (ii) The control budget shows the gross profit expected from the actual mix of sales but using budgeted gross profit percentages.

   (iii) Actual recorded gross profit is finally stated.
3. Variance calculations. These are shown on the statement and are self explanatory from a calculation point of view. Variances for individual menu divisions may be listed as required.

Exhibit 7–4

VARIETY RESTAURANT: GROSS PROFIT CONTROL STATEMENT

	Original Budget				*Adjusted for Turnover*	*Control Budget*				*Actual*	
	Sales		Gross Profit		Gross Profit	Actual Sales		Gross Profit		Gross Profit	
Menu Divisions:	Mix (%)	£	%	£	£	Mix (%)	£	%	£	%	£
Starters	10	10,000	75	7,500	9,000	13	15,600	75	11,700	77	12,012
Main Course	40	40,000	50	20,000	24,000	50	60,000	50	30,000	45	27,000
Vegetables	5	5,000	65	3,250	3,900	5	6,000	65	3,900	62	3,720
Sweets and Cheese	12	12,000	70	8,400	10,080	9	10,800	70	7,560	66	7,128
Coffee and Tea	10	10,000	70	7,000	8,400	9	10,800	70	7,560	70	7,560
Wines and Spirits	23	23,000	75	17,250	20,700	14	16,800	75	12,600	75	12,600
	100	100,000	63·4	63,400	76,080	100	120,000	61·1	73,320	58·35	70,020
		(a)		(b)	(c) (b)+20%		(d)		(e)		(f)

(c) − (b): £12,680
(e) − (c): (£2,760)
(f) − (e): (£3,300)
£12,680 + (£2,760): £9,920
£9,920 + (£3,300): £6,620

Summary:

		£
(c–b)	Sales margin quantity variance	12,680
(e–c)	Sales margin mix variance	(2,760)
(e–b)	Sales margin volume variance	9,920
(f–e)	Food cost variance	(3,300)
(f–b)	Total gross profit variance	6,620

Comments on the Statement:

1. A 20% increase in turnover has produced additional gross profit of £9,920 (sales margin volume variance). However, had the increase been evenly spread across the board the increase would have been £12,680. A change in sales mix lowered the profit by £2,760. The main reason being the lower sales of highly profitable wines and spirits.
2. Food costs rose by £3,300 above expectations after allowing for the increased business. This was largely associated with the main course. It has been assumed that there had been no change in prices charged compared with budget.
3. It is likely that if interim statements, e.g. quarterly, had been produced, some adverse trends might have been corrected and the year end profit improved further.
4. Cumulative turnover figures, 'year to date', with budgeted gross profit percentages would be important additional sales information.
5. A danger of viewing this statement without reference to wages and expenses is that additional expenses may have been incurred to achieve the improved turnover. Reference to Exhibit 7–9 completes the picture, showing that other expenses rose by £7,000 resulting in the actual net profit being £380 below the original budget.

Standard Costing: Standard Dish Selling Price and Cost

The fast food restaurant lends itself to tight cost control, for with a fast turnover of a limited number of dishes, standardization is the keynote of the operation. Whenever there is standardization and repetition of operations, standard costing in some form can play a part in cost control. Standard costing is the name given to the technique whereby standard costs and selling prices are predetermined and subsequently compared with the actual recorded costs and revenues. The difference between the total standard cost of meals or dishes in a period and their actual cost, is known as the cost variance. Other variances are associated with sales and may be called sales margin variances. Each variance is a profit variance in that it helps to explain why actual profit differs from profit budgeted at the start of the period.

To illustrate this procedure, Exhibit 7–3 will be expanded, first to take account of standard dish prices and costs, and then the more detailed standard food prices and food usage standards. Finally sales margin variances will be considered.

Additional information made available:

	Dish A	Dish B
Budgeted number of dishes	1,000	2,000
Actual number of dishes	1,643	1,222
Standard dish price	£2·80	£1·80
Standard dish cost	£1·20	£1·00
Standard food cost %	43%	56%

Exhibit 7–5

STANDARD RESTAURANT

GROSS PROFIT CONTROL STATEMENT (FOOD)

	Original Budget[1]						*Control Budget*[2]						*Actual*		*Variances*
Dish category	A		B		Total		A		B		Total		Total		
No. dishes	1,000		2,000		3,000		1,643		1,222		2,865		2,865		
	£	%	£	%	£	%	£	%	£	%	£	%	£	%	£
Sales revenue	2,800	100	3,600	100	6,400	100	4,600	100	2,200	100	6,800	100	6,600	100	(200)
Food cost	1,200	43	2,000	56	3,200	50	1,972	43	1,222	56	3,194	47	3,740	57	(546)
Gross profit	1,600	57	1,600	44	3,200	50	2,628	57	978	44	3,606	53	2,860	43	(746)

£406 £(746)

£(340)

Notes:

Symbol ( ) = adverse variance, otherwise variances are favourable

Control budget food costs are derived from food cost % to 2 decimal places viz. 42·86% (A)

Summary:

	£
Sales margin volume variance	406
Sales margin price variance	(200)
Food cost variance	(546)
Total Gross Profit Variance	(340)

[1]Sometimes referred to as a 'fixed budget'

[2]Sometimes referred to as a 'flexible budget'.

The preparation of the gross profit control statement (Exhibit 7–5) enables the main variances to be calculated and these can later be broken down into sub variances when food price and usage standards are available. Steps to construct the statement are as follows:

1. The original or fixed budget consists of the budgeted number of dishes multiplied by the standard dish price and standard food cost per dish.
2. The control or flexible budget indicates the revenue, costs and gross profit expected from the actual number of dishes served, assuming dish prices and food costs are as budgeted.
3. Actual sales revenue and food cost is taken from the original simple statement.

Comments on the statement:

1. Management would have expected budgeted profit to rise by £406 in selling 2,865 dishes, from £3,200 to £3,606.
2. Revenue from A and B was £200 short, and food cost £546 more than expected, together making a reduction of £746 in gross profit.
3. Introducing a control budget shows:
   (*a*) Food cost. Because of a change in sales mix, the rise in sales revenue of £400 was expected to result in virtually no change in food cost – falling from £3,200 to £3,194. Food cost however actually rose to £3,740 leaving an excess food cost of £546. This compares with a food cost variance of £440 inferred from Exhibit 7–2. At this stage it is unknown how much of this is attributed to food price changes and food usage.
   (*b*) Sales revenue. The actual sales should have produced revenue of £6,800. The fall from this figure would be due to sales price changes.

Standard Costing: Standard Food Price and Usage

To find out the reason for the extra food cost, standard food prices and usages need to be introduced and an enterprise using 'Standard food costing' would have this information available. The difference between the standard cost of meals or dishes in a period, and the actual cost, is known as the cost variance which can be broken down into its component parts of usage variance and price variance. These may be calculated as follows:

Usage variance = Standard price × (Standard quantity – actual quantity)

Price variance = Actual quantity × (Standard price – actual price)

The following figures are made available so that these variances may be calculated:

Standard Data

Dishes A and B consist of food Y and Z respectively and the standard food cost of each dish is:

A: 500 g of Y × £2·40 per kg = £1·20

B: 500 g of Z × £2·00 per kg = £1·00

Actual Data
In the period when 1,643 dishes of A and 1,222 dishes of B were served the following food was used:

800 kg of Y × £2·80 per kg
625 kg of Z × £2·40 per kg

For calculation purposes the following method is recommended:

(*a*) Standard food quantity × standard price	Usage variance
(*b*) Actual food quantity × standard price	
(*c*) Actual food quantity × actual price	Price variance

Applying this procedure to the example:

	Meal A – Food Y	£	£
(*a*)	1,643* dishes × 500g of Y = 821·5 kg × £2·40 =	1,972	52 Usage
(*b*)	800 kg × £2·40 =	1,920	
(*c*)	800 kg × £2·80 =	2,240	(320) Price
	Total food cost variance (a – c) =		(268)

Variances for meals A and B may be summarized:

	A	B	Total
	£	£	£
Usage variance	52	(28)	24
Price variance	(320)	(250)	(570)
	(268)	(278)	(546)

The food cost adverse variance of £546 initially discovered in the 'Gross Profit Control Statement' has now been shown to have been caused by price rises of £570 and the kitchen usage has been favourable to the extent of £24.

* Essential to the understanding of this control technique is that standard cost for a period is related to *actual* production/sales quantities achieved. Also, standard food cost coincides with the control budget figure, both being based on actual activity achieved.

More details concerning standard costing may be found in *A Standard System of Catering Accounting*.

Standard Costing: Sales Margin Variances
There are two main sales margin variances, margin referring to gross profit.

Sales margin price variance
Sales margin volume variance

Both are depicted in Exhibit 7–5 and Standard Restaurant figures will be used to show the appropriate calculations.

Standard Costing: Sales Margin Price Variance

This is the simplest of variances to calculate being the difference between actual sales quantities at standard selling prices and actual sales quantities at actual prices. The relevant figures for the Standard Restaurant are £6,800 and £6,600 leaving an adverse sales price variance of £200 indicating that on average, prices were below the standard set. If considered of value and the basic data being available, price variances could be calculated for each sale category.

Standard Costing: Sales Margin Volume Variance

This main variance as shown in Exhibit 7–5 is the difference between the budgeted gross profit (£3,200) and the gross profit expected from actual sales when selling prices and food costs are at standard (£3,606), giving a favourable variance of £406. Other methods of arriving at this figure are shown in Exhibit 7–7.

As restaurants sell more than one menu item, sales mix is important as noted elsewhere. Accordingly the sales margin volume variance may be broken down into two sub-variances:

Sales margin quantity variance
Sales margin mix variance

Standard Restaurant figures have been restated in Exhibit 7–6 and variance calculations made in Exhibit 7–7. These are referred to in the next paragraphs.

Standard Costing: Sales Margin Quantity Variance

The approach with all variance analysis is to vary one factor at a time, as in a controlled experiment. With the sales margin quantity variance, other variables such as selling price and sales mix are assumed to be as in the budget. The sales margin quantity variance reflects the extra gross profit from any sales above budget, ignoring deliberately any change in selling price or sales mix. As average gross profit % is assumed to remain at 50%, the extra sales of the Standard Restaurant of £400 produces an extra gross profit of £200 which is the favourable sales margin quantity variance. This can be seen in Exhibits 7–6 and 7–7.

Standard Costing: Sales Margin Mix Variance

This variance reflects the change in gross profit arising from any change in mix compared with budgeted mix. Standard Restaurant's actual sales mix shows an average gross profit of 53·03% compared with 50% in the budget. The extra gross profit is therefore the sale of £6,800 × 3·03% = £206 which is the sales margin mix variance. This variance quantifies the profit from the improved mix. The sales mix has improved because:

(i) Dish A is the more profitable with a gross profit of 57% compared with B's gross profit of 44%.

(ii) The sales mix in the budget was A 43·75% and B 56·25%. The actual results show a change of mix in A's favour with A's share rising to 67·65% and B falling to 32·35% of total sales.

Exhibit 7–6

STANDARD RESTAURANT
PRELIMINARY CALCULATIONS TO PROVIDE SALES MARGIN QUANTITY AND MIX VARIANCES

(*a*) BUDGET

Dish	*Sales Quantity*	*Standard Selling Price*	*Sales Revenue*		*Gross Profit*	
		£	£	%	£	%
A	1,000	2·80	2,800	43·75	1,600	57·14
B	2,000	1·80	3,600	56·25	1,600	44·44
			6,400	100	3,200	50

(*b*) ACTUAL SALES IN BUDGETED MIX

	Dish	*Sales Revenue*		*Gross Profit*	
		£	%	£	%
Sales of £6,800 in the budgeted mix of 43·75% and 56·25%	A	2,975	43·75	1,700	57·14
	B	3,825	56·25	1,700	44·44
		6,800	100	3,400	50

(*c*) ACTUAL

Dish	*Sales Quantity*	*Standard Selling Price*	*Sales Revenue*		*Gross Profit*	
		£	£	%	£	%
A	1,643	2·80	4,600	67·65	2,628	57·14
B	1,222	1·80	2,200	32·35	978	44·44
			6,800	100	3,606	53·03

Exhibit 7–7 STANDARD RESTAURANT
SALES MARGIN VARIANCE ANALYSIS: TOTAL METHOD

	£
(*a*) Budgeted total gross profit	3,200
(*b*) Actual total sales in budgeted sales mix × standard gross profit % for each item	3,400
(*c*) Actual total gross profit	3,606

VARIANCES

		£
$(b-a)$	Sales margin quantity variance	200
$(c-b)$	Sales margin mix variance	206
$(c-a)$	Sales margin volume variance	406

SALES MARGIN VARIANCE ANALYSIS: DIFFERENTIAL METHOD

Sales margin quantity variance £

Difference in total sales × standard average gross profit %
=(£6,800 − £6,400) × 50% = 200

Sales margin mix variance

Difference in average gross profit % × actual total sales
=(53·03% − 50%) × £6,800 = 206

Sales margin volume variance

Difference in sales	× standard gross profit %		£	
=A + £1,800	× 57·14%	=	1,028	
B − £1,400	× 44·44%	=	(622)	406

Or Difference in sales quantities × standard gross profit per unit

=A + 643	× £1·60	=	1,028
B − 778	× £0·80	=	(622)
			406

Sales Margin Variances: Summary of Calculation Methods

The calculation of the sales margin volume variance is relatively simple; separating it into quantity and mix can be a problem and other methods are worth considering which might help in the understanding of the concept. Two methods are shown in Exhibit 7–7 and there are other methods, all providing the same variance figures. The total method is worth mastering first because it can be the basis of understanding the differential method.

With the total method it is important to calculate a gross profit figure based on actual total sales in budgeted mix in order to separate the volume variance into its constituent parts. This can be done:

(i) As in Exhibit 7–6, the actual total sales of £6,800 are put into budgeted proportions and each item multiplied by budgeted gross profit %.

(ii) Work out the actual total sales as a percentage of budgeted total sales. $\frac{£6,800}{£6,400} \times 100 = 106{\cdot}25\%$. As sales are 106·25% of budget, the budgeted gross profit of each item is expected to increase accordingly viz:

A £1,600 × 106·25% = £1,700
B £1,600 × 106·25% = £1,700

£3,400

A full reconciliation statement can now be prepared (Exhibit 7–8) and compared with Exhibit 7–5 showing the additional variance information. Food cost variance, adverse £546, is shown to have been due to food price rises (£570) and that £24 has been saved by efficient usage of ingredients. The extra gross margin expected of £406 was almost equally divided between improvement in the mix of sales – £206 – and greater quantity of sales of £200.

Exhibit 7–8 STANDARD RESTAURANT

STATEMENT RECONCILING BUDGETED WITH ACTUAL GROSS PROFIT

	£	£
Budgeted gross profit		3,200
Apply: Sales margin variances		
Price	(200)	
Quantity	200	
Mix	206	
	206	
Apply: Food cost variances		
Price	(570)	
Usage	24	
	(546)	
Total variances		(340)
Actual gross profit		2,860

Inflation and the Cost Price Variance

In times of rapid inflation some organizations may feel the need to have more information available on prices of commodities and services to help ensure their own costs are not rising more than they should. Budgeting for inflation was mentioned in the previous chapter and here is considered the control aspect of food prices under inflation, using standard costing.

To control the efficient usage of any food it is best to use initially, measurements such as weight. However, it is advisable to incorporate such controls into the management accounting system and this can only be done by using the common measurement of money. Converting a weight variance to cost helps to establish whether the loss or gain is significant and worthy of reporting and investigating.

Price rises should not mask production performance in the kitchen as demonstrated in the previous section, so a standard or expected price is used to value losses or gains in usage of food. A standard purchase price should be set for the year which reflects an efficient, expected buying price. Price variances therefore reflect inaccurate expectations and may in some instances be used to assess the success of the buying policy.

Care should be used in interpreting the price variance because it may be advantageous to buy extra for stock at a high price because of even higher expected prices. The adverse price variance here might be regarded with some favour. On the other hand the cost of holding the extra stock should be considered, which may be as high as 25% of the total cost of the stock held for 12 months. An adverse price variance which follows from better quality purchases may be acceptable if a saving in consumption results. Relationships between variances found in this way may encourage a change in policy to reduce total costs.

It should be noted that in the price variance calculations used here it has been assumed that purchases and usage of food has been concurrent. In practice however the price variance is best calculated every time a purchase is made rather than as food is used, and this means that for the purpose of management accounts, stock is valued at standard prices.

By using published indices it is possible to provide information on price rises to indicate two matters:

1. How successful was buying management in forecasting price rises of food and commodities?
2. How successful was buying management in the face of rising prices in keeping costs down?

Some important foods or commodities may need close control and the following indicates how the inflation factor may be incorporated into standard food costing.

Let it be assumed that food Y on page 88 needs additional control because of rising prices. Data already given is summarized as follows:

Food Y

Standard price £2·40 per kg
Actual price paid (average) £2·80 per kg
Standard quantity allowed for actual number of dishes 821·5 kg
Actual quantity used 800 kg

The existing procedures have evaluated the saving in usage of food to be £52, (21·5 kg × £2·40) and the adverse price variance to be £320, (800 kg × 40p), a total adverse variance of £268. The standard price for the year of £2·40 had been calculated in the following manner. The actual price when the standard was set at the beginning of the year was £2·212. Average price rise expected during the year was 8½% to give the standard of £2·40 (£2·212 × 1·085). However, at the end of the year, using published statistics, the price index for this food in fact rose by an average of 17% giving an average price of £2·588 (£2·212 × 1·17). The 17% rise might have been determined from indices such as 183 for January and 245 for December. This gives a rise of 34% for the year (245/183 = 1·34) although as it is assumed that purchases are made at fairly regular intervals and inflation itself is regular throughout the year, an average rise of 17% is taken to represent the buying conditions.

A variance related to the uncontrollable price rise due to inflation can now be isolated. What may be done is to regard the price which reflects the inflated food price, as a revised standard price. This enables the calculation of:

(*a*) The cost of errors in price forecasting. This is the difference between the expected or standard price set at the beginning of the year and the inflated (revised standard) price multiplied by the standard usage quantity. This is an uncontrollable variance.
(£2·40 – £2·588) × 821·5 kg = £154 adverse.

(*b*) The cost saving in using less food than standard. This is evaluated at the revised standard price.
(821·5 kg – 800 kg) × £2·588 = £56 favourable.

(*c*) The extra cost of purchases above the price reflecting the price index for the food. This is the difference between the revised standard price and the actual price multiplied by the actual quantity purchased and used. This may reflect inefficient buying.
(£2·588 – £2·800) × 800 kg = £170 adverse.

In a format already used:

		£	*Variance* £	
(*a*) Standard cost for the year	: 821·5 kg × £2·400 =	1,972	(154)	Price
(*b*) Revised standard cost	: 821·5 kg × £2·588 =	2,126		revision
(*c*) Actual purchases (usage)	: 800 kg × £2·588 =	2,070	56	Usage
(*d*) Actual cost	: 800 kg × £2·800 =	2,240	(170)	Price
Total food cost variance (*a*) – (*d*)			£(268)	

Much of the value of this additional information depends upon the reliability of the index or price used to establish, at the end of the period, what should have been an efficient average buying price. The Central Statistical Office publishes many indices to help organizations make adjustments for inflation, one booklet being *Price index numbers for Current Cost Accounting*.

The revised standard price can of course be used at any time during the year if it is felt revision of standard dish costs is needed.

Wages and Expenses Control

Food, liquor and gross profit is capable of fairly close control. Most other costs – overheads – are either fixed or semi-variable and are not so easily controlled. Exceptions are costs which are optional such as staff training and may be regarded as policy costs. There are however, few costs in this category.

The alternatives for controlling wages and other costs are the budget *v* actual statement or a more detailed statement that takes account of those costs which vary to some extent with activity, as with food cost control.

Budget v Actual

Management of hotels and restaurants where most costs other than food and drink are fixed, or where activity varies little, would accept a control system which compared budget with actual as Exhibits 10–3, 10–4 and 10–5 (pages 162–164).

Flexible Budget Statement: All Costs Either Fixed or Variable

If detailed overhead expenses can be easily placed into fixed and variable categories, then besides the important gross profit control statement, a summary control statement covering net profit can be prepared as Exhibit 7–9. This example completes the Variety Restaurant financial picture which showed Gross Profit in Exhibit 7–4. Additional figures have been assumed for fixed and variable costs. The Variety Restaurant showed an improvement in gross profit from a budget of £63,400 to £70,020. However, since other variable and fixed costs are seen to have risen by more than the gross profit increase, a drop in net profit has resulted.

Flexible Budget Statement: Including Semi-variable costs

Large organizations needing close control of expenses produce a flexible budget taking into account cost behaviour patterns which are neither fixed nor variable with sales activity. Exhibit 7–10 shows semi-variable expenses such as laundry. It can be seen that semi-variable expenses have been adjusted to take account of the rise in sales, leaving variances due to price or usage of the item, which require separate explanations. As with food control statements the difference between the original budget and the control or flexible budget is a volume variance caused entirely by sales activity change.

Recommended statements in the standard accounting systems can be adapted to accept this extra control measure where considered appropriate.

By admitting that certain costs must rise in sympathy with activity, due allowance is given for these and attention is directed to changes which were not foreseen either because of difficulty in determining cost behaviour, change in price, or because of poor cost control.

Exhibit 7–9

VARIETY RESTAURANT

Summary Operating Statement

	Original Budget (1) £	*Control Budget* (2) £	*Actual* (3) £	*Controllable Profit Variances* (2–3) £
Sales	100,000	120,000	120,000	—
Less				
Food cost	36,600	46,680	49,980	(3,300)
Gross profit	63,400	73,320	70,020	
Less				
Other variable costs	15,000	18,000	20,000	(2,000)
	48,400	55,320	50,020	
Less				
Fixed costs	25,000	25,000	27,000	(2,000)
Net profit	23,400	30,320	23,020	(7,300)
Apply: Expected extra profit from actual sales (£30,320 – £23,400)				6,920
TOTAL NET PROFIT VARIANCE				(£380)

Summary of Variances

	£	*Profit Variance* £
Gross Profit Variances		
Sales margin volume	9,920	
Food cost	(3,300)	6,620
Expected increase in other variable costs		(3,000)
Overhead Expenditure Variances		
Variable cost	(2,000)	
Fixed cost	(2,000)	
		(4,000)
Total net profit variance		(£380)

Exhibit 7–10

ROOM DEPARTMENT COST CONTROL STATEMENT
(6 months ended ....)

	Cost Class	(1) Fixed Budget	(2) Flexible Budget	(3) Actual	(4) Variance (Col. 3 – 2)	(5) Remarks
		£ %	£ %	£ %	£	Increased turnover caused by......
Guest accommodation		20,000	22,000	22,000		
Room Hire		1,000	1,100	1,100		
TOTAL SALES		21,000	23,100	23,100		
Gross Pay						
N.I.						
Holiday Pay						
Staff Meals						
Staff accommodation						
TOTAL WAGE & STAFF COST	S.V.	7,000	7,100	7,100	—	
NET MARGIN		14,000	16,000	16,000	—	
Department supplies	S.V.	1,500	1,600	1,700	(100)	Minor equip. for rooms
Flowers & decorations	F.	300	300	320	(20)	Price increase
Magazines & periodicals	F.	100	100	90	10	
Printing & Stationery	S.V.	400	430	420	10	
Laundry & dry cleaning charges	S.V.	700	750	800	(50)	Under est. in quantity of dry cleaning
Cleaning Contracts	F.	500	500	500	—	
Linen	S.V.	100	105	105	—	
Uniforms	S.V.	200	200	200	—	
Utensils	F.	200	200	200	—	
TOTAL ALLOCATED EXPENSE		4,000	4,185	4,335	(150)	
DEPARTMENTAL OPERATING PROFIT		10,000	11,815	11,665	(150)	

SUMMARY	£
Profit variance due to volume (Col. 2 – 1)	1,815
Profit variance due to price/usage (Col. 3 – 2)	(150)
TOTAL PROFIT VARIANCE FROM BUDGET (Col. 3 – 1)	1,665

It should be noted that the flexible budget costs are not part of the double entry accounting system but are memorandum figures prepared as and when required. It is necessary however, to record information on cost behaviour to enable reasonably accurate flexible budgets to be prepared and also to provide a basis for the annual budget.

Cost Control Principles

There is no question that costs have to be controlled in a business, for it is natural that without some control mechanism in force, costs would surely rise. It is in the nature of things to spend money if no restraint is put on money available. The problem arises in a business as to the method used to control cost, and the cost of running the cost control system. Undoubtedly, there comes a time when the cost control system outweighs the benefits derived therefrom, so that a compromise usually results. However, the commonsense approach usually prevails and this dictates:

(*a*) It is a waste of effort to attempt to control costs which defy control. Effort should be put to determine whether the service for which the cost is incurred is necessary and, if so, whether alternative and cheaper means are available for supplying the service.

(*b*) Of the costs which are controllable, those constituting the highest cost should receive most attention from the control point of view.

In the first category such costs as local rates, maintenance, insurance and telephone rental are included and may be termed 'fixed costs' as they tend to remain unaffected by changes in turnover.

In the hotel and catering industry, the costs which represent the highest percentage of sales are cost of food, liquor and tobacco. It is also true that these are about the only true 'variable costs' of a business.

Balance Sheet Control

Whilst attention has been paid to profit control, it should not be forgotten than Budgetary Control covers other financial areas of the business. The two main areas are cash and the liquid position generally, and capital expenditure. Cash is controlled on a day to day basis whilst capital expenditure is compared with the budget as a check that authorized amounts for projects are not exceeded without full knowledge and good reason.

Other balance sheet items are controlled not by variance accounting but by ratios, for instance working capital. Long term liabilities are a matter of policy and involved more with financial management planning than control.

Administering Budgetary Control

Basic requirements for administering budgetary control include appointment of a budget officer, a budget committee and the compilation of a budget manual. A *budget officer* is assigned responsibility for the preparation of budgets and dealing with technical matters. He is likely to be an accountant. A *budget committee* is formed of top managers to co-ordinate budgeting activities. It would make recommendations to the board regarding acceptance of the master budget and would review periodic budget reports. A *budget manual* would be prepared by the budget officer and would serve as a rule book and reference for the implementation of procedures. The budget timetable would be an important item contained in the manual.

Responsibility Accounting

Cost control is best achieved when personnel accept responsibility for costs under their control even if they do not have the 100% control over some costs that they would like.

Routine reports may be constructed to show separately those costs which the recipient is required to control, and those he cannot control (non-controllable costs). The organization must be divided into responsibility centres – defined as an organizational unit having a single head accountable for activities of the unit. A budget centre often coincides with a responsibility centre.

A responsibility accounting system is operated within the budgetary control system and its requirements are:

(*a*) the individual in charge is held to be responsible for the activities within his jurisdiction, and the effort used in attaining his objectives is to be measured in terms of Controllable and Non-Controllable costs.

(*b*) the organization chart of the firm, supported by a schedule of cost responsibilities is the basis on which reports are prepared and recognition of controllable and non-controllable costs and revenue made.

Exhibit 7–11 gives an example

Exhibit 7–11

Hotel Organization Chart (Extract)

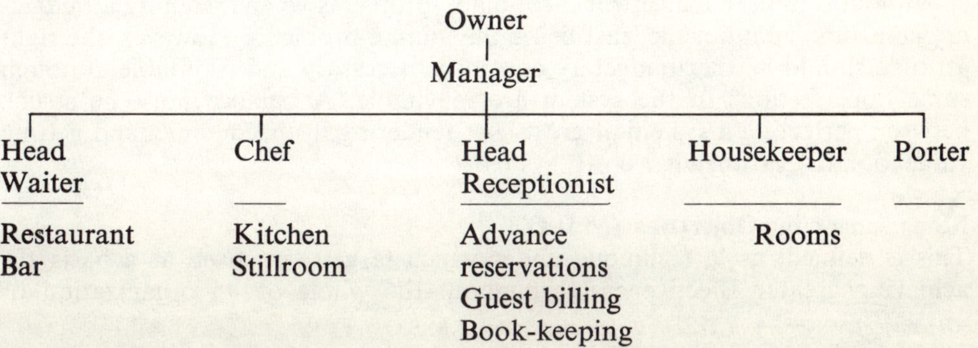

Schedule of Cost Responsibilities (Extract)

	Head Waiter	*Manager*	*Owner*
Wages of waiters	C	C	C
Flowers	C	C	C
Laundry	C	C	C
Breakages	C	C	C
Music	N/C	C	C
Repairs	N/C	C	C
Stationery	N/C	N/C	C
Cleaning Contract	N/C	N/C	C

C = Controllable
N/C = Non-controllable

All costs are controllable by the proprietor in the sense that he has the choice to incur them in the first instance.

Human Relations Aspects of Cost Control

Human factors involved in budgetary control are generally more difficult to deal with than the technical matters of quantifying budgets and preparing control statements. Far from motivating personnel to take the right decision in the company's interest, an ill-conceived budget and budgetary control system can have the opposite effect. The very name 'budget' may be associated with imposition, dictation from top management, and niggardly allowances. If such attitudes are not eliminated by proper education at the start of a budget programme, and good communications in the budget operation, then the objective of improved profit may not be attained.

A large percentage of supervisors in industry generally regard budgetary control as having an important impact on performance of their activity. If this influence is in the wrong direction then serious financial consequences could occur. Budgetary control may not be making a full contribution if supervisors see the budget as being too rigid in operation or, on the other hand, too often altered, or if they find performance reports badly presented to them. Since supervisors are basically concerned with the present and with handling immediate problems, budget figures may be ignored in order to solve pressing difficulties.

Without doubt, management faces many problems when installing a budgetary control system not the least being the human problems. However, the right attitude should be that budgetary control is necessary and profitable although some imperfections in the system are inevitable. A balance must be struck between perfecting a system at great cost rendering it uneconomic, and getting value for money from a less costly system.

Management by Objectives (M.B.O.)

This is defined[1] as 'a technique under which targets are fixed as a basis for achieving greater effectiveness throughout the whole of an organization or

[1]*Glossary of Management Techniques*, published by H.M.S.O.

part of an organization'. It differs from budgetary control in two major ways in that targets may be non-financial such as a percentage increase in output or sales, and it may be applied to only a part of the organization.

It is claimed that since managers participate in setting their own objectives a system of self-control replaces one of imposed control. In general M.B.O. is concerned with the individual more so than is budgetary control and ideally there should be close links between the operation of both techniques.

Divisional Performance

If a manager of a subsidiary company, division or operating unit has control over costs and revenue, the unit may be regarded as a profit centre, and the manager's performance measured in financial terms. With an increasing amount of delegated responsibility being placed on managers' shoulders it is important to measure their contribution to corporate profit. No standard measure is available although where feasible some relationship to capital employed would appear appropriate, the obvious method being a target return on investment incurred by the unit of say 50% increase over the next three years. A method recommended by Professor David Solomons is a residual profit target, that is the profit remaining after deducting the cost of capital invested in the unit. Both these methods involve determining the capital employed of a unit, say a large hotel, but the assessment of this figure is not a simple matter, for each year the market value of the hotel rises and a higher profit is required to maintain the same return on capital as before.

Questions and Problems

7–1 What is the basic limitation of an original/fixed budget when it comes to control of trading activities?

7–2 What is a control/flexible budget and how might it be applied to an hotel or catering organization?

7–3 'There is only one kind of budget which is any use for monitoring purposes and that is a control/flexible budget'.
You are required to:
(*a*) comment on this quotation;
(*b*) discuss the factors which you would take into account in deciding the volume base e.g. meals, sales, revenue etc., you would select for measuring changes in activity; and
(*c*) state what factors, other than the changes in the level of activity, would cause costs to vary.

7–4 Explain, in brief, the following terms:
(*a*) standard cost
(*b*) standard price
(*c*) food price variance
(*d*) food usage variance
(*e*) sales margin variance
(*f*) sales mix variance

7–5 Select a particular type of hotel or catering establishment and suggest which departments, and who within the departments, are concerned with setting standards.

7–6 Enumerate the likely causes of food cost variances and sales margin variances.

7–7 Explain the relationship between the food price variance and the food usage variance. Is it feasible for a favourable result achieved from one variance to contribute to an adverse result in another variance?

7–8 Distinguish between controllable and non-controllable costs giving examples of each.

7–9 Explain what you understand by 'responsibility accounting'.

7–10 The following information relates to the Food and Beverage Budget of the Berkshire Banqueting Suite for 1st quarter of 1977:

Budgeted number of meals	Menu A	3,000
	Menu B	4,000
	Menu C	5,000
Budgeted selling prices per meal	Menu A	£4
	Menu B	£5
	Menu C	£3
Budgeted food cost per meal	Menu A	40%
	Menu B	30%
	Menu C	50%

Semi-variable cost behaviour attributable to various levels of activity are estimated to be:

£25 per 100 meals from 100– 4,000
£20 per 100 meals from 4,001– 8,000
£15 per 100 meals from 8,001–12,000

Fixed costs for the quarter are £20,000. Budgeted activity is 60% of capacity.

Actual results were:

Number of meals sold (sales mix)	Menu A	12%
	Menu B	40%
	Menu C	48%

Food cost £15,700
Semi-variable costs £2,100
Activity was 50% of capacity at budgeted selling prices.

You are required to prepare a cost control statement for 1st quarter, 1977, to include:

(*a*) an original/fixed budget;
(*b*) a control/flexible budget;

(*c*) actual results; and
(*d*) variances
Comment on the results you have produced.

7–11 The Kingsley Restaurant budgeted in respect of the year ended 30 April, 1978 for sales of £300,000, and an average spending power of £2·50. The budgeted differential profit margins were as follows:

	Sales Mix	*Gross Profit*
	%	%
Soups and appetizers	10	65
Meat and fish	40	50
Vegetables	10	60
Sweets	10	60
Teas and coffees	10	70
Alcoholic beverages	20	65

Budgeted labour costs and overheads were £80,000. Of these, fixed costs were £40,000 and variable costs £40,000.

At the end of the budget year it was found that actual sales and the average spending power were as budgeted. The actual sales mix and differential profit margins were as given below:

	Sales Mix	*Gross Profit*
	%	%
Soups and appetizers	10	65
Meat and fish	50	45
Vegetables	5	60
Sweets	10	60
Teas and coffees	5	70
Alcoholic beverages	20	60

Actual labour costs and overheads were as budgeted but of the total of £80,000, £50,000 was fixed and £30,000 a variable cost.

(*a*) Prepare a statement of budgeted and actual results for the year.
(*b*) Comment on the result. (Scotec HND)

7–12 The following information relates to Friar's Restaurant for the first quarter of 1979:

Menu divisions	*Budget* Sales Mix	Gross Profit	*Actual* Sales Mix	Gross Profit
	%	%	%	%
Starters	15	70	20	75
Main courses	40	50	50	55
Vegetables	10	60	15	50
Sweets	20	40	10	40
Coffee and teas	15	70	5	60

Budgeted sales revenue for the quarter was £100,000 but the actual sales revenue achieved was £80,000.

You are required to:

(*a*) calculate the total variances detailed below:

(i) sales margin quantity;

(ii) sales margin mix;

(iii) sales margin volume;

(iv) food cost;

(v) overall gross profit; and

(*b*) explain briefly the information derived from the variances.

(HCIMA)

7–13 A medium-sized provincial restaurant operates a system of standard food costing. From the information given below, you are required to:

(*a*) calculate the ingredient cost variances;

(*b*) calculate the sales variances;

(*c*) reconcile the restaurant's budgeted and actual gross profit; and

(*d*) comment briefly on the variances.

Number of covers budgeted was 12,000. The actual number of covers realized was 10,800 and the sales achieved from these were £11,400. The average spending power was expected to be £1·05 per head.

The standard cost per dish is:

Standard Recipe Cost Card

Ingredients	£
A 250 g @ £1·60 per kg	0·40
B 125 g @ £1·20 per kg	0·15
Total food cost per portion	0·55

Actual figures relating to the ingredients were:

Ingredient	*Food used* kg	*Food price per kg* £
A	2,600	1·70
B	1,400	1·30

7–14 The Restview Restaurant prepared a budget from which standards are established. For a week in June 1978 the budgeted standards set, and the actual results achieved are as follows:

	Budgeted £		*Actual* £
Sales: 1500 dishes		1560 dishes	
at £1·06	1,590·00	at £1·10	1,716·00
Less cost of sales	795·00	*Less* cost of sales	783·20
Gross Profit	795·00		932·80

The standard cost per dish (only two ingredients are used) were calculated as follows:

		Standard cost per dish
Ingredient A	500 g at £0·50 per kg	£0·25
Ingredient B	250 g at £1·12 per kg	£0·28

The actual costs were as follows:

	Actual Price	*Actual food used*
Ingredient A	£0·52 per kg	800 kgs
Ingredient B	£1·02 per kg	360 kgs

You are required to:

(*a*) calculate the following variances:
 (i) Sales variances,
 (ii) ingredient price variances, and
 (iii) ingredient usage variances.

(*b*) reconcile the budgeted profit with the actual profit, and

(*c*) briefly comment on the significance of the variances.

(HCIMA, adapted)

7–15 The sales and cost budget for a fast food establishment for the month of November is as follows:

Food Item	*Units*	*Sales Value*	*Standard Cost*
		£	£
'Artie Berger'	10,000	10,000	9,000
'Brunchie'	5,000	8,000	6,000
'Crunchy'	10,000	12,000	10,800
'Dunkie'	5,000	18,000	14,200
		£48,000	£40,000

After completion of the sales analysis for November, the following statement of actual values is compiled:

Food Item	*Units*	*Sales Value*
		£
'Artie Berger'	9,200	9,200
'Brunchie'	7,000	11,000
'Crunchy'	12,000	14,600
'Dunkie'	2,000	7,800

Calculate the variation in profit from that budgeted, and show how much is due to the factors of sales price, quantity and mix.

7–16 'Hot Pot' is a fast food establishment which offers a choice of two light meals. Management have introduced a system of standard costing and presented overleaf is the data relating to one quarter's expected and actual results:

	Standard	Budget	Actual
Number of meals sold:			
'Wee-bite'		30,000	33,500
'Lite-bite'		40,000	39,000
Selling price:			
'Wee-bite'	£1·20		£40,200
'Lite-bite'	£1·50		£62,400
Ingredient quantity:			
'Wee-bite'	150 g		5,192·5 kg
'Lite-bite'	160 g		6,630 kg
Ingredient price:			
'Wee-bite'	£3·50 kg		£3·25 kg
'Lite-bite'	£4.50 kg		£4·75 kg

You are required to:

(*a*) calculate: (i) sales variances
(ii) food cost variances

(*b*) reconcile the budgeted and actual gross profit; and

(*c*) comment on the variances you have prepared.

Further Reading

1. Burke, W. L., and Smyth, E. B., *Accounting for Management*, Sweet and Maxwell; chapters 3 and 4.
2. Fay, C. T., Rhoads, R. C., Rosenblatt, R. L., *Managerial Accounting for the Hospitality Service Industries*, W. C. Brown Company Publishers; chapters 16 and 18.
3. Horngren, C. T., *Cost Accounting, a managerial emphasis*, Prentice-Hall; chapters 7, 8 and 26.
4. *A Standard System of Catering Accounting*, Hotel and Catering EDC, HMSO.

CHAPTER EIGHT

COST – VOLUME – PROFIT ANALYSIS

BEFORE finalizing a profit plan, account should be taken of feasible alternative plans or forecasts to ensure that the best planned use is made of available resources. Alternative plans might consider such factors as pricing policy, food supply and prices, advertising, and standards for portion control.

When additional capital is included in a forecast, a number of methods might be used to assess the profitability of the investment, ranging from average rate of return to the more elaborate net present value method using the discounted cash flow technique. This chapter will deal only with the planning of profit from existing resources, leaving the subject of appraising further investment to be dealt with separately in Chapter 15.

Profit Relative to Turnover

Planning improvements in profit is not merely an exercise in figure-work: it requires practical, feasible ideas to come from management so that there is something to quantify in financial terms. One factor in the industry crying out for improvement, is the percentage capacity or occupancy of existing establishments, and fortunately there is evidence that the marketing minded manager in particular is achieving success in this area. Fortes for instance took over an hotel and within 3 years were able to double the turnover and treble the profit with negligible extra investment, and there was still a large gap between actual and potential turnover which they worked on and reduced.

Considering that an extra £1½ million turnover from an hotel group could well contribute more than £½ million extra profit without additional facilities and that when an hotel moves from 70% to 80% occupancy the additional turnover is almost completely extra profit it can be seen how important it is to acquire an understanding of how changes in level of activity such as turnover affects profit. This understanding can come from simple examples illustrated by charts.

The first example is of a stallholder at a market, similar in many ways to the restaurant but relieved of all the complication of food production and variety of dishes.

The stall has been hired for £12 covering a short period when it is planned to sell articles at £5 each which have cost £3 on a sale or return basis. The target is to sell all 12 articles that are available.

Analysis of costs involved in the enterprise shows two clear categories, namely a fixed or period cost of £12 which has to be paid regardless of how many articles are sold and a variable cost of £3 which varies in total directly with changes in sales level. No other costs are incurred.

Break-even Chart

To obtain a picture of all possible results taking into account the constraints of cost, selling price and maximum quantity, the break-even chart shown in Exhibit 8–1 has been prepared. This form of chart clearly portrays the quantitative factors of the situation, indicating for instance that when six articles have been sold or £30 cash received from sales any possibility of a loss has passed, and any further sales will provide a profit. Profit or loss expected at any sales level can be found by measuring the distance between revenue and total cost against the vertical scales, for example a profit of £8 is measured at the 10 unit level.

Exhibit 8–1

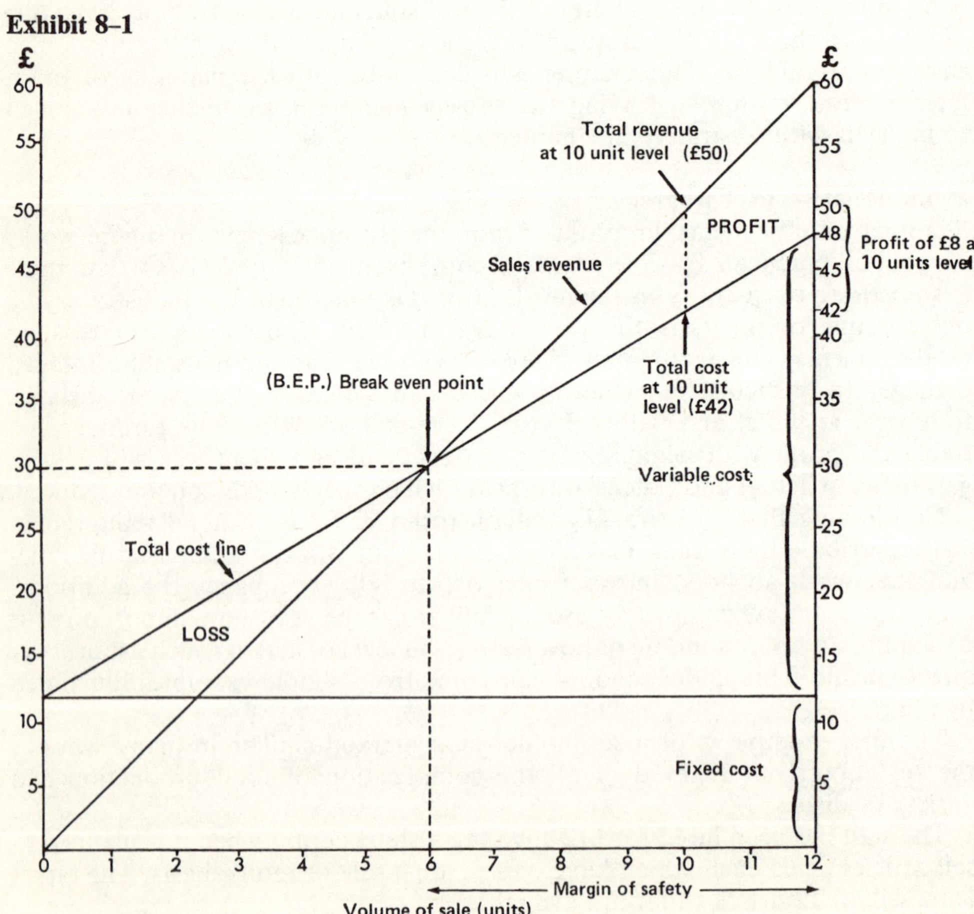

Exhibit 8–1a

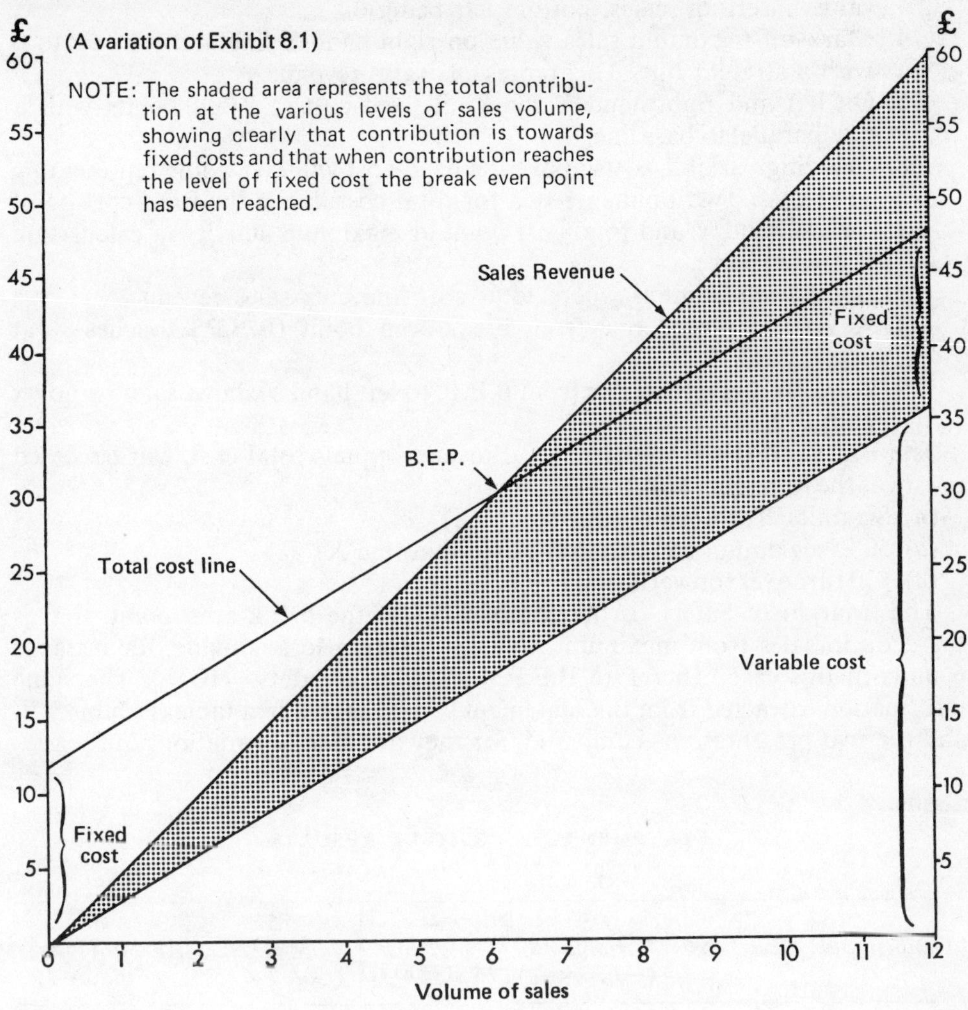

DRAWING A BREAK-EVEN CHART (EXHIBIT 8–1)

1. Calculate values of maximum sales revenue and maximum activity, activity being measured in units, covers, hours, etc.
2. Determine X (horizontal) and Y (vertical) scales taking into account:
   (*a*) Y scale represents £s
   (*b*) X scale represents activity
   (*c*) maximum sales and activity
   (*d*) the larger the scale the more accurate will be results
   (*e*) wherever possible multiples of 5 or 2 in the scale
   (*f*) a chart may cover 1 month, 3 months or 1 year according to the problem.

3. Draw in X line and two Y lines, one from 0 and one from maximum X value, inserting scales, bottom left being 0.
4. Mark off maximum sales value on right hand Y line and join up to 0 with a straight line. This represents sales revenue.
5. On left and right hand Y mark off fixed cost and join points with a line parallel to base line.
6. Inserting variable costs above the fixed cost will give a line representing total cost. Two points needed for total cost line is the fixed cost point on left hand Y and total cost point at maximum activity (a calculation is needed here).
7. Break-even point is where total cost line cuts sales revenue.
8. A vertical dotted line from break-even point (B.E.P.) touches X at activity B.E.P.
9. A horizontal dotted line from B.E.P. to left hand Y shows sales turnover at B.E.P.

The B.E.P., at the level where total revenue equals total cost, can be stated in any of the following terms:

(*a*) Six units of sale (on horizontal line X)
(*b*) 50% maximum capacity (on horizontal line X)
(*c*) £30 turnover (on vertical line Y)

The 'Margin of Safety' is the complement of the break-even point, that is the drop in sales from maximum capacity before a loss is made, for instance 6 units in this case. Therefore B.E.P. + Margin of Safety = 100%. The same information extracted from this statement can be shown in a table (Exhibit 8–2) and the two presentations compared, for they are merely variations in form.

Exhibit 8–2

STATEMENT OF POSSIBLE RESULTS
TOTAL COST APPROACH

1 Number sold	*2* Fixed cost	*3* Variable cost (Col. 1 × £3)	*4* Total cost (Col. 2+3)	*5* Sales revenue (Col. 1 × £5)	*6* Profit/(Loss) (Col. 5−4)
	£	£	£	£	£
0	12	0	12	0	(12)
1	12	3	15	5	(10)
2	12	6	18	10	(8)
3	12	9	21	15	(6)
4	12	12	24	20	(4)
5	12	15	27	25	(2)
6	12	18	30	30	0
7	12	21	33	35	2
8	12	24	36	40	4
9	12	27	39	45	6
10	12	30	42	50	8
11	12	33	45	55	10
12	12	36	48	60	12

Contribution

An important concept in profit planning is the term 'contribution' which is the sales revenue less variable cost. The stallholder receives a contribution of £2 for each article sold (£5–£3). A period when no sales were made at all would involve him in £12 loss (stall hire), but every article sold would contribute £2 towards reducing this loss, until the £12 had been balanced by contributions.

Exhibit 8–3 shows this approach in table form. It can be seen that articles sold 'contribute' towards the fixed cost, and when this has been 'recovered' all additional contributions represent profit, e.g. at 7 unit level profit = 1 contribution @ £2. Where the only significant variable cost is food, liquor, etc., then for practical purposes, contribution may be regarded as gross profit.

Exhibit 8–3

STATEMENT OF POSSIBLE RESULTS
CONTRIBUTION APPROACH

1	*2*	*3*	*4*	*5*	*6*	*7*	*8*
Number sold	*Sales revenue (Col. 1 × £5)*	*Variable cost (Col. 1 × £3)*	*Contribution (Col. 2 – 3)*	*Fixed cost*	*Loss (Col. 4 – 5)*	*Profit (Col. 4 – 5) or (Col. 8 × £2)*	*Units sold above B.E.P. of 6*
	£	£	£	£	£	£	
0	0	0	0	12	(12)		
1	5	3	2	12	(10)		
2	10	6	4	12	(8)		
3	15	9	6	12	(6)		
4	20	12	8	12	(4)		
5	25	15	10	12	(2)		
6	30	18	12	12		0	
7	35	21	14	12		2	1
8	40	24	16	12		4	2
9	45	27	18	12		6	3
10	50	30	20	12		8	4
11	55	33	22	12		10	5
12	60	36	24	12		12	6

Profit-Volume Chart

The profit-volume chart in Exhibit 8–4 is drawn to show this characteristic of the contribution. Two clear advantages can be claimed for this chart compared with the break-even chart:

(*a*) Profit or loss at any level can be read off more easily.

(*b*) Because of its simplicity in appearance, variations in contribution and fixed cost can be shown on one chart.

Exhibit 8–4

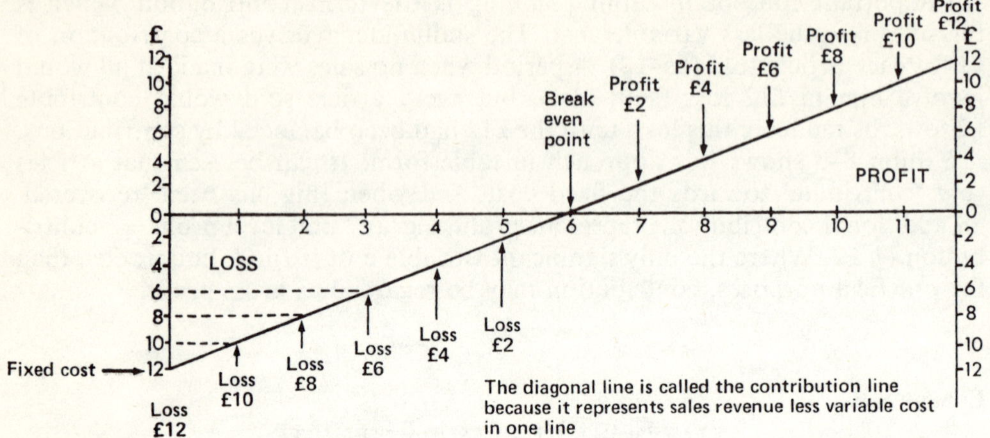

Instructions for preparation of the profit-volume chart are as follows:

1. Calculate profit at maximum sales level. This added to the fixed cost is the maximum value of the vertical (Y) line.
2. Draw the vertical line to scale and insert 0 value so that above it represents profit and below it fixed cost.
3. Draw in the horizontal (X) line to a scale to represent sales units.
4. The 'contribution' line starts at the fixed cost point on the vertical line and needs one more point to fix its position. This point can be either the break-even point or the profit at any particular sales level, and each involves calculation.
5. The fixed cost is joined to, say, the B.E.P. and the profit graph is completed.

Should the stallholder be faced with a £16 charge for the period the profit volume chart representing this situation – Exhibit 8–5 indicates a break-even point of 8 units and a profit of £8 if all 12 articles were sold.

Exhibit 8–5

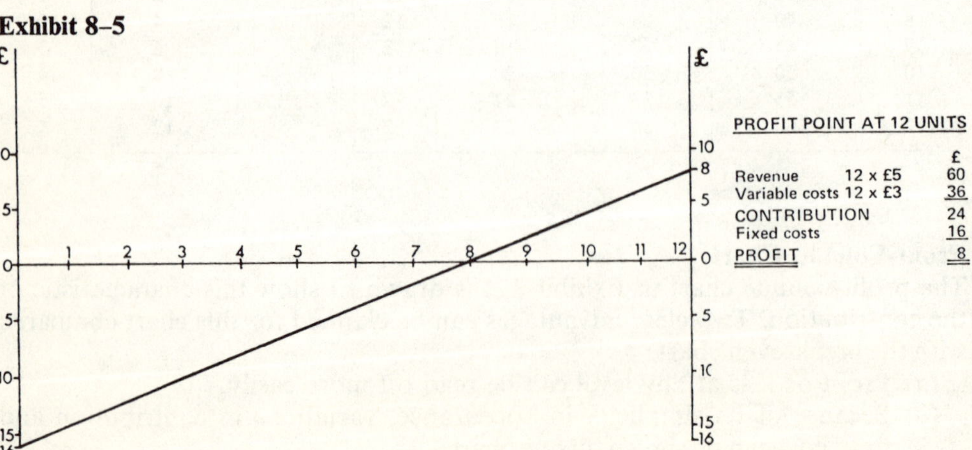

If he then increased his selling price to £5·5 to counter the increased fixed cost, with cost remaining at £3 each a further chart – Exhibit 8–6 shows a break-even point of 7 (6·4) and a profit of £14 if all 12 articles were sold.

Exhibit 8–6

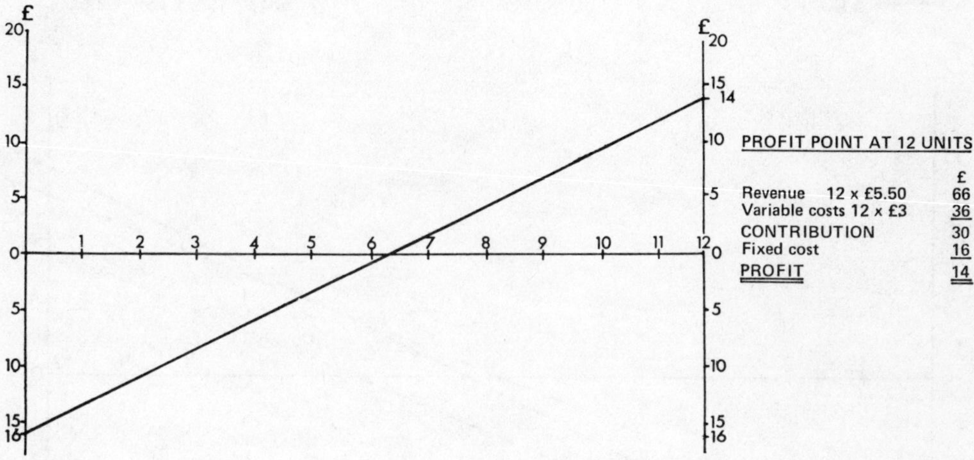

All three situations may be shown on a single chart (Exhibit 8–7) facilitating useful comparisons. Comparing the 3rd situation with the 1st he would improve profit by £2 if he sells all 12, but if business were poor he would be £1 out of pocket instead of breaking even, if only 6 were sold. From Exhibit 8–4 it can be seen that the calculation of break-even point in units is:

$$\text{Total fixed cost for period} \div \text{contribution per unit}$$

Using the original figures in Exhibit 8–1 the break-even point is calculated by this formula:

$$£12 \div £2 = 6 \text{ units}$$

More useful may be to know how many articles have to be sold to achieve a profit target, and the following formula gives the answer:

$$\frac{\text{Total fixed costs} + \text{profit}}{\text{Contribution per unit}}$$

Suppose £10 profit is wanted, then 11 units have to be sold:

$$\frac{£12 + £10}{£2} = 11 \text{ uni}$$

Exhibit 8–7

	Selling Price	Variable Cost	Contribution	Fixed cost	Break even Point in Units	Break even Point Calculation
	£	£	£	£		
1——	5.00	3	2.00	12	6	£12 ÷ £2.00
2-----	5.00	3	2.00	16	8	£16 ÷ £2.00
3——	5.50	3	2.50	16	**7 (6.4)**	£16 ÷ £2.50

Contribution to Sales Ratio[1]

Another variation of using the contribution for planning profit is to relate the contribution to sales revenue in terms of percentage of sales. This important percentage is called the Contribution to Sales Ratio (C/S) and is similar to the gross profit percentage used so excessively in the industry. If percentage figures are put alongside figures just used, the following results:

	£	%
Selling price	5	100
Variable cost	3	60
Contribution	2	40

The gross margin is 40%, or in other words the contribution to sales ratio is 40%. This can be used to determine BEP in value and also the turnover value to achieve a particular profit, the formulae being:

[1]Formerly known as profit volume ratio (P/V ratio).

$$\text{Fixed cost} \div \text{C/S ratio}$$

and

$$\frac{\text{Fixed cost} + \text{profit}}{\text{C/S ratio}}$$

Using again the original example,

$$\text{BEP in £ turnover} = £12 \div 40\% = £30$$

$$\text{£ turnover for £10 profit} = \frac{£12 + £10}{40\%} = £55$$

It can be seen that if cost behaviour is predictable then numerical tables and charts may be prepared to show the effect on profit of variations in plans, and especially in volume changes.

Multi-Activity Profit-Volume Chart

A profit-volume chart can be drawn to depict how each product, service or department contributes to profit, and for convenience they are drawn in order of profitability with the highest contribution to sales product first (C). Total fixed cost for the enterprise is marked as with a profit chart, and a line drawn showing C's contribution, then B and A.

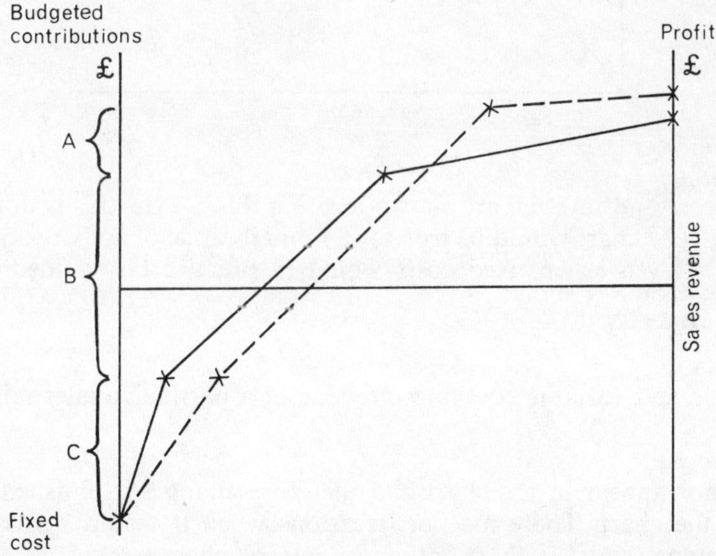

In the illustration the dotted line is actual and the other the budget. It can be seen that C's contribution was the same as budgeted but from higher sales. B's contribution to sales on the other hand improved and boosted profits but A's fell as did its sales.

Break-even Charts Review

Economics break-even chart

Accurate break-even charts in the form described earlier depend upon costs and revenue being represented by straightlines (are linear). The chart is nevertheless useful if the picture provided is an approximate representation of the data. An economics break-even chart generally shows average selling price falling as extra sales meet more competition, and the law of diminishing returns increasing the variable unit cost.

Two break-even points result from these factors:

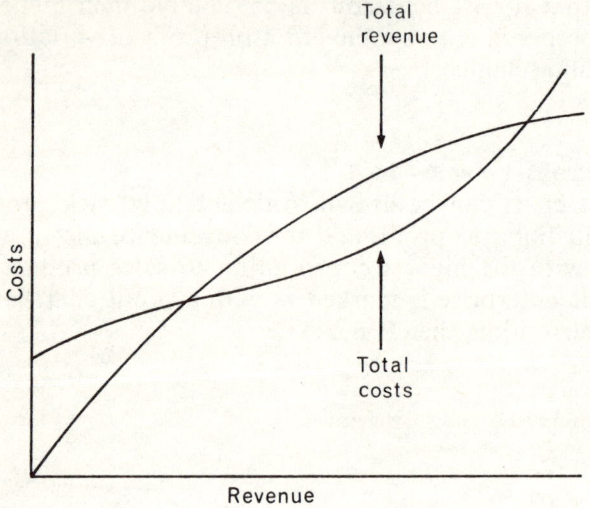

Relevant range

Although cost and revenue are shown meeting the Y axis, this is done for ease of drawing. The chart would be true for a limited range of activity and certainly not for low levels when fixed costs would in practice be avoided by closing facilities.

Product mix

The revenue and variable cost lines are true of a particular sales mix only.

Finished stocks

These do not appear in the chart and therefore changes in finished stocks do not affect the chart. There may be occasions when it would be dangerous to make decisions using the chart but ignoring stock changes.

Cash break-even charts

Two forms of cash break-even chart are available to management, one in which cash payments and cash receipts for a year replace costs and revenue in the orthodox form.

The other covers any relevant period with cumulative cash being shown. It gives a profile of cash associated with an investment project and shows how many years will elapse before the investment is recovered in cash. It takes the form of a profit chart if cash inflow is constant.

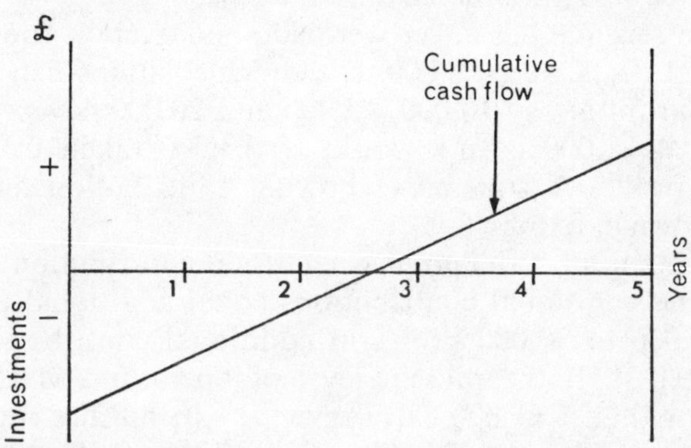

Simple Profit Planning

Operation of vending machines provides another simple profit planning example where costs again are either fixed or variable.

Let the machine be sighted outside a greengrocer's shop on a piece of ground useless for other purposes, and let it dispense drinks at 5p each. Mr. G. the greengrocer decides to load both channels with the same powder to produce drink A. Costs associated with the operation are estimated to be:

Annual hire charge and maintenance			£95
Electricity and water per annum			£5
Cost of cups £5 per 1,000	(£0·5 per 100)	} =	£2 per 100
Cost of powder £1·43 per 100 }	(£1·5 per 100)		
Estimate wastage 5% }			or 2p each

Mr. G. reckons that for every drink he sells he will receive 3p (5p – 2p) and this will contribute to the £100 annual charge. To find out how many drinks he will need to sell to recover his annual charge he divides £100 by 3p to give 3,333 drinks. He estimates that 4,000 would be his first year's sales and since this is 667 in excess of his break-even point of 3,333 his profit should be 2,000p (667 × 3p). If his sales proved to be 5,000 he would expect a profit in the year of 5,000p or (5,000 – 3,333) × 3p.

A simple profit planning exercise has been described which, magnified many times, and complicated by other factors, is the sort of work hotel and restaurant managements carry out.

Progressing to the restaurant, the contribution approach can be used to assess the expected profit for different number of covers.

Suppose for some particular reason the restaurant has persuaded an extra guest to join a party of three. The value to the business of this fourth guest is simple to estimate because it is the cash received from him – say 80p – less the food cost of the dishes served – say 50p – leaving additional profit of 30p. It might be said that the extra guest contributed 30p to the profits of the business being selling price less variable cost of the sale.

If the average revenue per cover were 80p and average food cost were 50p, and annual fixed costs were £3,000, speedy calculations can be made to discover expected profit at say 10,000, 15,000 and 20,000 covers per annum. For instance profit at 20,000 covers would be £3,000 taken from 20,000 × £0·3, leaving £3,000 profit. A statement showing contribution and profit at the three levels is shown in Exhibit 8–8.

It can be seen that after the point where total contribution equals fixed cost (10,000 level), the additional contributions equal additional profit. Increasing covers from 15,000 to 20,000 brings in additional contribution and profit of £1,500 (5,000 × £0·3). If the present level of operations is 15,000 covers per annum it is clear that if £1,000 extra revenue expenditure such as advertising were to increase turnover to 20,000 covers without affecting either present contribution (gross profit) per cover or fixed costs, then £500 extra profit could be expected.

Exhibit 8–8

Profit Statement showing contribution over a range of covers

Covers (No.)	10,000	15,000	20,000
	£	£	£
Sales @ £0·8	8,000	12,000	16,000
Less variable costs @ £0·5	5,000	7,500	10,000
CONTRIBUTION @ £0·3	3,000	4,500	6,000
Less fixed cost	3,000	3,000	3,000
PROFIT	NIL	1,500	3,000

The concern here has been with the average price for the average meal which is required to achieve a total contribution and profit. However, policy often suggests that certain dishes, for instance starters and vegetables, can accept a higher than average mark up, compensating for a low gross margin on some main dishes. Several reasons could be put forward for accepting on some dishes a lower than average gross margin for the business, varying from competition restricting the price, to a deliberate policy of low prices to attract customers who would be likely to take also speciality dishes which gave above average margins.

Contribution per Unit of Limiting Factor

In circumstances where there is opportunity to change the limits of operated departments it may be advisable to enlarge the most profitable department at the expense of another department. Accordingly the floor space may be regarded as the limiting factor and a calculation made to discover which department has the highest contribution per sq. metre of floor space.

Listing departments in order of contribution per sq. metre is the start-point in a profitability study.

Forecast Profit Statement year ended . . . .

Eg.		*Dept. A*	*Dept. B*	*Dept. C*	*Total*
1	Contribution	£2,000	£4,000	£5,000	£11,000
2	Square metres	1,000	1,000	2,000	4,000
(1 ÷ 2)	Contribution per sq. metre	£2	£4	£2·5	
	Order of profitability	3	1	2	

On the face of it, if say 500 square metres of Dept. A were to be used to expand Dept. B and B's sales increased by ½ without dropping selling prices total contribution would be:

		Dept. A	*Dept. B*	*Dept. C*	*Total* £
1	Contribution per sq. m.	£2	£4	£2·5	
2	Square metres	500	1,500	2,000	
(1 × 2)	New total contribution	£1,000	£6,000	£5,000	12,000
	Former contribution				11,000
	Increased annual contribution				1,000

This change in contribution takes account of changes in the total cost of food and drink caused by new sales levels. If no additional fixed costs such as salaries, equipment and advertising were involved then the additional contribution of £1,000 would become the additional profit. If equipment costing £3,000 were required, depreciation of £600 per annum over 5 years would mean the increase in profit was only £400 p.a.

Other factors to be considered would be the effect on profit if any sales in Dept. A influenced sales in Dept. B. A very small contribution by one department might be the cause of a large contribution in another department, a state of affairs which might be acceptable because in the final analysis it is *total* contribution and *total* profit that counts.

A restaurant in a departmental store may show only a small contribution, but may attract customers to sales departments where good contributions are being made.

Clearly the contribution per unit of limiting factor is a useful start for a plan to increase profitability, indeed it should precede the preparation of the sales budget.

Linear Programming

If there are two different products, services or departments competing for two or more limited resources then the linear programming 'graphical technique' will provide the answer in terms of the optimal activity mix which maximizes profits. An example will illustrate the technique.

A speciality restaurant offers two groups of dishes known as 'frieds' and 'grills', which have average contributions of £1 per dish.

	'frieds'	*'grills'*
Average labour times per dish:		
Food preparation	2 mins	3 mins
Restaurant service	5 mins	2 mins

Total food production and service available per day:

Kitchen staff	30 hours
Restaurant staff	40 hours

Current ingredient scarcity allows only 500 'grills' to be available per day.

Determine graphically the dish mix which maximizes contributions.

The solution is best commenced by laying out the relevant facts in mathematical form:

(*a*)[2] Kitchen limiting factor	$2f + 3g \leqslant 30$ hours
(*b*) Restaurant limiting factor	$5f + 2g \leqslant 40$ hours
(*c*) Food scarcity factor	$g \leqslant 500$ dishes
(*d*) Maximize contributions	£1f + £1g

As negative production is not possible f and g must be each $\geqslant$ zero.

The first three expressions may now be graphed as illustrated in Exhibit 8–9. For example, with the kitchen limiting factor the maximum number of dishes which could be produced is:

$$\text{'frieds'} \quad \frac{30 \text{ hrs} \times 60 \text{ mins}}{2 \text{ mins}} = 900$$

or

$$\text{'grills'} \quad \frac{30 \text{ hrs} \times 60 \text{ mins}}{3 \text{ mins}} = 600$$

Similarly either 480 'frieds' or 1200 'grills' could be served in 40 hours. These alternatives may be plotted on the graph together with the 500 'grills' food

[2] f = 'frieds' and g = 'grills'.

Exhibit 8–9

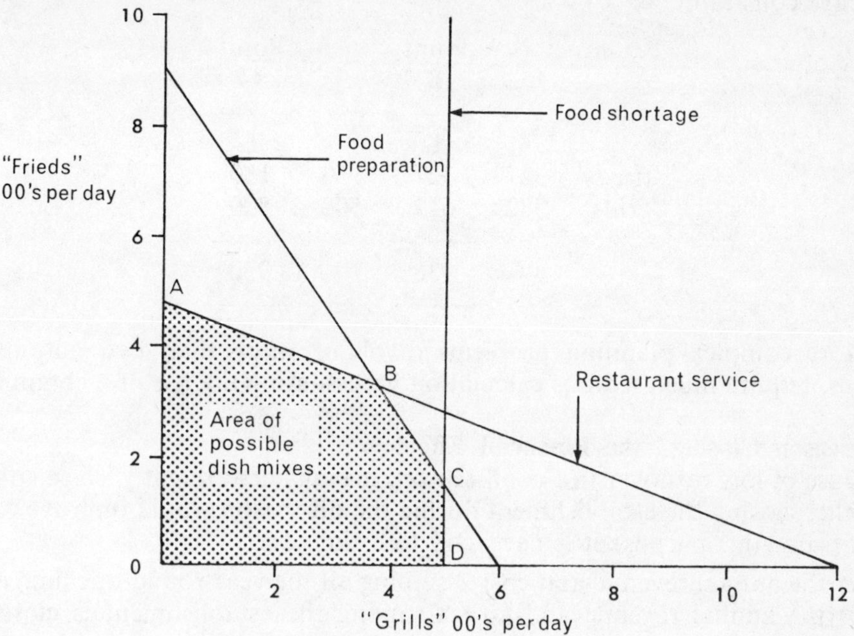

shortage. Points A, B, C, and D become the possible combinations of dishes. A ruler joining 200 'frieds' with 200 'grills' will represent all combinations of dishes to give a total contribution of £200 e.g. 200 'frieds' or 200 'grills' or 100 'frieds' and 100 'grills' etc. Keeping the slope constant and moving the ruler outwards from O, which represents increasing the total contribution, point B is the last to be reached. This point is where 327 'frieds' and 382 'grills' are produced. Maximum contribution is therefore:

					£
'frieds'	327	@	£1	=	327
'grills'	382	@	£1	=	382
					709

This is better than point C which gives:

					£
'frieds'	150	@	£1	=	150
'grills'	500	@	£1	=	500
					650

It will be noted that the food shortage is not a constraint on the optimum mix. However, if the contribution were 'frieds' . . £1 and 'grills' @ £1.60, then C would represent the best mix and the food shortage factor would become an effective constraint.

		Point B		Point C
		£		£
'frieds'	327	327	150	150
'grills'	382	611	500	800
		938		950

More complex planning problems involving more than two outputs e.g. dishes, require much tedious calculation necessitating the use of a computer.

Off-season Closing – the Financial Effect

Because of low turnover in the off-season, management might wish to consider whether closing the establishment during the off-season would improve overall profit. For this purpose it is necessary to estimate:

(*a*) the annual revenue and cost assuming all the year round opening, and
(*b*) the annual revenue and cost assuming the establishment is closed for a period.

Clearly the alternative with the highest profit would, on the face of it, be the best course of action. Different presentations may be used to show the financial comparison, but it is wise in each case to classify costs according to their behaviour, namely, variable, semi-variable and fixed.

Given the costs and revenues for a 12-month opening and an 8-month opening. Exhibit Nos 8–10 and 8–11 are examples of recommended presentations.

Exhibit 8–10

Presentation 1 – 'Total approach'

		(a) 12 months		(b) 8 months		(c) 'difference'
	£	£	£	£	£	£
Sales		50,000		45,000		5,000
Food & drink costs		20,000		18,000		2,000
GROSS MARGIN		30,000		27,000		3,000
Semi-variable costs						
Wages	10,000		8,000		2,000	
Light, heat & power	2,000		1,600		400	
Maintenance & repairs	1,500		1,300		200	
Laundering	1,000		900		100	
Telephone	250		200		50	
Depreciation	1,500		1,000		500	
Other expenses	2,750		2,700		50	
		19,000		15,700		3,300
		11,000		11,300		300
Fixed costs						
Lease	1,000		1,000			
Local rates	1,000		1,000			
Other expenses	3,000		3,000			
		5,000		5,000		nil
		6,000		6,300		300
Apply 12 months opening profit				6,000		
Additional profit from 8 months opening				300		

Note: Column (*c*) has been introduced to facilitate the 'Differences' approach of presentation 2.

Exhibit 8–11

Presentation 2 – 'Differential approach'

Effect of closing for four months	£
Savings in annual costs (detailed)	3,300
Less: Gross margin lost	3,000
Additional profit per annum	300

It should be noted that fixed costs are not relevant to the decision.

It must be remembered that statements such as these assist in decision making, but that some factors such as goodwill are difficult to quantify and may not be brought into the financial statement. The decision in this case might be to remain open all the year if at least £300 in goodwill, affecting future profits to this extent, were considered.

Questions and Problems

8–1 Explain the following terms:
(*a*) contribution
(*b*) break-even point
(*c*) margin of safety.

8–2 What is the 'contribution to sales ratio'?

8–3 Below is an outline break-even chart:

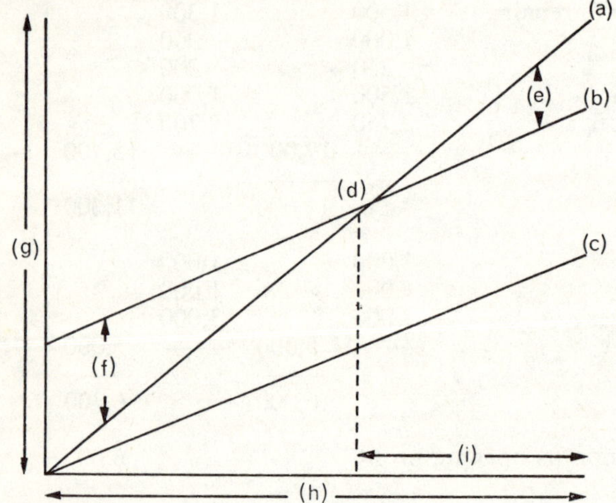

Name the various points indicated by the letters. What is the name of the area taken in by the 'origin', (*a*) and (*c*)?

8–4 Below is the outline of a profit volume break-even chart.

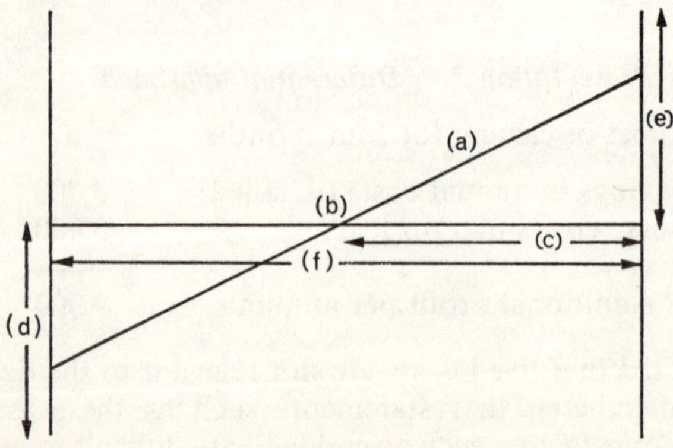

Name the various points indicated by the letters.

8–5 Accounting and economics break-even charts differ. Describe the principal differences between the charts and indicate the extent to which one is justified in using the accounting kind of chart.

8–6 Complete the following tabulation:

Annual fixed costs	*Contribution per unit*	*Break-even point*
£	£	*Units*
10,000	0·50	*
*	0·85	9,000
30,000	*	20,000

8–7 The budgeted sales of three companies are as follows:

	Company 1	*Company 2*	*Company 3*
Budgeted sales in units	10,000	10,000	10,000
Budgeted selling price per unit	£2·00	£2·00	£2·00
Budgeted variable costs per unit	£1·50	£1·25	£1·00
Budgeted fixed expenses total	£3,000	£5,500	£8,000
Budgeted capacity	80%	80%	80%

From the above information you are required to compute for each company:

(*a*) budgeted profit;
(*b*) the budgeted break-even point in unit sales;
(*c*) the budgeted margin of safety expressed as a percentage of total capacity; and
(*d*) the impact on profits of a ± 10% deviation in sales.

Comment briefly on the effect of this in relation to the distribution between the company's fixed and variable expenses.

8–8 A new restaurant is to be opened for which equipment is purchased costing £12,000 and additional working capital of £5,000 is provided.

Expected annual costs are rent and rates £2,500, salaries £3,000, insurance £100, and depreciation is to be 10% per annum of the cost of the equipment. Variable costs other than food will be 30% of sales.

It will be the policy of the management to add 200% to the food cost to give selling price which will be £1·50 per cover.

From this information you are required to determine by both calculation and break-even chart:

(*a*) the break-even point in number of covers per annum, and
(*b*) the number of covers necessary per annum to make a return of 20% on capital employed.

8–9 Silvermere Developments Ltd has the opportunity of opening a restaurant in Brightsea which would be called 'Silversea Chef'. Silvermere

Developments Ltd would have to pay £36,000 for the fixed assets and provide £4,000 working capital. A feasibility study has been completed and the results indicate annual costs (exclusive of VAT) as follows:

(i) food costs of between 35% and 45% of sales
(ii) wages £14,000, and
(iii) other costs £16,000.

Although the 'Silversea Chef' would be able to cater for 30,000 customers per annum, the feasibility study forecasts a demand of between 20,000 to 25,000 customers per annum with an average spending power of £2·70 (inclusive of VAT at 8%) per customer. The wages and other costs will cover the range of demand forecasted.

You are to prepare a report for the Board of Directors of Silvermere Developments Ltd (which expects a return on capital of 15%) on the viability of financing the opening of the 'Silversea Chef' to include a statement of the forecast of the range of profit or loss per annum and a break-even (or contribution) chart. (HCIMA)

8–10 The following information relates to three alternative forecasts A, B and C each of which has the same price and the same potential level of sales but only one can be included in the next period's budget. Present this information in a suitable graphical form and comment on it in respect of the particular problem under consideration.

	A	*B*	*C*
Selling price	£1	£1	£1
Contribution to sales ratio	20%	15%	10%
Fixed costs	£9,500	£6,000	£3,750
Estimated sales	60,000 (covers)	60,000 (covers)	60,000 (covers)

8–11 The following information is taken from the accounts of the Linda Restaurant.

	Sales £	*Total costs* £
Year 1	60,000	54,000
Year 2	64,000	56,400
Year 3	70,000	60,000

(*a*) From this information calculate the net profit to be achieved in Year 4 if sales are £80,000 as estimated and fixed costs increase by £4,000.

(*b*) Calculate also the break-even point when sales are £80,000.

8–12 A food processing job is done manually by employees who can each carry out 1,500 jobs in a week, and whose wages are £90 each per week. The cost of food supplies required in this task is £500 per 1,000 jobs.

As a result of a work study investigation it is found that the task can be undertaken by a piece of equipment costing £32,500 with a capacity of up to 9,000 jobs per week. The operator would be paid £120 per week but would not be available for other work as he is a specialist operator. The present employees on this work are moved to other work should the need arise.

Costs associated with the equipment are:

Maintenance per week £30
Operating costs £20 per 1,000 jobs
Food supplies £500 per 1,000 jobs
The machine would be depreciated over 5 years of 50 weeks on a straight line basis with no residual value

You are required to ascertain the weekly level of activity beyond which there would be a cost saving to the company by having the work mechanized.

Your answer should be arrived at by each of the following methods:
(*a*) Tabulation;
(*b*) Calculation;
(*c*) Break-even chart.

8–13 It is possible to prepare a profit/volume break-even chart from successive sets of past sales and profit figures and then to use the chart to predict future results. For any volume of sales, a figure for total costs can then be read off the chart and the fixed and variable elements of total costs isolated.

You are required to:

(*a*) draw a break-even chart from the following figures:

	Sales	*Profit*
	£	£
Year 1	3,200,000	80,000
Year 2	3,500,000	200,000

(*b*) predict the variable cost, contribution, fixed cost and profit associated with £5,000,000 sales volume, and set out your predictions in the form of a profit statement; and
(*c*) state the main assumptions underlying predictions such as these.

8–14 Go-Ahead Hotels Ltd. offer a package holiday which during the current year has sold for £40, the variable cost being £25. The company's accountant has estimated the profit for the year at £150,000 after allowing for fixed costs of £120,000.

During discussion on the 1979 budget the hotels' controller said he anticipated a unit variable cost rise of £1 following a recent wage award. The accountant expects fixed costs to rise by £5,000 this being due, in the main, to increased rental payable under the company's leases which are currently being re-negotiated. The marketing manager thought the market was buoyant but also owing to rising costs, competitors would increase the prices of their holidays in 1979. He expressed the views that:

(*i*) with the price remaining at £40, the number of holidays sold next year would increase by 10%; and

(*ii*) if the price could be reduced by £1, increase in sales of 25% could be expected.

You are required to:

(*a*) present a statement to show which of the marketing manager's proposals provide the greater amount of profit;

(*b*) calculate in respect of each alternative the break-even point in terms of sales volume; and

(*c*) under alternative (*ii*) how many holidays would the company need to sell to earn a profit of £160,000?

8–15 A company which produces two food products has annual fixed costs of £12,000:

	Food product A	*Food product B*
	£	£
Selling price	5	4
Less: Variable costs	2	2
Contribution	3	2

The desired product mix is two of A for every one of B. You are required to show by both calculation and break-even chart how many of each food product need to be sold to break even.

8–16 Precise Limited has prepared the following budget for the forthcoming year:

	Restaurant	*Canteen*	*Total*
No. of meals	40,000	120,000	160,000
	£	£	£
Sales	80,000	360,000	440,000
Expenses:			
Food	20,000	80,000	100,000
Direct labour	4,000	140,000	144,000
Overheads	40,000	90,000	130,000
	64,000	310,000	374,000
Profit	16,000	50,000	66,000

The overhead figures contain both fixed and variable overheads. The variable element is estimated to be 30% of the direct labour expense.

You are required to:

(*a*) Ascertain by calculation the break-even point assuming sales remain constant; and
(*b*) Draw a multi-activity profit volume chart and explain why the break-even point differs from your calculations in (*a*) above.

8–17 A catering company has decided that its profit on turnover is insufficient and after investigation, has concluded that it must attempt to change its mix of sales.

Budgeted data for the year:	£
Total budgeted sales value	5,000
Total fixed overhead	800

Sales of individual products

Food product	Mix %	Total variable costs £
K	40	1,500
L	10	600
M	30	1,200
N	20	600

Proposed budget for the year:
The sales director is faced with severe competition in his market, so does not believe that he can increase total sales. However, he believes that if he discontinues product L he can increase sales of the remaining food products, so that the original total budgeted sales value would be unchanged. His recommendation is based on an estimate that the sales mix should be:

Food product:		%
	K	40
	M	20
	N	40

You are required to:

(*a*) present on graph paper a profit-volume graph to show:
 (i) the results of the budgeted sales mix for the year; and
 (ii) the expected results if the sales mix were changed to that recommended by the sales director;
(*b*) comment on the results shown on your graph.

8–18 The Premier Catering Company offers four menus, details of which are as follows:

	Menus			
	W	X	Y	Z
	£	£	£	£
Selling price	3	10	6	5
Less: Variable costs	1	4	4	2
Contribution	2	6	2	3

Each menu absorbs units of a limiting factor per cover i.e. Menu W, 4 units; Menu X, 10 units; Menu Y, 2 units; Menu Z, 4 units. The sales manager has carried out a market research study which has resulted in the following forcast of the maximum covers per menu for the coming period: Menu W, 20,000; Menu X, 8,000; Menu Y, 15,000; Menu Z, 12,000. Further, the total amount of limiting factor estimated to be available during the next period is 108,000 units. You are required to calculate the optimum sales mix and the total contribution which results.

8–19 A large hotel has 500 rooms divided into 200 suites and 300 double bedrooms. The hotel is full for nine months of each year but from January to March business is fairly quiet. Room tariffs, costs etc., are as follows:

	Suite	*Double room*
Selling price	£20	£12
Variable costs (including room servicing)	£9	£5
Room servicing times	1 hour	$\frac{1}{2}$ hour

Experience has shown that during the three-month period the maximum number of room lets that can be made are 4,000 suite room nights and 9,000 double room nights. The total number of room servicing hours available is estimated to be 7,000 hours.

Using the linear programming graphical technique determine the combination of suite/room lets which will yield the greatest profit.

8–20 Your company is considering the purchase of an hotel in Torquay. On the basis of past years' trading results, the estimated figures for future years' trading results are as follows:

	1st April to 30th September	*1st October to 31st March*
	£	£
Sales	43,000	15,000
Other income	4,000	700
Cost of sales	23,000	8,000
Wages	14,000	4,000
Heat and light	600	700
Repairs and maintenance	500	250
Rates	1,000	1,000
Other expenses	400	50
Depreciation:		
Premises	2,000	2,000
Fittings	900	900
China, cutlery etc.	300	100

If the hotel closed during the off season, then the depreciation on fittings would be reduced to £500 and China, Cutlery, etc., £Nil.
You are required to:

(*a*) prepare financial statement(s) to illustrate the advisability of remaining open (or closing) during the off season periods; and
(*b*) if it is the company's policy to achieve a return on investment of 12%, what is the maximum price it could offer for the hotel?

8–21 In April 1975, the budget committee of The Lawrence Hotel Ltd., formulated the master budget for the year ended 31st May 1976, on the basis of information then available. A summary of the master revenue accounts follows:

THE LAWRENCE HOTEL LIMITED

Master trading, profit and loss account for the year ended 31st May, 1976

	Total		Season		Off-season	
	£	£	£	£	£	£
Sales		100,000		80,000		20,000
Variable costs	44,000		32,000		12,000	
Fixed costs	40,000		33,000		7,000	
Total costs		84,000		65,000		19,000
Net profit		16,000		15,000		1,000

Additional information:

(*a*) Normally the hotel opens all the year. The season is regarded as June to September inclusive.

(*b*) Variable costs are:
  (i) 40% of sales in the season; and
  (ii) 60% of sales in the off-season.

(*c*) The actual results for the 3 months June to August 1975 inclusive show:

	£	£
Sales		50,000
Variable costs	20,000	
Fixed costs	24,750	
Total costs		44,750
Net profit		5,250

(*d*) Bookings for the rest of the year are down and the forecast sales for September is £10,000, and for the off-season is £12,000.

(*e*) The marketing director recommends an advertising campaign to the Board of Directors which can only be launched for both September and the off-season. This offers a reduction in charges which will increase the sales forecasts in (*d*) by 50% and effectively increase the variable costs in September to 50% of sales and in the off-season to 65% of sales.

(*f*) Other hotels in the area are in a similar position. The Grand Hotel has offered to take over all the off-season business of The Lawrence Hotel at the current rates charged by the Lawrence Hotel and to give it agents commission of 15% of sales. The September bookings will have to be honoured.

You are required to prepare:

(*i*) the forecasted trading, profit and loss accounts for September and the off-season assuming the Company makes no changes at all;

(*ii*) the revised forecast, for the same periods if the marketing director's proposal IS accepted; and

(*iii*) the revised forecast, for the same periods if the offer from the Grand Hotel is accepted; and

(*iv*) a report for the Board of Directors indicating, *with reasons*, which of the alternatives it should accept (HCIMA)

8–22 Feasts Ltd. own and operate the Elizabethan Rooms which specialize in medieval-style banquets.

The average cost and profit structure per cover for the current year, based on 50,000 covers, has been prepared:

	£
Food	2·00
Direct labour	0·60
Variable overhead	0·40
Fixed overhead	1·20
Profit	0·80
Average spending	5·00

At present the directors are considering alternative courses of action for the coming year:

Alternative 1
To continue with the existing method of operation. If this alternative is adopted, then it is anticipated that the current year's costs will increase as follows:

	%
Food	11·5
Direct labour	15·0
Variable overhead	20·0
Fixed overhead	10·0

Alternative 2
To modernize the system of food production and service by introducing convenience foods and a limited degree of self-service. An analysis has been carried out and, if this alternative is adopted, the new system will have the following effect on the current year's costs:

Decrease in total variable cost per cover	£0·20
Increase in fixed cost per annum	£45,000

Irrespective of which alternative is selected, the directors estimate that:

(*i*) the volume of business will increase during the coming year to 70,000 covers;

(*ii*) a 6% price rise, effective from the beginning of the coming year, is unlikely to affect the estimated level of demand.

You are requested to:

(*a*) calculate, for each alternative, the number of covers that would have to be sold in order to maintain the current year's profits at their present level;

(*b*) calculate (or determine graphically) the number of covers beyond which it would prove more profitable to introduce the modernized system; and

(*c*) comment briefly on the financial implications of the alternatives and recommend to the directors which alternative should be adopted. (HCIMA)

8–23 The Cozy Restaurant has made a loss of £3,636 over the first six months of the year although it had been estimated that a profit of £10,000 would be made for the year.

Various proposals have been made to rectify the situation. You are required to evaluate and comment upon each of these proposals.

Figures for the six months show:

	£
Sales revenue	100,000
Cost of food used	60,000
Labour cost	25,000
Overheads	18,636

The average spending is exactly £2 per customer. The full capacity of the restaurant is twice the occupancy which has been achieved.

However, labour costs have been analysed and it has been ascertained that £5,000 is constant but the remainder is proportionate to the level of sales.

Of other overheads, £8,636 is fixed. This figure would be increased, however, if the restaurant was working above 75% capacity constantly, as additional plant would be required.

Proposal 1 Spend £1,000 on advertising to increase sales.

Proposal 2 Introduce a scheme for bulk buying of food used. It is estimated that this will reduce costs by 9% but fixed overheads will be increased by £1,000.

Proposal 3 To reduce prices by 15% to achieve 100% capacity utilization.

Proposal 4 For the foreseeable future to plan only to break even and to reduce variable costs other than cost of goods used to achieve this. (HCIMA)

Further Reading

1. Bell, A. L., Break-Even Charts Versus Marginal Graphs, (DeCoster, D. T., Ramanathan, K. V., Sundem, G. L.) *Accounting for Managerial Decision Making*, Melville Publishing Company; pp. 147–157.

2. Fay, C. T., Rhoads, R. C., Rosenblatt, R. L., *Managerial Accounting for the Hospitality Service Industries*, W. C. Brown Company Publishers; chapter 11.
3. Horngren, C. T., *Cost Accounting, a managerial emphasis*, Prentice-Hall Inc.; chapters 3, 11 and 25.
4. Sizer, J., *An Insight into Management Accounting*, Penguin Books; chapter 8.

CHAPTER NINE

PRICE DETERMINATION

Pricing decisions form one of management's most important tasks. The success or failure of an undertaking may depend on the ability of management to develop acceptable prices for goods and services. Formulating an effective price policy is a complex and delicate matter and one which calls for a knowledge of economic, market, financial and psychological factors. However, the subsequent discussion is concerned with the more practical financial aspects of pricing in relation to hotel, catering and institutional activities.

There appear to be two basic ways of pricing with numerous variations of each.

Traditional Cost-plus Pricing

In essence, this approach consists of adding a predetermined amount, termed 'mark-up', to an estimated product or service cost to arrive at a selling price. Normally mark-up is applied in the form of a percentage and this may be expressed as a simple equation:

$$\text{Cost} + \text{Mark-up} = \text{Selling price}$$

The composition, in terms of the proportion of cost to mark-up, gives rise to the cost-plus pricing variations.

The basic approach, known as 'full' or 'total' cost pricing, entails establishing the total cost of individual products to which is added an anticipated amount for net profit. Thus, referring to the basic cost-plus equation the cost component represents total cost, and mark-up depicts net profit.

A variation, termed 'direct cost pricing', requires the ascertainment of product prime costs i.e. direct material, direct labour and direct expenses, to which is added a margin sufficient to cover indirect costs (overhead) and provide an adequate net profit. Reference to the cost-plus equation indicates that the cost element represents total direct costs whilst mark-up comprises overheads plus net profit.

Another variation, referred to as 'gross margin pricing' calls for an expected amount for gross profit to be added to the direct material cost i.e. food and beverages. This should normally be sufficient to cover all remaining costs plus an acceptable net profit. Again, referring to the cost-plus equation, it will be seen that the cost component consists solely of direct material while the mark-up element embraces all other costs plus net profit. Below is an example of gross margin pricing:

Market research indicates that a proposed new restaurant has an annual sales volume potential of 80,000 covers at a selling price between £1·50 and £2·50 per cover. Estimated annual costs are food £64,000, labour £55,000, and all expenses £21,000. The directors expect the restaurant to achieve a net profit of £20,000 per annum. Determine a pricing policy, in terms of the average mark-up percentage to be added to the food cost per cover which will realize the directors' objective:

	£
Net profit required	20,000
Labour	55,000
Expenses	21,000
Gross profit	96,000
Food cost	64,000
Total sales revenue	160,000

$$\therefore \quad \text{Mark-up pricing policy} = \frac{£96,000}{£64,000} \times \frac{100}{1} = 150\%$$

This establishes that an average mark-up being 150% of cost requires to be added to the food cost in order that the £76,000 labour and expense costs are recovered and the net profit of £20,000 achieved.

It is worth mentioning that in absolute terms mark-up and gross profit are the same figure. However, gross profit becomes gross profit percentage when related to selling price, but mark-up when related to cost. Therefore, if the pricing policy of the previous example had been expressed in terms of an average gross margin (profit) percentage then the result would have appeared as follows:

$$\text{Gross margin pricing policy} = \frac{£96,000}{£160,000} \times \frac{100}{1} = 60\%$$

This in turn indicates that an average of 60% of the selling price must be added to the food cost so as to cover other costs and provide the desired net profit. The traditional cost-plus pricing variations are summarized in Exhibit 9–1 (overleaf).

Exhibit 9–1

TRADITIONAL COST-PLUS PRICING VARIATIONS

	Cost base				Mark-up	
'Full cost pricing'	Direct material	Direct labour	Direct expenses	Indirect Cost	Profit	= Selling price

	Cost base			Mark-up		
'Direct cost pricing'	Direct material	Direct labour	Direct expenses	Indirect cost	Profit	= Selling price

	Cost base	Mark-up				
'Gross' margin pricing'	Direct material	Direct labour	Direct expenses	Indirect cost	Profit	= Selling price

A further variation of cost-plus pricing is 'rate of return pricing'. In this case net profit is established from the rate of return on capital employed laid down by top management. Having ascertained the net profit figure any of the preceding methods may then be adopted to apply to the average dish cost. Below is an example of pricing using the rate of return approach:

A catering company is investigating the possibility of investing £200,000 in a new restaurant venture from which the directors would require a return of at least 15% per annum. The average spending per customer is anticipated to be £5. Activity is estimated to be in the region of 40,000 covers per annum and associated labour and overhead costs of £100,000. Determine the gross margin pricing policy which will give the return required by the directors.

$$\text{Net profit to achieve desired return on investment} = \frac{£200{,}000 \times 15}{100} = £30{,}000$$

Estimated gross profit:

	£
Net profit	30,000
Labour and overheads	100,000
	130,000

$$\text{Anticipated sales turnover} = 40{,}000 \times £5 = £200{,}000$$

$$\therefore \text{ Gross margin pricing policy} = \frac{£130{,}000 \times 100}{£200{,}000} = 65\%$$

Providing the sales and cost levels occur as planned then the gross profit percentage of 65% will ensure that the required net profit, and therefore return on investment, is achieved.

In practice it is the gross margin variation (with or without the rate of return element) which is normally adopted and this is usually applied to food and beverages. The reason stems from the nature of catering activities. In contrast to those of manufacturing, catering undertakings experience what may be described as 'short-run' or 'erratic' activity cycles. For instance, take the case of a table d'hôte restaurant in an hotel. In order to provide meals for breakfast, luncheon and dinner services the restaurant has to engage in three distinct production cycles per day, each of which comprises a relatively small number of different dishes. It therefore becomes impractical to build up full or total product (dish) costs by allocating and apportioning associated costs, and as a result the gross margin pricing variation is employed to facilitate the recovery of wages and other indirect costs and provide a net profit. A similar kind of situation occurs with beverages in that although there is no production activity and the length of the service cycle is not so significant, the wide variety of low value drink items available also renders total cost ascertainment impractical.

As total and even prime cost ascertainment often proves an uneconomic exercise it becomes apparent that the material cost of food and beverages provide the only suitable base on which mark-up or gross profit percentage may be applied. This means that by comparison with manufacturing undertakings the link between cost and price is relatively tenuous. Moreover, the further up-market the undertaking the weaker the link becomes, as the tendency is for the material cost to pale into insignificance.

In larger catering organizations where centralized food production may be employed it sometimes becomes possible to ascertain a higher proportion of total unit cost. This normally occurs through specialization derived from the division of labour and this permits, in addition to food cost, the identification of direct labour cost. The use of convenience food provides a similar example. In this case the price paid for the food will include the processor's material, labour and expense costs plus an element of net profit. Therefore, in both instances, the amount of unit cost that may be identified increases and subsequently has a stronger bearing on selling price.

Turning to accommodation, the case for traditional cost-plus pricing is even less convincing than for food and beverages. Room sales effectively constitute a rental or hire charge and by their nature do not involve material cost. This, coupled with the fact that other identifiable costs are normally insignificant in relation to selling price, stretches the already tenuous link between cost and price to a point where for practical purposes the relationship becomes meaningless.

Contribution Pricing[1]

Whereas traditional cost-plus pricing aims to cover total cost and a target profit, contribution pricing seeks to achieve a target contribution towards fixed costs and profit. This necessitates the identification of fixed and variable cost be-

[1]Sometimes referred to as 'marginal cost pricing'.

haviour patterns and is based on the premise that prices are set using variable cost as the floor and what the market will bear as the ceiling. The general philosophy behind this approach is that although individual sales may not achieve a net profit the sum total of contributions from all sales will be sufficient to cover fixed costs and provide an adequate net profit.

Where this approach is implemented fixed costs are treated as 'period costs' and subsequently written off against profit at the end of the accounting period. They may be allocated to products and services or departments for planning purposes, but this should be in total for an anticipated volume and sales mix and not per unit. The reason being that unit costs are valid only at a given sales volume and mix.

Contribution pricing can serve as a particularly useful approach in service industries such as hotel and catering where a relatively high proportion of fixed cost to total cost is apparent. For instance, assume the variable costs and selling price of an hotel room night is as indicated below:

	Room	
	£	£
Selling price		18
Less: Variable costs		
Direct labour	2	
Variable overhead	1	3
Contribution		15

Providing the room sale achieves a price in excess of the amount of the variable cost i.e. £3, then a contribution will be generated towards fixed cost and net profit for the period as a whole. The extent of the price latitude, what economists call price discretion, is equal to the difference between the variable cost and the normal selling price, or viewed another way, equal to the contribution which in either case is £15. This provides the high fixed cost undertaking with considerable scope in which to develop an imaginative (flexible) pricing policy that will increase capacity utilization and net profit.

Cost-plus v Contribution

A considerable amount of controversy surrounds the issue of the most suitable pricing approach to adopt.

Arguments for cost-plus pricing:

- it forms a logical basis on which to recover total costs.
- compared with other approaches, which require the separation of fixed and variable costs, it is simple to understand and 'safe' to use.
- it provides what business men describe as a 'fair' profit.
- it encourages price stability, whereas constant short-term price changes may prejudice long-term objectives.

Criticisms of cost-plus pricing:

- demand is ignored in terms of what the customer is prepared to pay, and it erroneously suggests that the correct price is the sum of all costs plus an assumed mark-up.
- it involves circular reasoning in that cost depends on volume, but volume is influenced by price.
- as the combination of cost and mark-up in respect of competitors is unlikely to result in a similar price, sales will normally go to the lower priced product or service.
- it is misleading in that it exaggerates the precision by which costs may be allocated.

Arguments for contribution pricing:

- it provides the scope for an imaginative (even aggressive) pricing policy.
- in cases where demand is elastic the price that maximizes contribution, and therefore profit, may be more or less than total cost plus mark-up.
- the presence of multi-product/service undertakings renders the allocation of fixed cost meaningless and therefore cost-plus pricing unreliable.
- as opposed to current costs marginal costs are said to more accurately reflect the future.

Disadvantages of contribution pricing:

- the practical difficulties encountered in locating the demand curve of a particular undertaking.
- the problems associated with the determination of fixed and variable costs.
- the fact that many businessmen are not familiar with cost-volume-profit techniques and therefore, are unable to make full use of such aids.
- the fear that if prices are set at a level which will maximize contribution, constant price changes could adversely affect price stability.
- in certain situations competition may prove so severe as to reach a climax where no individual undertaking is able to generate sufficient contribution to cover fixed costs and achieve a reasonable profit.

Where the traditional cost-plus pricing approach is operated in respect of normal business, contribution pricing can still be used to good effect for what Sizer[2] describes as 'secondary pricing decisions'. Examples of these include low season holidays, special weekends, prestige functions and so on. In fact the support role is particularly useful in those establishments which experience marked demand fluctuations, a characteristic that is inherent in many sections of the industry.

Pricing Hotel Accommodation

A time-honoured rule of thumb method of pricing rooms is known as the 'rule of a thousand'. This provides for an average room rate of an hotel to be ascertained on the basis of £1 for each £1,000 of capital cost. Initially, capital cost included only the cost of construction but this now appears to embrace the total investment per room.

[2]John Sizer *An Insight into Management Accounting* Penguin Books

The rule was established a number of years ago and founded on prevailing occupancies, operating costs, interest rates and acceptable profit margins. Since then, however, the variables and their relationships have changed and although for practical purposes it remains a broad guide, this rule of thumb must be used with full knowledge of its severe limitations.

An additional method of accommodation pricing is based on the rate of return variation of the cost-plus pricing approach. This yields a minimum average room rate sufficient to earn a stated rate of return on capital employed. Essentially this requires an estimate of total unallocated costs and costs of the accommodation department together with the desired return on investment, less contributions/profits from other operating departments. The amount is divided by the estimated number of rooms sold for the year to obtain the average room rate. As for all cost based pricing computations this has a number of deficiencies. Cost allocation is an accounting technique used mainly for internal management control purposes and since the allocations are not able to be measured in a true economic sense, such substitutions for real economic value subsequently lead to inaccuracies in the result.

This method has been used in various forms in this country for some years but in the United States the procedure has been formalized for the American Hotel and Motel Association and is known as the 'Hubbart Formula'.[3] However, it is considered more appropriate to illustrate a Hubbart style rate of return pricing method that conforms to the general structure of the standard system of hotel accounting prescribed for British hotels (see Exhibit 9–2). It should be noted that as the formula results in an average, an accommodation price structure will require to be developed for different kinds of rooms.

Exhibit 9–2

AVERAGE ROOM RATE COMPUTATION (100 ROOM HOTEL)

Net assets:	£
Hotel fixed assets	1,450,000
Working capital	50,000
	1,500,000
Capital employed:	£
Ordinary share capital	1,000,000
12% Debentures	500,000
	1,500,000
	£

[3]An application of the 'Hubbart Formula' may be found in C. T. Fay, R. C. Rhoads and R. L. Rosenblatt *Managerial Accounting in the Hospitality Services Industries* 2nd edition W. C. Brown Company Publishers (USA)

Required return on capital employed at 10%	150,000
UK Corporation tax at 50%	150,000
Required NET PROFIT before tax	300,000
12% Debenture interest	60,000
Required HOTEL NET OPERATING PROFIT	360,000
Repairs, rates, depreciation etc.	160,000
Required HOTEL OPERATING PROFIT	520,000
Service departments and general expenditure:	
Administration	50,000
Sales, advertising and promotion	30,000
Heat, light and power	40,000
General expenditure	20,000
	140,000
Required HOTEL OPERATING INCOME	660,000
Estimated departmental operating profit (excluding rooms)	
Food	150,000
Liquor and tobacco	100,000
Other	10,000
	260,000
Required rooms department operating profit	400,000
Estimated rooms department expenses	110,000
Required rooms department revenue	510,000
Number of room nights per annum at an average occupancy of (say) 70%	25,500
Required average room rate (£510,000÷25,550)=£19·96 or	£20

Pricing Food and Beverages

Earlier it was stated that food and beverage selling prices are normally based on the cost-plus approach using either the gross margin or rate of return variations. Where this is so a general procedure should be adopted in order to evolve individual prices for dishes, meals and drinks. One way is to develop what may be described as a 'multi-stage approach' that comprises a number of distinct steps commencing with the estimated sales for a period and ending with individual food and beverage selling prices, as illustrated in Exhibit 9–3 (overleaf).

Exhibit 9–3

FOOD AND BEVERAGES
Multi-stage approach to cost-plus pricing

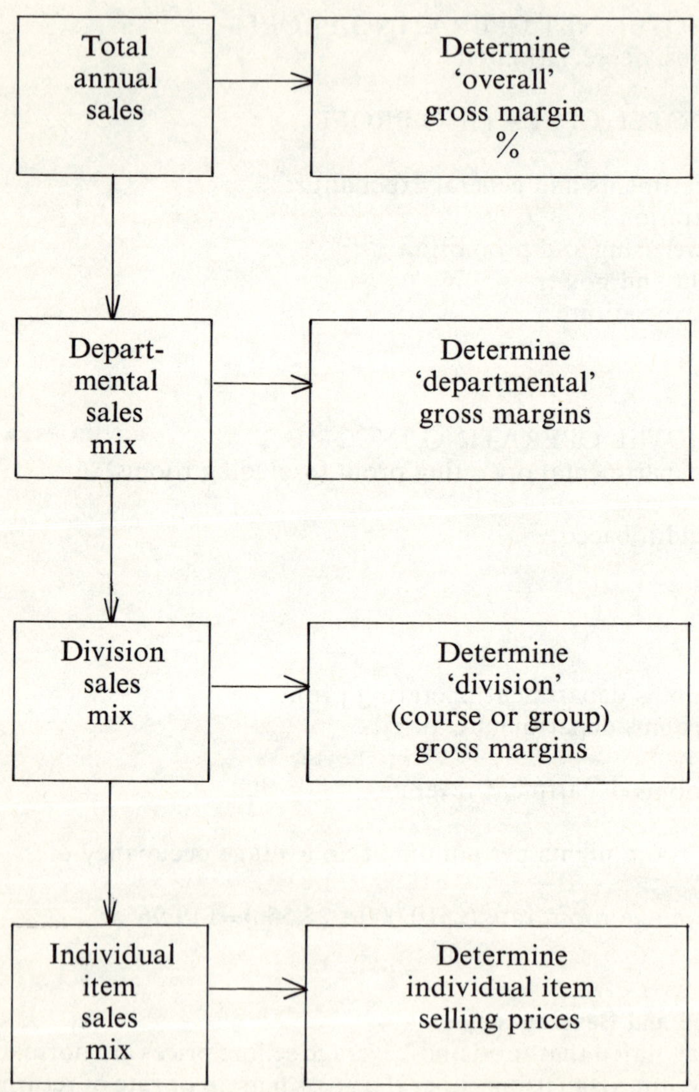

In the initial stage it is necessary to determine the annual sales and average gross margin percentage that will provide a desired return on capital employed. For example, the details of a proposed catering undertaking are as follows:

Capital employed	£175,000
Desired return	20%
	£
Target net profit	35,000
Plus: Fixed costs	27,000
Estimated gross profit	62,000

Average gross margin 62% ∴ Estimated sales $= \frac{£62{,}000}{62} \times \frac{100}{1} = £100{,}000$

The second stage requires the estimation of departmental sales mix together with the anticipated gross margin percentages. On the assumption that the proposed catering establishment will contain four departments: à la carte restaurant; buttery; cocktail bar; and shop, the analysis might appear as follows:

Estimated departmental analysis

	Sales mix		Gross margin	
	£	%	£	%
Restaurant	50,000	50	35,000	70
Buttery	25,000	25	15,000	60
Bar	20,000	20	11,000	55
Shop	5,000	5	1,000	20
	100,000	100	62,000	62

The departmental gross margin percentages are a matter of policy and may be checked against the overall percentage. This is carried out by weighting each gross margin percentage by the sales mix percentage, as follows:

Sales mix		Gross margin		
%		%		%
50	×	70	=	35
25	×	60	=	15
20	×	55	=	11
5	×	20	=	1
100				62

Stage three comprises the departmental division sales mix estimates i.e. starters, main course etc. for food, and wine, spirits, beers etc. for beverages, again with the respective gross margin percentages.

Take the à la carte restaurant:

Estimated division analysis

	Sales mix		Gross margin	
	£	%	£	%
Starters	9,000	18	7,650	85
Main course	25,000	50	16,250	65
Vegetables	5,000	10	3,750	75
Sweets	8,000	16	4,800	60
Coffee	3,000	6	2,550	85
	50,000	100	35,000	70

The final stage consists of estimating individual food and drink items and determining the selling prices which will ultimately appear on the menus, wine lists and bar tariffs. In the final stage it is also necessary to take into account minor adjustments in respect of operational factors, market influences and price roundings.

Where appropriate the procedure may be reversed. Thus, selling prices are set for each dish or drink whilst the overall gross margin for the department and business becomes a residual matter.

Total Pricing

In developing a pricing policy an important aspect to consider is the relationship, if any, that exists between products and/or services produced by an undertaking. Firms in some industries manufacture or process products that from the consumer point of view are self contained items, independent of each other. Where this is evident pricing structures must be aimed at maximizing profit from the individual products themselves. However, due to its nature, the hotel and catering industry experiences a relatively high degree of product and service interrelationship. In many undertakings, such as hotels, the interdependence of facilities is two dimensional. For instance, an à la carte menu contains a number of courses which are interdependent in so much as they constitute a complete meal. The meal cannot however be seen in isolation, as the restaurant in which it is served is itself an interdependent component of the hotel in that it forms part of the total service offered to a guest. Therefore, as far as a customer is concerned the facilities provided are regarded as a 'composite' product. Where this is so then on no account should departmental price structures be determined independently, but prepared as a 'total' pricing effort. In this way departmental gains will not be made at the cost of overall results. This is based on the synergy doctrine which suggests that the outcome of combined effort is greater than the sum of individual action.

Mark-up and Gross Profit

The percentage added to food or drink cost for determining selling price is known sometimes as mark-up. The figure added is gross profit and becomes gross profit percentage when it is related to the selling price. The mark-up and gross profit are the same figure in absolute terms, but are different percentages because the figure is related to different bases, viz. mark-up percentage relates to cost and gross profit percentage relates to selling price.

If food costs 50p and the customer is charged 75p then there has been a mark-up of 25p. If 25p is expressed as a percentage of cost (50p) the result is a 50% mark-up. However, if the mark-up of 25p is expressed as a percentage of selling price there results a gross profit percentage of 33⅓%. To establish the mark-up when the cost and gross profit percentage are known:

Gross profit % required	=	Mark-up of	
50%	=	$\frac{50}{(100-50)} \times 100$	$= 100\%$
33⅓%	=	$\frac{33\frac{1}{3}}{(100-33\frac{1}{3})} \times 100$	$= 50\%$
25%	=	$\frac{25}{(100-25)} \times 100$	$= 33\frac{1}{3}\%$

Questions and Problems

9–1 Compare 'full cost-plus pricing' with 'gross margin pricing'.

9–2 Is the 'rate of return' method of pricing a variation of cost-plus pricing? Explain.

9–3 Give a critical analysis of the full cost-plus pricing approach, with your suggestions as to how any short comings may be overcome.

9–4 'Gross margin pricing is frequently used in the hotel and catering industry for pricing food and beverages'. Discuss.

9–5 What reasons can you advance for and against having a pricing policy in a restaurant based on a fixed percentage mark-up on the food cost of each dish? Explain briefly two other methods of establishing the menu price of a dish.

9–6 Distinguish between 'cost-plus pricing' and 'contribution pricing'.

9–7 'Contribution pricing can serve as a particularly useful approach in service industries . . .' Do you agree? Explain.

9–8 Distinguish between the 'rule of a thousand' and the 'Hubbart Formula' methods of pricing hotel room rates.

9–9 Explain briefly how you would approach a total pricing policy for either an hotel or a university hall of residence.

9–10 Real Estate Investments Ltd. are investigating the possibility of building and operating a 300 bedroom hotel in a large city centre. The construction cost has been estimated at £4·5m of which £3m will be borrowed at an interest rate of approximately 12% per annum and the balance from an issue of ordinary shares.

Tentative operating forecasts have been prepared as follows:

Average annual occupancy (assuming a 365 day year)	70%
Food and beverage department contributions per room/night	£3
Annual operating expenses	£1·5m
Room servicing costs per room/night	£4

The company requires a minimum rate of return on shareholders investment of 15% after tax (Corporation tax may be assumed at 50% of net profit).

You are required to calculate the average room rate using the Hubbart Formula.

9–11 The management of Titanic Catering Ltd. has been researching its pricing policy for the Table d'Hôte menu in a new floating restaurant which will operate for 50 weeks of the year.

The capital cost of the venture will be £120,000 and the management requires an annual net profit of 15% of this figure. The restaurant is expected to turn over 200 covers per week.

Labour costs, mooring charges, maintenance and other fixed costs will total £330 per week when open.

From their research of other establishments of this type, the management proposes the following menu structure together with anticipated food cost and sales mix percentages.

	Food cost % of selling price of dish	*Sales mix % of total sales revenue*
Appetisers	40	15
Main Courses	45	50
Selection of vegetables	33⅓	9
Sweets	40	10
Coffee	25	4
½ carafe of wine (optional)	50	12
		100

(*a*) Calculate the annual net profit required by the management.
(*b*) From the above figures, estimate the overall gross profit percentage achieved.
(*c*) Set prices for the whole meal and the individual courses based on the expected number of customers and the required net profit. (Ignore VAT and assume all covers take wine).

(HCIMA)

9–12 The Serenity Club intends to hold a dinner which will be attended by an estimated number of 200 members. The Grand Hotel has been approached with a possible menu and is in process of calculating costs, bearing in mind the club's hope that the charge could be kept down to £1·75 per head. The costs of the function have been apportioned as follows:

Food cost (exclusive of meat)	£80	
Other direct costs:		
Trio with soloist	£40	
Sundries (menu cards, flowers)	£20	
Extra labour		20% of sales
Extra overheads		10% of sales

Fixed cost per day of the function suite is £40.

Meat weighing 60 kg (exclusive of bone and waste) has been purchased by the piece costing £75. The comparative cost of the meat bought retail by the separate cuts would work out at £90. Roasting meat which is to be used from the piece has a retail cost of £1·80 per kg. It is estimated that there will be a 40% cooking loss. It is intended to serve a meat portion of 120 g.

(*a*) Calculate the charge per head necessary to make a 10% net profit on sales.
(*b*) Taking into account the fact that no other function has been booked for that day, consider, with calculations, the advisability of offering the dinner at the club's price of £1·75 per head.

(Scotec HND)

9–13 The Royal Highway Hotel Ltd., which consists of 100 double bedrooms, is planning to introduce a 'Break-a-Way Weekend' special offer during the first quarter of the new year.

The offer provides inclusive terms (with the exception of afternoon tea) from a Friday dinner time until Sunday after luncheon with a standard of facilities comparable to normal paying guests.

Details regarding the daily costs incurred by the hotel in respect of inclusive terms are shown overleaf.

Direct material, i.e. food:

	per cover
	£
Breakfast	0·60
Luncheon	1·00
Afternoon tea	0·40
Dinner	1·40

Direct labour:

	£	
Food	9·00	serving 30 covers per day
Accommodation	8·00	servicing 16 rooms per day

Direct expenses, i.e. laundry, etc.: £0·70 per day
The current inclusive terms are an average rate of £20 per person per day.

Additional advertising for the weekend offer has been agreed at £1,800.

The hotel usually only achieves a low room occupancy during the quarter, but the resident director and his manager are quietly confident that the offer will attract a further 600 guests over the quarter, thus raising the average occupancy to a more respectable level.

Annual fixed overheads of £90,000 are applicable to an average room occupancy level of up to 100%. The average annual occupancy is currently 65%. Assume that there will be two persons in each room and that demand will accrue evenly over the quarter.

The price charged to the special offer customers is in no way expected to influence the normal clientele pricing policy.

You are required to:

(*a*) recommend a pricing policy for the 'Break-a-Way Weekend' offer which will return 10% profit on sales;

(*b*) prepare a statement, based on (*a*) above, indicating the effect on the hotel's profit for the quarter if the offer comes up to expectations; and

(*c*) explain to the director the principles you have applied in arriving at your results, in (*a*) and (*b*) above.

9–14 Magnet Ltd. operate a staff dining hall for the provision of meals to their employees. They serve an average of 500 meals per day, 5 days per week for 50 weeks of the year, several choices being offered each day.

The annual cost of food is £37,500, wages £34,000, overheads £27,500.

The company wish to provide meals at an average charge of £0·50 each, and are willing to subsidize the canteen to the extent of £25,000 p.a.

The company occupying an adjoining factory have approached Magnet Ltd. and asked if they would be prepared to serve their employees with meals (400 per day) of the same quality and price. They are prepared to take meals at a different time to the Magnet employees, so there would be no difficulty regarding accommodation. Additional labour costing £7,000 p.a. would be required in the canteen.

The catering manager has been asked to suggest a pricing policy (i.e. the percentage to be added to the cost of each dish) and to give his recommendation as to whether the company should be prepared to supply meals to the neighbouring firm on the terms suggested.

You are asked to advise the catering manager on the course of action he should recommend, taking into account financial implications. You should state any assumptions you have made.

9–15 The South Down University offers various 'Educational Holidays' on a normal commercial basis during the vacations.

Each holiday was sold at the price of £30 per person last year and a total of 5,000 guests were accommodated. The costs incurred in producing the various holidays offered are the same.

The variable cost of producing a holiday last year was:

	£
Food	10·00
Direct labour	9·00
Variable overheads	2·00
	21·00

The fixed overhead relevant to the holidays during the year was £20,000.

During the coming year, the costs of the holidays are expected to increase by the following:

	%
Food	10·00
Direct labour	16·67
Variable overheads	25·00
Fixed overhead	5·00

Market research carried out by a firm of hotel and catering consultants has shown that when the university increases the price of its holidays to its guests, so long as the increase is kept below 11%, this is unlikely to have an effect on the number of units sold. However, for every 1% prices are raised above an 11% increase, the number of holidays sold can be expected to fall by 2%.

The following is required for the coming year:

(*a*) the selling price of the holidays if the number sold and the annual profits are to remain the same as in the previous year;

(*b*) the number of holidays that the university would have to sell if it did not change the price charged for these, but maintained the profit level attained in the previous year; and

(*c*) a brief analysis of a situation where, when prices are changed, the number of units sold is affected. The data provided in the above example can be used to illustrate your analysis.

Further Reading

1. Dean, J., *Managerial Economics*, Prentice-Hall Inc.
2. Greer, H. C., *Cost Factors in Price-Making*, Harvard Business Review; July–August, 1952; pp 33–45.
3. Baxter, W. T., and Oxenfeldt, A. R., Costing and Pricing: The Cost Accountant versus the Economist, *Studies in Cost Analysis* (edited by Solomons, D.), Sweet and Maxwell, pp 293–312.
4. Rogers, H. A., *Price Formation in Hotels*, HCIMA Review, Spring 1976.
5. Savage, C. I., and Small, J. R., *Introduction to Managerial Economics*, Hutchinson and Co.; chapter 6.
6. Sizer, J., *An Insight into Management Accounting*, Penguin Books; chapter 9.
7. Tucker, S. A., *Pricing for Higher Profits*, McGraw-Hill.

CHAPTER TEN

STANDARD SYSTEMS OF ACCOUNTING

STANDARD classification systems of accounts have operated in some industries for many years and a most important project undertaken in 1965–6 by the University of Strathclyde's Scottish Hotel School set out, after much research, a standard classification of accounts for the British hotel industry, forming the basis of the development of a system of standard hotel accounts. Responsibility for this development was accepted by the Hotel and Catering Economic Development Committee (EDC) and after further work a standard system of hotel accounting was prepared for publication in 1969 and promoted by the National Economic Development Office following the view of the Advisory Committee on Uniform Accounts for Hotels that the system was likely to be acceptable to a majority of hoteliers. For administrative convenience the booklet is printed and published through Her Majesty's Stationery Office.

Hotel Accounting

The recommended system is designed for use by all sizes of hotel to give the hotelier a very informative appreciation of his own operation. This *raison d'être* is sufficient in itself for an hotelier to use the classification of accounts recommended. However, the further advantage is the facility it affords hoteliers of taking part in the inter-hotel and inter-motel comparison schemes organized by the Centre for Hotel and Catering Comparisons at the University of Strathclyde. Although uniform accounting and inter-hotel comparison are independent the one internal looking, the other outward looking, they have been so designed to improve the two-way communication of data between the hotel and the Centre.

The main aim of this system is to assist hotels towards more profitable operation. This is done in two ways. First, the system applies the principles of management accounting to hotels, and it can therefore provide hotel management with the information required to plan and control hotel operations and improve their understanding of their own business. Secondly the system provides a standard of classification of accounts and so can facilitate the collection and presentation to management of control information in a form which for all practical purposes is common throughout the hotel industry. Reporting to management is in the form of monthly reports comprising: a summary operating statement showing profit at various levels of control, compared with budget; a summary balance sheet; and control ratios.

Collecting Information

To understand the recommended classification and coding of revenue items it is useful to consider the two-dimensional aspect of expenses. A primary expense is defined as one which cannot be divided into two or more types of expenditure so that a primary expense account can hold only one type of expenditure.

A cost centre has been defined as the smallest accounting unit for which costs will be collected, for example a physical location, an activity or merely a convenient resting place for certain primary expenses not falling naturally into any other cost centre.

An accounting statement is in subjective form when expenditure is listed according to the total of each kind of primary expense. An example is the traditional profit and loss account in which primary expenses are listed according to the 'subject' or nature of the expenditure such as salaries, wages and electricity.

On the other hand, a statement is in objective form when expenditure is grouped according to the object or function of the expenditure. An example is the statement presented to management in which expenses are grouped in cost centres in line with responsibilities for such expenses.

It can be seen that all revenue items may be arranged to fit into a matrix as follows:

Type of Expense Accounts	Department (Cost Centre) Accounts			

This basis has been used for all costs, income and departmental accounts. Decisions taken in standardizing the system were:

(*a*) Is the objective analysis to be determined by physical location or activity? As the activity of supplying rooms, food, etc. is common to all hotels, this method was chosen. The departments are:

Operated departments:	01	Rooms
	02	Food
	03	Liquor and tobacco
	09	Other income
Service and other departments:	11	Administration
	12	Sales, advertising and promotion
	13	Heat, light and power
	19	General Expenditure
	21	Repairs and Maintenance

22 Plant and machinery
23 Property
31 Non-operating income and expenditure

As can be seen, the departments are in effect cost centres by definition.

(*b*) What happens to primary expenses which might require to be apportioned between departments? The system allows expenses to be charged directly to more than one department, for instance laundering expenses. However, as the system is tied in with responsibility for expenses, service and other departmental expenses are not apportioned over operated departments whose heads have no direct control over such expenses.

Classification of capital account items simply follows the order of items in the balance sheet.

Exhibit 10–1 shows a summary of the recommended classification and coding of accounts with four examples using the coding system. Example 1 shows a credit to 03041, a revenue account. Example 2 shows a debit to 19221 a cost account. Example 3 shows a debit to an asset account 52625, and example 4 is a credit to a liability account. In each case only one of the double entries is stated.

Exhibit 10–1

	Revenue Items		*Capital Items*	
		Departmental code		*Category code*
Main code	Departments	01... to 40...	Assets Liabilities	50... to 69... 70... to 99...
		Account code		*Account code*
Sub code	Income accounts Cost accounts	..001 to ..099 ..100 to ..599	Detailed accounts	..600 to ..999
Examples				
1. Tobacco receipts	Liquor & tobacco dept. Tobacco sales a/c	03... ..041 } 03041		
2. Carpet shampoo	General expenditure dept. Cleaning supplies a/c	19... ..221 } 19221		
3. Purchase of furniture			Plant, etc Furniture	52... 52625
4. Purchase from sundry trade creditors			Creditors Trade creditors	71... 71811

Presenting Routine Hotel Accounting Information

Regular information is the life blood of management. The effectiveness of this information in the planning and control of operations is dependent largely on the form and timing of its presentation.

The most common forms of presentation are:
(*a*) Operating Statements (*b*) Ratios

Operating Statements:
A Standard System of Hotel Accounting contains recommended forms of operating statement prepared monthly, consisting of a summary operation statement supported by more detailed departmental operating statements.

Exhibit 10–2 shows examples of the two forms and the relationship between them. The full statement in each case is headed:

THIS PERIOD				*CODE*	*ACCOUNT DETAIL*	*YEAR TO DATE*			
BUDGET		*ACTUAL*				*ACTUAL*		*BUDGET*	
£	%	£	%			£	%	£	%

Ratios:
A ratio is the result of dividing a number (the numerator) by another number (the denominator) and may be expressed in various forms. When both numerator and denominator are in money terms it is common to express the relationship:

(*a*) as a percentage when the numerator is generally smaller than the denominator

$$\text{e.g.} \quad \frac{\text{Cost of sales}}{\text{Net sales}} \quad \frac{£1{,}990}{£6{,}000} = 33{\cdot}2\%$$

(*b*) as 'number of times' when the numerator is generally greater than the denominator

$$\text{e.g.} \quad \frac{\text{Annual cost of sales}}{\text{Stock}} \quad \frac{£36{,}000}{£6{,}000} = 6 \text{ times}$$

However, other ratios, operating ratios in particular, relate money to physical units, giving a further common form of £ per room, £ per meal, £ per guest, etc.

$$\text{e.g.} \quad \frac{\text{Restaurant sales}}{\text{Meals served}} \quad \frac{£2{,}460}{565} = £4{\cdot}35 \text{ per meal}$$

Ratios recommended in the standard system are:

Exhibit 10–2

Exhibit 10–2 showing sample hotel operating statements. £ and % columns are omitted for simplicity. Columns are as catering operating statements Exhibits 10–3 and 10–4.

FOOD OPERATING STATEMENT

CODE	ACCOUNT DETAIL
011	Restaurant sales
031	Banquets
	TOTAL SALES
091	Allowances to guests
	NET SALES
101	Food purchases
109	Food stock inc./Dec.
125	Stock losses
126	Sale of kitchen waste (Cr.)
127	Cost of staff meals & liquor (Cr.)
128	Cost of entertaining (Cr.)
	COST OF SALES
	GROSS PROFIT
131	Gross pay
133	N.I.
134	Holiday pay
135	Staff meals & liquor
136	Staff accommodation
	TOTAL WAGES & STAFF COSTS
	NET MARGIN
201	Department supplies
202	Flowers & decor
211	Printing & stationery
232	Kitchen fuel
271	Laundry & dry cleaners' charges
272	Cleaning contracts
282	Music & entertainers
324	Trade licences
411	Linen
412	Uniforms
413	Plate & cutlery
414	Glass & china
415	Utensils
	TOTAL ALLOCATED EXPENSE
	DEPARTMENT OPERATING PROFIT

SUMMARY OPERATING STATEMENT

CODE	ACCOUNT DETAIL
	OPERATED DEPARTMENTS
	Net sales
01	Rooms
02	Food
03	Liquor & tobacco
	TOTAL NET SALES
	Gross profit
01	Rooms
02	Food
03	Liquor & tobacco
	TOTAL GROSS PROFIT
	Wages & staff costs
01	Rooms
02	Food
03	Liquor & tobacco
	TOTAL WAGES & STAFF COSTS
	Net margin
01	Rooms
02	Food
03	Liquor & tobacco
	TOTAL NET MARGIN
	Department operating profit
01	Rooms
02	Food
03	Liquor & tobacco
	TOTAL DEPARTMENT OPERATING PROFIT
09	OTHER INCOME
	HOTEL OPERATING INCOME
	Service departments & general expenditure
11	Administration
12	Sales advertising & promotion
13	Heat, light & power
19	General expenditure
159	Staff accommodation adjustment
	TOTAL SERVICE DEPARTMENTS & GENERAL EXPENDITURE
	HOTEL OPERATING PROFIT
21	Repairs & maintenance
22	Plant & machinery
23	Property
	HOTEL NET OPERATING PROFIT
31	Non-operating income & expenditure
	NET PROFIT, before TAX

	Form
A *Accounting Profitability Ratios*	
$\dfrac{\text{Operating profit}}{\text{Operating assets}}$	%
$\dfrac{\text{Gross profit}}{\text{Sales}}$	%
$\dfrac{\text{Net profit}}{\text{Sales}}$	%
B *Accounting Liquidity Ratios*	
$\dfrac{\text{Current assets}}{\text{Current liabilities}}$	times
$\dfrac{\text{Current assets less stock}}{\text{Current liabilities}}$	times
$\dfrac{\text{Stocks}}{\text{Daily cost of sales}}$	days stock
$\dfrac{\text{Debtors}}{\text{Daily credit sales}}$	days credit
C *Operating Ratios (Capacity Utilization)*	
$\dfrac{\text{Rooms occupied}}{\text{Rooms in hotel}}$	%
$\dfrac{\text{Number of guests}}{\text{Guest capacity}}$	%
$\dfrac{\text{Meals served}}{\text{Restaurant seating capacity}}$	%
D *Operating Ratios (Average Prices)*	
$\dfrac{\text{Room sales}}{\text{Rooms occupied (times no. days occupied)}}$	£ per room per day
$\dfrac{\text{Room sales}}{\text{Number of guests (times no. days stayed)}}$	£ per guest per day
$\dfrac{\text{Restaurant sales}}{\text{Meals served}}$	£ per meal

Accounting ratios are explained in detail in the next chapter whilst operating ratios are self-explanatory.

Appendices to the Report

A Glossary of accounting terms including the following term:

Accounts classification. An arrangement of accounting records for a definite purpose. In this report the purpose of classification is to provide accounting information for hotel management, and to provide it in a manner which is uniform to the hotel industry. A classification specifies the accounts to be used, their contents, and the sequence in which they are to be arranged.

B Basic classification of profit and loss accounts comprising:

1. List of departments (reproduced on page 140).
2. List of account names and their allocation to departments.
3. An example accounts code.

C Basic classification of balance sheet accounts comprising:

1. List of account categories (reproduced below).
2. List of account names provided in each category together with an example accounts code.

List of account categories

Category code	*Category title*
50–58	FIXED ASSETS
51	Property
52	Plant and machinery
55	General equipment
56	Investments and loans
58	Goodwill
59	OTHER ASSETS
60–69	CURRENT ASSETS
61	Stocks
65	Debtors
68	Current investments
69	Bank balance and cash
70–79	CURRENT LIABILITIES
71	Creditors
79	Bank overdrafts
80–88	PROVISIONS
81	For renewal of fixed assets
82	Other provisions
89	DEFERRED LIABILITIES
90–99	CAPITAL & RESERVES
91	Share capital
92	Reserves
93	Loan capital

List of account names (e.g.)

Account code	*Account name/or type*
Property	
51601	Freehold land and buildings
51602	Depreciation of freehold buildings
51611	Leasehold – long term
51612	Amortization of long term leaseholds
51616	Leaseholds – Short term
51617	Amortization of short term leaseholds

D Example operating statements and summary balance sheet.

Summary operating statement and food department operating statement are shown as Exhibit 10–2.

E Alphabetical list of accounts provided in the basic classification comprising:

1. Account names, in alphabetical order.
2. Allocation of accounts to departments or balance sheet categories.
3. Example account codes.
4. Examples of transactions allocated.

e.g. *Account*	*Allocation*	*Code*	*Examples*
Laundry and dry cleaners' charges	Rooms	01271	For linen and soft-furnishings in guest, public and cloakrooms and uniforms of rooms staff.
	Food	02271	For kitchen and table linen, and soft-furnishings in kitchens, restaurants and banquet rooms, uniforms of food staff.
	Liquor and tobacco	03271	For linen and soft-furnishings in bars, and uniforms of liquor staff.
	General expenditure	19271	For laundry and dry cleaning costs not allocated to departments.

F Accounts dictionary comprising:

An alphabetical list representing commodities, services, etc., commonly purchased/sold and their allocation in the basic classification.

e.g. Under the letter L

Expense item	*Code*		*Account name*	*Department or group of accounts to which allocated*
Laundry charges	01 02 03 19	271	Laundry and dry cleaners' charges	Rooms/Food/Liquor and tobacco/General expenditure

Catering Accounting

A standard system of catering accounting was published in 1971 as the catering equivalent to the hotel system, recommendations being along similar lines. This system is a natural extension wherever a catering activity is carried out within the wider sphere of an hotel operation. The basic operating functions, regarded as separate activities are:

Food preparation
Food Sales (restaurant, bar, banquet), with the addition of
Liquor sales
Liquor stockholding (cellar)

The common factor of these activities is the ability in practical terms, to identify labour with an activity and to produce a profitability statement for each. As with the hotel system other types of activity are regarded as service activities. Going beyond the hotel system, a standard costing system is now recommended to help in the control of food preparation costs. The food preparation activity is credited with the number of dishes supplied multiplied by the standard cost of each dish. This is the standard food cost for the period and the procedure enables comparison to be made with the actual food costs incurred so that the difference can be analysed into such detailed variances as are warranted. Examples of such variances were given in Chapter 7 on pages 95 and 96.

It has been considered worthwhile to reproduce three operating statements in full (Exhibits 10–3, 4 and 5) as well as extracts from them to show their inter-relationship (Exhibit 10–6).

Questions and Problems

10–1 Explain the difference between a subjective and an objective accounting statement.

10–2 What advantages are likely to accrue to an hotel owner who uses the standard classification of accounts recommended by the National Economic Development Office?

10–3 Outline the main objectives and features of the Standard System of Catering Accounting.

Exhibit 10–3

FOOD PREPARATION OPERATING STATEMENT

THIS PERIOD						*YEAR TO DATE*			
BUDGET		*ACTUAL*			*ACCOUNT DETAIL*	*ACTUAL*		*BUDGET*	
£	%	£	%	*CODE*		£	%	£	%
					NET SALES				
9,500	74·8	9,850	74.7		Restaurant	31,220		29,700	
3,200	25·2	3,330	25·3		Banquets	10,080		9,700	
12,700	100·0	13,180	100·0		*NET FOOD SALES*	41,300	100·0	39,400	100·0
					ACTIVITY CENTRE COSTS				
3,100		3,220		101	Food purchases at standard	10,050		9,700	
120		130		109	Food stock inc./dec.	440		400	
20		20		125	Stock losses	80		70	
(40)		(60)		126	Sale of kitchen waste (Cr)	(290)		(150)	
(420)		(460)		127	Cost of staff meals (Cr)	(1,380)		(1,410)	
(400)		(360)		128	Cost of entertaining (Cr)	(1,020)		(1,140)	
2,380	18·7	2.490	18·9		*STANDARD COST OF FOOD*	7,880	19·1	7,470	19·0
2,000		2,050		131	Gross pay and other staff costs	6,420		6,200	
40		40		135	Staff meals and liquor	130		140	
150		150		136	Staff accommodation	400		420	
2,190	17·3	2,240	17·0		*TOTAL WAGES AND STAFF COSTS*	6,950	16·8	6,760	17·2
70		60		201	Supplies	180		200	
30		30		251	Kitchen fuel	90		90	
110		90		271	Laundry and dry cleaners 'charges	260		300	
70		50		411	Linen and uniforms	140		150	
80		60		413	Kitchen utensils	190		220	
340	2·7	290	2·2		*TOTAL ALLOCATED EXPENSE*	860	2·1	960	2·4
4,910		5,020			*FOOD PREPARATION COSTS*	15,690		15,190	
—		100	·7	102	Materials price variance	270	·6	—	
4,910	38·7	5,120	38·8		*TOTAL FOOD PREPARATION COSTS*	15,960	38·6	15,190	38·6
				104	Food transfer charge(s) (to other activity centres)				
3,150	33·2	3,270	33·2		*022 Restaurant* } Activity centre codes	10,370	33·2	9,860	33·2
1,760	55·0	1,830	55·0		*060 Banquets*	5,540	55·0	5,330	55·0
4,910	38·7	5,100	38·7			15,910	38·5	15,910	38·6
—		20			*FOOD PREPARATION COSTS UNDER/OVER RECOVERED*	50		—	

Extracts from food preparation operating statement

	£
Total food preparation costs	15,960
Food transfers (standard cost)	
022 Restaurant	10,370
060 Banquets	5,540
	15,910
Food preparation costs under recovered	50

Exhibit 10–6 showing

xhibit 10–4

RESTAURANT OPERATING STATEMENT

THIS PERIOD						*YEAR TO DATE*			
BUDGET		*ACTUAL*			*ACCOUNT DETAIL*	*ACTUAL*		*BUDGET*	
£	%	£	%	*CODE*		£	%	£	%
600		9,980		011	Food sales	31,600		30,000	
100		130		091	Allowances to customers	380		300	
,500	100·0	9,850	100·0		*NET FOOD SALES*	31,220	100·0	29,700	100·0
,150	33·2	3,270	33·2	103	Cost of sales	10,370	33·2	9,860	33·2
,350	66·8	6,580	66·8		*FOOD GROSS PROFIT*	20,850	66·8	9,840	66·8
,140	100·0	3,250	100·0	021	Liquor and tobacco sales	10,430	100·0	10,000	100·0
,820	57·7	1,880	57·7	113	Cost of sales	6,020	57·7	5,770	57·7
,320	42·3	1,370	42·3		*LIQUOR AND TOBACCO GROSS PROFIT*	4,410	42·3	4,230	42·3
,670	60·6	7,950	60·7		*RESTAURANT GROSS PROFIT*	25,260	60·6	24,070	60·6
,500		2,440		131	Gross pay and other staff costs	7,460		7,500	
550		600		135	Staff meals and liquor	1,890		1,700	
450		410		136	Staff accommodation	1,480		1,500	
,500	27·7	3,450	26·3		*TOTAL WAGES AND STAFF COSTS*	10,830	26·0	10,700	26·9
,170	32·9	4,500	34·4		*RESTAURANT NET MARGIN*	14,430	34·6	13,570	33·7
130		140		201	Supplies	450		400	
80		90		271	Laundry and dry cleaners' charges	260		250	
100		130		282	Music and entertainment	340		300	
60		50		411	Linen and uniforms	210		200	
50		40		413	Cutlery, glass and utensils	110		150	
420	3·3	450	3·4		*TOTAL ALLOCATED EXPENSE*	1,370	3·3	1,300	3·3
,750	29·6	4,050	31·0		*RESTAURANT OPERATING PROFIT*	13,060	31·3	12,270	30·4

Extracts from restaurant operating statement	£
Cost of sales	10,370
Restaurant operating profit	13,060

Extracts from summary operating statement	
Restaurant operating profit	13,060
Food preparation costs under recovered	(50)

transfers of actual year to date figures

Exhibit 10–5

SUMMARY OPERATING STATEMENT

THIS PERIOD						*YEAR TO DATE*			
BUDGET		*ACTUAL*			*ACCOUNT DETAIL*	*ACTUAL*		*BUDGET*	
£	%	£	%	*CODE*		£	%	£	%
					NET SALES				
12,640	45·2	13,100	44·8	022	Restaurant(s)	41,650	46·3	39,700	46·5
6,000	21·5	6,280	21·5	032	Bar(s)	19,400	21·6	18,000	21·1
9,300	33·3	9,830	33·7	060	Banquets	28,830	32·1	27,700	32·4
27,940	100·0	29,210	100·0		*TOTAL NET SALES*	89,880	100·0	85,400	100·0
					ACTIVITY OPERATING PROFITS				
3,750	29·6	4,050	31·0	022	Restaurant(s)	13,060	31·3	12,270	30·4
1,150	19·2	1,250	19·9	032	Bar(s)	3,700	19·1	3,450	19·2
2,460	26·5	2,530	25·7	060	Banquets	7,360	25·5	7,320	26·4
7,360	26·3	7,830	26·8		*TOTAL ACTIVITIES OPERATING PROFITS*	24,120	26·8	23,040	27·0
					ACTIVITY CENTRE COSTS OVER/UNDER RECOVERED				
—		(20)		021	Food preparation	(50)		—	
—		30		031	Cellar	110			
—		—		100	Distribution	—		—	
7,360	26·3	7,840	26·8		*NET ACTIVITIES OPERATING PROFITS*	24,180	26·9	23,040	27·0
980	3·5	1,040	3·6	090	*OTHER INCOME*	2,990	3·3	2,980	3·5
8,340	29.8	8,880	30·4		*CATERING OPERATING INCOME*	27,170	30·2	26,020	30·5
					EXPENDITURE				
3,710	13·2	3,860	13·2	190	General expenses	11,460	12·8	10,960	12·9
4,630	16·6	5,020	17·2		*CATERING OPERATING PROFIT*	15,710	17·4	15·060	17·6
770	2·8	900	3·1	210	Repairs and maintenance	2,940	3·3	2,360	2·7
540	1·9	500	1·7	220	Plant and machinery	1,450	1·6	1,610	1·9
250	·9	250	·8	230	Property	760	·8	750	·9
1,560	5·6	1,650	5·6			5,150	5·7	4,720	5·5
3,070	11·0	3,370	11·6		*CATERING NET OPERATING PROFIT*	10,560	11·7	10,340	12·1
(140)	·5	(210)	·7	310	Non-operating income and expenditure	(440)	·5	(350)	·4
3,210	11·5	3,580	12·3		*NET PROFIT BEFORE TAX*	11,000	12·2	10,690	12·5

10–4 The Hotel and Catering E.D.C. has recently introduced a Standard System of Hotel Accounting which it sees as being useful, among other benefits, in the compilation of inter-hotel comparison.

(*a*) List three other benefits which it is claimed will accrue if the system is widely adopted.

(*b*) Distinguish between an accounts classification and an accounts dictionary in the context of a standard system of hotel accounting.

(*c*) What do you understand by inter-hotel comparison?

(*d*) How will uniform accounting help? (HCIMA)

10–5 The Manor Park Ltd., a medium sized hotel, has recently introduced the

'Standard System of Hotel Accounting' recommended by the Hotel and Catering EDC. The system has apparently worked so well as to induce the General Manager to request you to draw up the end-of-year accounts in the style of the 'Standard System'.

The trial balance for the year ended 31st March, 1976, has been extracted and agreed:

	£000's	£000's
Sales: Rooms		550
Food		250
Drink		200
Administration	70	
Sales Promotion	30	
Heat, light and power	30	
General expenses	60	
Departmental costs:		
Rooms	130	
Food	60	
Drink	60	
Repairs and maintenance	20	
Accumulated depreciation on equipment and fittings (31st March, 1975)		20
Wages and staff costs:		
Rooms	140	
Food	50	
Drink	20	
Cost of sales:		
Rooms	—	
Food	100	
Drink	100	
Loan interest	20	
Retained profit (31st March, 1975)		17
Freehold property	700	
Equipment and fittings	100	
Stock (31st March, 1976)	10	
Debtors	135	
Cash	5	
Creditors		6
Overdraft		4
Ordinary share capital (Authorized £1,000,000)		600
General reserve		43
Loan		150
	£1,840	£1,840

The following is relevant:

(*a*) UK Corporation Tax on the year's profits is estimated at £50,000 payable before the end of the next financial period.

(*b*) Depreciation on equipment and fittings is £10,000.

(*c*) A dividend on Ordinary shares of 10% is proposed.

(*d*) There are no prepaid or accrued expenses.

You are required to:

(*a*) prepare the departmental trading, profit and loss account for year ended 31st March, 1976 (see note below); and

(*b*) prepare the balance sheet as at that date.

Note: In answering (*a*) above you should include the following profit levels:

(*i*) GROSS PROFIT;
(*ii*) NET MARGIN;
(*iii*) DEPARTMENT OPERATING PROFIT;
(*iv*) HOTEL OPERATING PROFIT;
(*v*) HOTEL NET OPERATING PROFIT;
(*vi*) NET PROFIT before TAX;
(*vii*) NET PROFIT after TAX;
(*viii*) RETAINED PROFIT c/f.

Further Reading

1. *A Standard System of Catering Accounting*, Hotel and Catering EDC, HMSO.
2. *A Standard System of Hotel Accounting*, Hotel and Catering EDC, HMSO.
3. *Hotel Accounting – Introduction to a Standard System*, Hotel and Catering EDC; HMSO

CHAPTER ELEVEN

MEASURING FINANCIAL PERFORMANCE

'RATIOS are the basics of the business. From the beginning we have always known what we were doing, and have always compared one place with another by the use of percentages or ratios. The system has been refined into more statistics, into graphs and so on, which are helping us to do better still.' These words are from that highly successful businessman who advocates the use of ratios, namely Sir Charles Forte.

It is usually a matter of convenience and custom that some accounting relationships are expressed as percentages and others as ratios, although all tend to come under the heading of ratios.

Two major uses of accounting ratios are:

(*a*) Making comparisons with other businesses to provide the basis for setting targets aimed at improving results.

(*b*) Making comparisons of internal results over a period of time. By this means, favourable and adverse trends are illuminated so that forecasts may be made, for instance on the basis of adverse trends being corrected.

Accounting ratios may be classified as follows:

(*a*) Profitability (*b*) Liquidity (*c*) Investment

Profitability Ratios

Return on Capital Employed (%)

Without doubt the most important ratio of any business is profit (return) related to capital employed (investment), although each of these two terms cover a number of particular meanings. The purpose of the ratio determines which measure of profit and of capital employed to use, but once selected, the choice should be used consistently.

Three of the more common interpretations are:

(*a*) *Measurement of management's use of total funds*

$$= \frac{\text{Profit before loan interest and tax for the year} \times 100}{\text{Capital employed (at the end of year or the average)}}$$

Capital Employed = total assets less current liabilities.

Measurement of management's use of equity funds

$$= \frac{\text{Earnings for the year} \times 100}{\text{quity capital employed (at the end of the year, or the average)}}$$

Earnings = profit after tax, interest and preference dividend.
Equity capital = Ordinary share capital plus reserves.

(*c*) *Measurement of management's operating efficiency*

$$= \frac{\text{Operating profit for the year} \times 100}{\text{Operating assets (at the end of the year, or the average)}}$$

Operating profit = Profit before interest and tax, from normal operations, i.e. excluding income from investments outside the business.

Operating assets = Total assets less investment outside the business.

The performance of individual business units such as a factory or hotel is more difficult to assess because of the problem in determining the value of capital employed. which revolves around valuing the main asset, namely premises in the case of an hotel. The University of Strathclyde do not calculate this ratio in their inter-hotel comparison scheme because it has proved to be as yet impractical to prepare a fair valuation for all participating hotels which would not lead to distorted ratios. This valuation problem will eventually be overcome, but in the meantime the problem exists of valuing on a common basis, without great expense, hotels old, new, owned and leased. However, the inter-motel scheme does include this ratio as the investment in motels has been of fairly recent date, and therefore an acceptable valuation of investment has been used for comparison.

For internal planning purposes an hotel group may value each unit as it thinks fit. A comparison between hotels within a group indicates the extent to which each unit is contributing to the company return, and if one hotel's return on investment is very low, consideration would be given to improving it, using it for some other more profitable purpose, or even selling it.

Inflation is an important factor to take into account when evaluating capital employed. In the manufacturing industry, processing plant valued at cost less accumulated depreciation, gradually reduces capital employed if some profit is not retained and reinvested. Accordingly a similar profit each year on a reduced capital employed would result in an improved return, giving a false impression of improved profitability. On the other hand, freehold hotels tend to appreciate considerably in value due to inflation and other factors such as being in an area favoured by a tourist demand, and periodic revaluation of properties increases capital employed, leading to a reduced return on investment with similar annual profits. Even increased profit in a year when existing properties are revalued could well result in a considerable drop in the return on investment compared with the previous year. However, in this case, from an operating viewpoint, the position might be regarded as satisfactory. For internal purposes it is clearly important to make annual adjustments to capital employed figures to take account of inflation.

The British Institute of Management publish in their Journal *Management Today* an annual profitability league table designed to assess the profitability of the top 200 British companies. To illustrate the limitations of the return on capital employed in judging performance, some exceptional profitability changes from 1969 to 1970 give rise to the following comment in the journal, 'comparison between these two years rub in emphatically . . . that the return on investment made by a company is only one measure of management performance – and, moreover, a measure that applies only to a historical period'.

To show with what care the particular return on investment should be chosen, the table gives four different measures, the figures for J. Lyons and Co. Ltd. ranging from 4·7% to 10·7%, and an exceptional company ranging from 20·4% to 108·7%!

Profit to Sales (%)

This is the most used ratio in the industry and is not unduly influenced by valuation and inflation problems because higher costs caused by inflation are passed on through selling price increases. In businesses with unchanged capital employed this ratio would be the most important, for an increase in this ratio would mean an increase in return on capital employed, assuming a constant total sales. The relationship between profit and sales may be determined at any profit level such as departmental gross profit, departmental net margin (after wages and staff costs), departmental operating profit, and hotel gross and net operating profit as shown in Exhibit 4–2.

Sales to Capital Employed (*times*)

This ratio is a measure of asset utilization; the number of times assets (capital employed) are turned over in the form of sales in a year.

The relationship between these three ratios is best demonstrated with figures as follows:

Forecast	*Profit/sales*		*× Sales/capital*		*Profit/capital employed*
A	$\frac{£10{,}000}{£100{,}000}$ (10%)	×	$\frac{£100{,}000}{£100{,}000}$ (1·0)	=	10%
B	$\frac{£12{,}000}{£100{,}000}$ (12%)	×	$\frac{£100{,}000}{£100{,}000}$ (1·0)	=	12%
C	$\frac{£12{,}000}{£120{,}000}$ (10%)	×	$\frac{£120{,}000}{£100{,}000}$ (1·2)	=	12%

The management might be considering next year's budget and be faced with the choice of three forecasts, each related to a different policy.

Forecast A would repeat current results.

Forecast B would result from economies in present operations, saving £2,000 in the year.

Forecast C would result from sales promotion increasing turnover. Although the extra cost would mean that the profit/sales percentage would remain unchanged, the extra turnover achieves an extra £2,000 net profit.

The three interlinking ratios give a useful picture of past or forecast results and the first of the ratios is capable of a more detailed analysis as Exhibit 12–1. Similarly sales may be related to individual assets such as stocks; in this manner sales/capital employed ratio may be further analysed.

Liquidity Ratios

Although the general level of profit of a business may be reasonable, cash may not be available to settle debts and a liquidity problem will have arisen. It is only right therefore that ratios should measure not only profitability but also cash and other current assets in relation to demands made by creditors. Profitability ratios cover business operations for a period of time. Liquidity ratios on the other hand use items from the balance sheet to measure the ability of a business at a particular point in time to finance its current trading activities out of its liquid or near liquid resources.

Current Ratio (*ratio*)

Sometimes called the working capital ratio, this is the most common indicator of the ability to settle short term debts. Whilst this ratio is useful for comparisons between firms, as working capital is reduced to a form (ratio) where size of firm does not hinder comparison, for periodic comparison within a business it is the absolute rather than the relative amount which is the more important figure to study and to act upon.

The current ratio is expressed:

$$\frac{\text{Current assets}}{\text{Current liabilities}}, \text{ the denominator arranged to be 1.}$$

E.g. Current assets £54,000
Current liabilities £42,000 giving a ratio of 1·3:1

As a rough guide, if the ratio is greater than 1:1 the business is solvent, whereas a ratio of less than 1:1, say 0·7:1 may indicate a danger of insolvency. There is however a possibility of drawing wrong conclusions from such secondary data as ratios if the primary data (absolute working capital) is not studied. For instance if an overdraft is regarded as a current liability the ratio may well be below 1:1 and yet the real liquid position may be satisfactory. Another acceptable reason for the position to be apparently bad would be the sure knowledge of immediate cash being received from a fixed asset sale.

A high current ratio of say 5:1 might be regarded as high in the hotel and catering industry, indicating, after studying further ratios of other firms, the stock holding to be unnecessarily high. However, another industry, say distilling, where stocks need to be held for several years to mature, may have an average current ratio of 5:1 because of high stock values which are essential to the business.

Current ratios give only a general indication of working capital relationships, with other ratios that now follow, providing the necessary detail.

Liquid or Acid Test Ratio (ratio)

This is also called the Quick or Quick Asset ratio. The ability of a business to meet its immediate obligations is measured by comparing its current assets, excluding stocks, with its current liabilities, and a ratio of at least 1:1 would be expected to show a satisfactory liquid position, for instance:

$$\frac{\text{Current assets (excluding stock)}}{\text{Current liabilities}} \quad \frac{£44{,}000}{£40{,}000} \quad \text{ratio} = 1{\cdot}1 : 1$$

Stocks are excluded on the grounds that the proceeds from sale of stocks will not be received for some little time. On the other hand quoted investments if not made for trade purposes, since they may be quickly sold for cash, may be included.

Again, too low a ratio may indicate insolvent conditions, and too high a ratio may mean liquid assets are too great and are being mismanaged.

For internal assessment of the very short-term position, absolute rather than the relative position is best considered, and if cash flows are forecast the ratio may be limited to items receivable and falling due within say 3 months.

Stock Ratio (days or times per annum)

This is more explicitly termed Stock Turnover Ratio. Of the several versions of this ratio, a common one for hotel and catering is in expressing cost value of stock at the year end relative to average daily costs of sales.

$$\text{E.g.}\ \frac{\text{End of year stocks of liquor}}{\text{Average daily cost of sales}} \quad \frac{£6{,}000}{£100} \quad \text{Ratio} = 60 \text{ days}$$

This indicates that it takes on average 60 days to turn stock over into sales. If this appears a slow turnover rate compared with other firms, either sales might be increased without increasing stock or if extra sales cannot be achieved, stock might be capable of some reduction. In the one case more profit should be earned from additional turnover, alternatively the saving in stock holding might be used elsewhere in the business to earn profit. If 50 days' stock were considered a target, this could be achieved by increasing turnover by 20% or by reducing stock by 16·7%.

$$\frac{\text{Stock}}{\text{Daily cost of sales}} \quad \frac{£6{,}000}{£120} = 50 \text{ days}$$

$$\frac{\text{Stock}}{\text{Daily cost of sales}} \quad \frac{£5{,}000}{£100} = 50 \text{ days}$$

Another version is the ratio of cost value of stock to cost of annual sales which gives the number of times stock is turned over per annum.

E.g. $\dfrac{\text{Annual cost of sales}}{\text{Stock}} \quad \dfrac{£36{,}000}{£6{,}000} = 6 \text{ times}$ improving to:

$\dfrac{\text{Annual cost of sales}}{\text{Stock}} \quad \dfrac{£36{,}000}{£5{,}000} = 7{\cdot}2 \text{ times}$ with a stock reduction

Average stock may be used if it is considered that year end stock figure is not representative of the average stock holding. If cost of Sales is not available then Sales Value may be used.

Debtors' Ratio (days)

This is more explicitly termed Debt Turnover Ratio or Collection Period for Debts, and indicates the average length of period of time for which credit is given by the company.

For internal analysis the amount of credit sales can be segregated from cash sales and only the former used to calculate the ratio, which is similar in some ways to stock turnover ratio.

E.g. $\dfrac{\text{Average debtors}}{\text{Average daily credit sales}} \quad \dfrac{£120{,}000}{£2{,}000} = 60 \text{ days}$

For external analysis where the two types of sale cannot be separated, the total sales are usually used as the distortion tends to be low although it does not imply that proportions of credit and cash sales are constant for firms being compared, and also constant over the periods studied.

Alternative ratios are in weeks and number of times per annum the debtors are turned over.

An increase in number of days over a period of time indicates longer credit is being allowed to customers and may call for better control.

Creditors' Ratio (days)

This ratio, also named Creditor Turnover Ratio, is the average creditors' relative to average daily credit purchases, and a low number of days indicates possibly that better credit terms may be negotiated. This ratio has much in common with the debtors' ratio.

Investment Ratios: Historical Performance

Three ratios give an indication of the past financial performance and dividend policy of a company at the end of a financial year. They are:

Earnings per share
Dividend per share
Dividend cover

Such ratios are an historical fact and not subject to day to day fluctuations since they use the three ingredients:

(*a*) *Earnings for the year*. This figure is the profit after tax and preference dividends but before taking into account such extraordinary items as goodwill written off, fire insurance claim and profit or loss on disposal of investments. Extraordinary items are those which relate to events outside the ordinary activities of the business and which are both material and expected not to recur.

(*b*) *Dividend per ordinary share*. This is the sum of the interim dividend paid and the proposed final dividend, and is quoted as pence per share.

(*c*) *Number of ordinary shares*. This is the number of shares in issue, that is, issued and fully paid, and ranking for dividend in respect of the period.

Example

(*a*) Earnings for the year: £10,000
(*b*) Dividend per ordinary share: 4p
(*c*) Number of ordinary shares: 200,000

Earnings per share

$$\frac{£10{,}000}{200{,}000} = 5\text{p per share}$$

Dividend per share = 4p per share

Dividend cover

$$\frac{\text{Earnings per share}}{\text{Dividend per share}} \quad \frac{5\text{p}}{4\text{p}} = 1{\cdot}25 \text{ times}$$

Investment Ratios: Present and Future Performance

Ordinary shares are very sensitive to expected future company performance. Investors expecting good trading results later in the year will increase demand for the shares, pushing their price up until anticipated results are reflected in the price. Should the results fall short of the standard set by investors the price will tend to fall, even though the results may have been good. Changes in share price reflect not so much management's past performance as expected future results.

Three ratios which help investors in this respect are:

Price earnings ratio
Earnings yield
Dividend yield

Given that a company has 200,000 shares, earnings per share of 5p, a dividend per share of 4p, and on one particular day the share price quoted on the stock exchange is 60p, the following ratios would be seen in the financial press:

Price Earnings Ratio (P/E Ratio)

This ratio is a way of stating the relationship between earnings and the market price of an ordinary share. It gives the market's evaluation of the share in terms of the number of years for earnings to match the share price.

$$\frac{\text{Market price of share}}{\text{Earnings per share}} = \frac{60\text{p}}{5\text{p}} = \text{P/E of 12}$$

Earnings Yield (%)

This is the reciprocal of the P/E ratio in percentage terms. It is the long term return on the share as it takes account of earnings, which include profit retained in the company.

$$\frac{5\text{p}}{60\text{p}} \times 100 = 8{\cdot}3\%$$

Dividend Yield (%)

This relates dividend per share to the market price of each ordinary share and indicates the present cash return in the form of dividend paid.

$$\frac{4\text{p}}{60\text{p}} \times 100 = 6{\cdot}7\%$$

It should be noted that as the share price changes, so each ratio will change. A price rise to 70p per share would change each ratio to 14, 7·1% and 5·7% respectively.

Working Capital Management

The primary object of management is to achieve profit targets – once set – over a number of years. To merely ensure the firm continues in operation, an important short-term target has to be met continually without fail, and that is the ability of paying debts and other obligations as they fall due, otherwise it becomes insolvent. Herein lies the function of working capital management. A balance should be struck between having too much and too little working capital, an objective that can only be achieved with any degree of accuracy through regularly updated forecasts and budgets of each element of working capital. Too much working capital means that opportunity is being lost of using long-term investment inside or outside the business simply because the surplus is not recognized. Too little working capital endangers the very existence of the firm, so that it is clear that to err on the high side is the better course.

The major elements of working capital within the control of management are stocks, debtors, short-term investments, cash at bank and in hand, bank overdrafts and creditors. Ratios involving working capital items are useful in forecasting the working capital level, mention having been made already of current ratio, liquid ratio, stock ratio, debtors ratio, and creditors ratio. A policy decision is needed to determine target levels of ratios of each item, for instance the number of days' stock holding and the number of days' credit allowable to customers. Whilst past experience and comparison with similar firms may be the only way of assessing target cash and stock levels, debtor and creditor levels can be more clearly defined using ratios.

Estimating Working Capital

Whether in respect of a proposed new undertaking or the extension of existing activities, the necessary level of working capital that will be required to fund trading operations must be identified. Below is an example of estimating the average working capital for a proposed catering establishment:

Forecast annual sales £130,000
Average gross profit on sales 70%

It is estimated that:

(*a*) food and drink stocks held will amount to 5 weeks supply
(*b*) of the sales $\frac{1}{4}$ will be on credit and debtors will be allowed a payment period of 7 weeks
(*c*) all purchases of stocks will be on credit and it is anticipated that suppliers will allow 4 weeks credit
(*d*) advance booking deposits will amount to 5% of 1 weeks sales
(*e*) a cash balance equivalent to $\frac{1}{2}$ of the other working capital requirements is to be maintained

Estimated Working Capital Requirements

	£	£
Food and drink stocks:		
5/52 × 30/100 × £130,000		3,750
Debtors: 7/52 × $\frac{1}{4}$ × £130,000		4,375
		8,125
Less: Creditors		
4/52 × 30/100 × £130,000	3,000	
Advance booking deposits		
1/52 × 5/100 × £130,000	125	3,125
		5,000
Plus: Cash balance		
$\frac{1}{2}$ × £5,000		2,500
Total working capital required		7,500

At first sight the computation appears straightforward but it does conceal several deficiencies. These arise as a result of the fundamental assumption in the estimate that sales and costs accrue evenly throughout the period. However, many catering concerns experience some degree of seasonal fluctuation and therefore the increase in business that occurs during the on-season will require additional working capital funds, that is if the undertaking is to continue to pay its way. The additional amount of working capital may be established in a manner similar to that used in the example, thereby treating the on-season period as an extension, albeit temporary, of business activities.

Stock, debtor and creditor levels tend to follow the general pattern of sales activity and thus it is the cash balance that is probably the most suspect element within the estimate. This is due primarily to ad hoc payments in respect of such items as taxation, dividends and purchase of assets in addition to the more regular payments to employees and creditors, which take place during a period. Even with the deficiencies outlined above the computation serves as a useful starting point from which the working capital level may be decided.

Overtrading

This is a shortage of liquid funds caused by expansion of sales without sufficient additional capital to back up the operation. Businesses which give credit to customers and hold large stocks are, however, more prone to overtrading than many hotel and restaurant concerns.

To expand sales usually demands a higher level of debtors and stocks, which if not completely offset by extra credit allowed from suppliers means holding more working capital investment. Where is this to be obtained? If overdraft facilities are fully stretched before expansion, difficulty is likely to arise in obtaining more cash with which to fund the difference.

A difficult situation usually arises in overtrading when through lack of cash, creditors are kept waiting for their money and they become reluctant to supply goods on credit, debtors are chased for earlier settlement and offered attractive discounts, or cash customers are offered cut price sales to turn over faster the stocks. In any case profit is likely to suffer.

Undertrading is the opposite of overtrading in that sales are too low in relation to capital resulting in low profits. However the cash position may be healthy unless too much is taken out of the business by shareholders.

Balance Sheet Limitations

Ratio analysis aids interpretation of the financial position of a business by concentrating attention on relationships of items making up the final accounts. As the balance sheet shows the financial position at one point in time, a few days' transactions could change the whole picture almost overnight, although this by no means invalidates the study of relative and absolute figures for the purpose of assessing the health of a business.

An overdraft shown and treated as a current liability could result in a liquid ratio of much less than 1:1 yet no liquidity problem may exist as the overdraft is unlikely to be withdrawn.

Valuation of land and buildings may take place only once in five years so that in the interim years they would be undervalued in a period of inflation. E.g. as in 1968 J. Lyons and Co. Ltd. revalued land and buildings adding some £25 million to the value of assets. Hotel companies owning their own hotels are constantly benefiting by inflation because these increasingly valuable assets do not in the short term need replacing. However, any plant and machinery owned needs to be replaced at some future time when inflation will have added to the cost of replacement. Unless the difference between original cost and replacement cost is set aside over the years and not distributed to shareholders, there may be a problem of finding the extra finance for the firm to stay in the same position.

In businesses where much replacement of assets is needed and all profits are distributed, then it may be said that capital is being eroded in that asset values and therefore capital employed is in real terms reducing in value.

Questions and Problems

11–1 Compare and contrast 'profitability' and 'liquidity' ratios.

11–2 The gross profit percentage is one of the most closely controlled ratios within the hotel and catering industry. Why do you think this is so?

11–3 What factors should a manager be aware of when reading a financial performance report containing various accounting and operating ratios?

11–4

Firm	*Sales*	*Net Profit*	*Capital Employed*	*Net Profit Ratio*	*Net Turnover*	*Return on Capital Employed*
	£	£	£	%	No. times	%
A	200,000	30,000	160,000	*	*	*
B	40,000	*	*	5	2	*
C	*	3,000	*	10	*	5
D	*	*	400,000	*	6	8
E	900,000	*	300,000	3	*	*

Compute the missing figures indicated by *.

11–5 Overleaf are the end-of- year accounts of the Bridge Hotel.
You are required to calculate the various profitability and liquidity ratios you consider to be relevant in assessing the financial performance of this hotel. Comment on your results.

Trading, Profit and Loss Account for year ended 31st December

	£	£
Sales		120,000
Opening stock	7,400	
Purchases	51,000	
	58,400	
Less: Closing stock	8,000	50,400
GROSS PROFIT		69,600
Less:		
Wages and staff costs	30,000	
Expenses	22,800	52,800
NET PROFIT		16,800

Balance Sheet as at 31st December

	£
Freehold premises	71,000
Kitchen plant (net)	5,450
Fittings	7,050
Stocks	8,000
Debtors	17,700
Bank balance	8,400
Cash balance	600
	118,200
Capital	68,200
Profit	16,800
Loan	20,000
Creditors	11,600
Accrued expenses	1,000
Advance bookings	600
	118,200

Other information

(*a*) Average daily cost of sales; food £60; liquor £80.
(*b*) Average daily credit sales £240 and credit purchases £150.
(*c*) Debtors and creditors at the beginning of the year were £13,500 and £8,400 respectively.
(*d*) Stocks at the beginning of the year; food £700; liquor £6,700.
(*e*) Stocks at the end of the year; food £1,100; liquor £6,900.

11–6 The following relates to Wheelers Catering Company:

Trading, Profit and Loss Account for year ended 31st March, 1977

	£
Sales (all on credit)	100,000
Less: Cost of sales	
Less: Labour and expenses	
Net profit before tax	

Balance Sheet as at 31st March, 1977

	£
Fixed assets (net)	
Stock	
Debtors	
Cash	Nil

Less: Corporation tax			£
Less: Dividend paid		Share capital	50,000
Retained profit c/f	Nil	Retained profit c/f	Nil
		Creditors	

Given the following ratios you are required to fill in the missing figures in the outline final accounts:

Turnover to capital employed	2:1
Average collection period*	18 days
Acid test ratio	1:1
Stock turnover period*	36 days
Gross profit	60%
Net profit before tax	15%
Corporation tax	50%
Ordinary share dividend	15%

*Assume a 360 day year

11–7 From the following information prepare a trading, profit and loss account and balance sheet:

Issued share capital	£36,000
Working capital	£6,000
Rate of turnover of capital employed	2
Rate of stock turnover (times)	12
Current ratio	1·6:1
Debtors' ratio	0·075:1
Acid test ratio	1·1:1
Labour and expenses in relation to sales	20%

Notes: 1. Capital employed is to be taken as issued share capital plus net profit.
2. Ignore depreciation and appropriation of profits.

11–8 The accounts for the City Luncheon Caterers is below.

Trading and Profit and Loss Account for the year ended 30 April 1974

1973		
£		£
48,000	Sales	60,000
17,000	Cost of Sales	20,000
31,000		40,000
14,000	Wages	18,000
17,000		22,000
13,000	Other expenses	16,000
£4,000	Net profit for the year	£6,000

Balance Sheet at 30 April 1974

£						£
			Fixed Assets			
20,000			Freehold property at cost			20,000
4,000			Equipment at cost less depreciation			6,000
24,000						26,000
	£		*Current Assets*		£	
	2,200		Stock		1,800	
	800		Debtors		1,000	
	1,950		Cash at Bank		400	
	4,950				3,200	
		£	*Less: Current Liabilities*	£		
		2,600	Creditors	2,500		
		200	Accrued expenses	100		
	2,800				2,600	
2,150						600
£26,150						£26,600
£						£
			Financed by:			
25,150			Capital			26,150
4,000			Add—profit for the year			6,000
29,150						32,150
3,000			Less—drawings			5,550
£26,150						£26,600

Additional information:

(i) The freehold property has increased in value from £20,000 at 30 April 1973 to £25,000 on 30 April 1974.

(ii) One third of the sales are credit: the balance is cash sales.

(iii) Cost of sales, 10% are of a perishable nature and are paid for in cash; the balance represents non-perishable stock which is purchased on credit.

(iv) Stock, on average 5% is perishable, the rest non-perishable.

(v) The return on owners capital for this type of establishment is 12%.

(vi) The restaurant provides lunches for office workers between 12 am and 3 pm. It is a non-seasonal city centre establishment and provides lunches on 250 days in the year for 120,000 customers p.a.

(vii) The service area has 40 tables, 4 covers to a table.

(viii) The owner employs 16 service staff and 9 kitchen staff.

(ix) Included in wages is £2,000 for the owners salary.

You are required to calculate and comment upon THREE statistics you regard as important from EACH of the following:

(*a*) the trading, profit and loss account

(*b*) the balance sheet, and

(*c*) the service area.

(Please explain any assumptions you have made in your answer).

(HCIMA)

11–9 Below are the financial results of The Classic Hotel Ltd. for the years 1977 and 1978. The hotel has been operating since 1970 and is accommodation sales biased.

Balance Sheets as at 31st December

	1977		*1978*	
	£	£	£	£
Fixed Assets (net)				
Freehold property		320,000		390,000
Equipment and furniture		70,000		100,000
		390,000		490,000
Current Assets				
Stocks of food and beverages	20,000		75,000	
Debtors	12,000		50,000	
Cash	53,000	85,000	2,000	127,000
		475,000		617,000

Financed by:				
Ordinary Share Capital		250,000		320,000
Retained profits		90,000		120,000
		340,000		440,000
10% Debenture (secured on property – 1985)		60,000		60,000
Current Liabilities				
Creditors	8,000		15,000	
Taxation	40,000		60,000	
Proposed dividend	25,000		30,000	
Overdraft	2,000	75,000	12,000	117,000
		475,000		617,000

Profit and Loss Accounts for Year ending 31st December

	1977		*1978*	
	£	£	£	£
Sales		500,000		700,000
Less: Cost of sales		100,000		140,000
Gross profit		400,000		560,000
Less: Labour	140,000		200,000	
Other expenses	180,000	320,000	240,000	440,000
Net profit before tax		80,000		120,000
Less: Corporation tax (50%)		40,000		60,000
Net profit after tax		40,000		60,000
Less: Proposed Ordinary Share dividend		25,000		30,000
Retained profits for the year		15,000		30,000

Of the sales half were on credit and all purchases were on credit.

You are requested to:

(*a*) calculate six key accounting ratios for 1977 and 1978; and

(*b*) comment on the strengths and weaknesses revealed by the ratios and any other information you consider relevant.

State clearly any assumptions you make.

(HCIMA adapted)

11–10 The following information relates to La Carte, an exclusive licensed restaurant, which has recently extended its facilities:

Last period results (prior to the extension)

	Meals	*Drink*
	£	£
Sales revenue	120,000	70,000
Less: Cost of sales	36,000	28,000
Gross Profit	84,000	42,000

It is estimated that:

1. Sales from meals and drinks will reach £160,000 and £100,000 respectively.
2. The amount of stocks held will be:
   Food 3 weeks
   Drink 6 weeks
3. Of the total sales 1/4 will be on credit and the debtors will take 5 weeks credit.
4. A cash balance of £200 will be required for floats.
5. Food suppliers will give 6 weeks credit but will not offer any discounts for early payment.
   Drink suppliers will give 8 weeks credit or offer 2½% cash discount for settlement within 4 weeks. (Assume that all the payments will be within the discount terms.)
6. Advance booking deposits, currently running at about 10% of 1 week's meal sales, will continue at the same rate.
7. Bank overdraft of £2,000 is expected to be little used leaving the average bank balance to be nil.

Assume that sales and costs accrue evenly throughout the period. You are asked to prepare a statement analysing the estimated average working capital necessary to fund the restaurant's increased activities.

Further Reading

1. Clarkson, G. P., and Elliot, B. J., *Managing Money and Finance;* Gower Press; chapter 7.
2. Wood, F., *Business Accounting* (Vol. II), Longman; chapter 47.

CHAPTER TWELVE

INTER-FIRM COMPARISONS

TO maintain financial control, internal performance targets must be set in various sections of the business and performance monitored for comparison with the targets. Targets so far considered are budgets, for instance a departmental sales budget; standards such as the quantity of food for a dish; and financial and liquidity ratios.

Although the level of these targets is for management itself to decide, assistance in setting them can come from a knowledge of the performance of similar firms, most industries having access to this information in some form of inter-firm comparison scheme. The Centre for Inter-Firm Comparison (CIFC) organizes schemes for many industries, whilst some schemes are run by trade associations or other interested bodies. Hotel and catering firms can avail themselves of the services of the Scottish Hotel School, University of Strathclyde which operates both an hotel and motel scheme.

The Inter-Hotel Comparison Scheme

This scheme is one whereby financial and operating figures are collected in strict confidence from a range of hotels, processed and used by the Strathclyde Centre to enable an hotelier to compare the performance of his hotel with others of like type. The first hotel scheme was instituted by the University of Surrey in 1967 with the aim of providing 'norms' or standards by which hoteliers could judge their own performance, such standards being in the form of a percentage, ratio, or index number. To assist hoteliers determine their own target standards, ratios of three (unidentified) participating hotels are published for each factor under consideration (e.g. profit per 1,000 sq. ft.), the particular ratios being named lower quartile, median and upper quartile. To determine which of the values from a number of hotels become these three, all values are placed in ascending order, known as an 'array', and the median value is the value of the middle item. The median is an average giving a better indication of the typical value than the more common arithmetic average which may be influenced unduly by extreme values. The median has the virtue that it must be one particular value from the whole range whereas an arithmetic average may not represent a specific hotel.

The value of the item halfway between the lowest valued item and the median is the lower quartile, and similarly the item halfway between the median and the highest valued item is the upper quartile. Half the items are therefore between the quartiles which therefore give some indication of the spread of values around the median. Percentiles are similar to quartiles but show the percentage figures instead of only the items at quarterly intervals.

Suppose the percentage profit on sales submitted by 11 hotels were:

Hotel	A	B	C	D	E	F	G	H	I	J	K
%	34·9	29·4	25·3	49·3	39·9	66·9	31·2	35·2	43·1	54·1	37·1

Placed in an array they would appear:

Hotel	C	B	G	A	H	K	E	I	D	J	F
%	25·3	29·4	31·2	34·9	35·2	37·1	39·9	43·1	49·3	54·1	66·9
Order	1	2	3	4	5	6	7	8	9	10	11

The hoteliers would be informed of the three values representing the median and the quartiles as follows:

Lower quartile (11 items +1) × $\frac{1}{4}$ = 3rd item = 31·2% (G)
Median (11 items +1) × $\frac{1}{2}$ = 6th item = 37·1% (K)
Upper quartile (11 items +1) × $\frac{3}{4}$ = 9th item = 49·3% (D)

Hotel owner K would know that he produced an average percentage because as many hotels submitted lower figures as produced higher ones. He would, know also, because of the quartiles, that the hotels with higher figures than his tended to be of relatively higher value than those below, the quarter below dropping only 5·9% (37·1–31·2) whilst the quarter above going up by 12·2%. If he aimed to reach the upper quartile and be near the top he would know he had 12·2% to go.

Hotel owner J with 54·1% would know that he produced a higher percentage than over three-quarters of the participating hotels, which may give him cause for satisfaction. However, another factor, say profit per 1,000 sq. ft., may show him to be near the bottom of the table accounting for only an average overall result.

Hotels in the scheme are classified by size, etc., so that fair comparisons may be made, but even so, variations within classes do exist and these are taken into account when interpreting data. The most profitable hotel will not have a top rating in every factor comparison, for it may have a high reputation for the supply of drinks and therefore hold large stocks as a matter of policy, putting it above the upper quartile for the number of days' supply in store. The aim generally here may be to be near the lower quartile.

Each hotelier, then, uses the published data to provide himself with a target figure for each percentage ratio and index, raising sights where he would expect to produce better relative results, and ensuring that results in other areas he regards as satisfactory are maintained.

Comparative data presented include:

(*a*) The Size and Composition of the Sample:

Proportion of hotels in the scheme owned by public company, private company, partnership/sole owner.

Number of hotels operated by participating companies – single unit, 2–5 hotels, over 5 hotels.
Sales mix of the hotels by department, size, price, location, bias.
Seasonality of hotels – seasonal, non-seasonal.
Breakdown of individual floor areas in total sample.

(*b*) Sales and Operating Statistics:
Sales trends using 1966 as index 100.
Moving annual total of bed occupancy as a percentage of last year.
Actual room sales as a percentage of maximum attainable room sales, also known as MAR – maximum attainable revenue.
Food sales per sq. ft. of kitchen and restaurant area.
Restaurant and kitchen: sq. ft. per cover.
Accommodation sales per room and per bed.
Departmental sales per employee.
Number of employees related to number of guests.
Average number of days' supply of food and drink.

(*c*) Cost and Profit Statistics:
Percentage cost and profit to sales, listing nearly 30 expense items.
Departmental analysis of goods sold and wage costs.
Wage per employee.
Departmental analysis of major costs by (*a*) sales bias (*b*) price of bedrooms (*c*) size of sleeper places.

Inter-Motel Comparison Scheme

In 1969 the first motel survey was conducted on similar lines to the hotel survey. A significant difference was the inclusion of a profit to capital employed ratio because of the relative ease with which capital costs can be calculated, having been incurred within the last few years.

Inter-firm Comparison in Other Industries

Originally inter-firm comparison schemes were based on a uniform costing system for the industry to assist in forming a common selling price policy, but more recently the emphasis, like the inter-hotel scheme, has been to aid management effectiveness.

The largest and oldest trade association is run by the British Federation of Master Printers dating from 1915 and whose 'Ratios for Management' scheme started in 1958. The Cotton Board Productivity Centre started a scheme in 1962.

The Centre for Inter-Firm Comparison (CIFC) was set up in 1959 by the British Institute of Management in association with the British Productivity Council to compare performance of firms in the same industry. They have had much success in installing and operating schemes within industries and in 1970 some 60 industries were covered by their schemes.

Exhibit 12–1

PYRAMID OF INCOME AND EXPENDITURE RATIOS

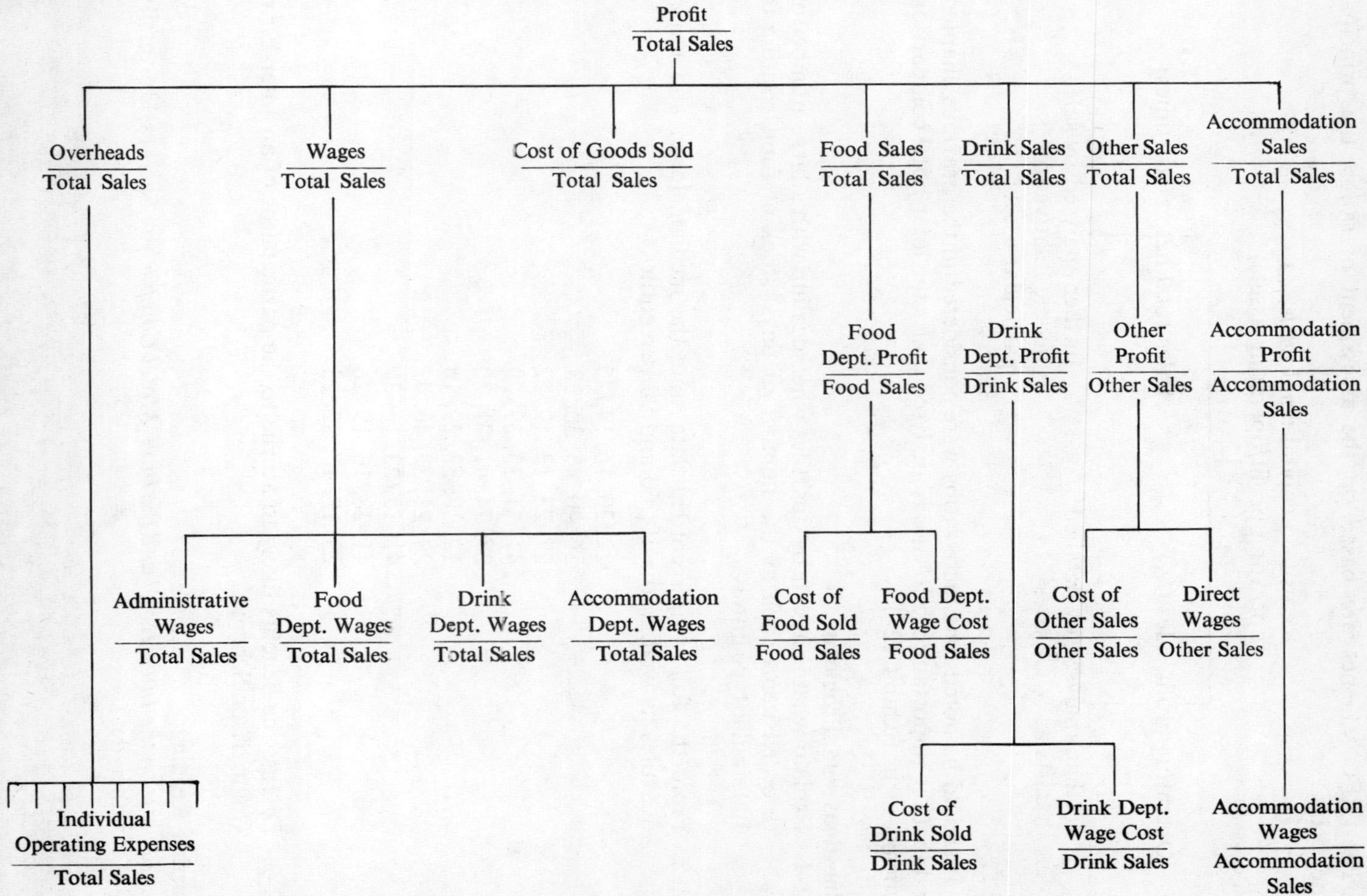

The CIFC schemes are based on the assessment of ratios, the principal ones being:

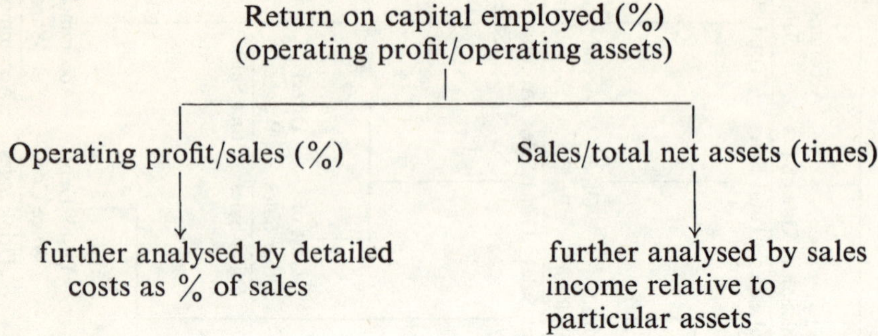

It should be noted that these ratios were considered in the previous chapter, and that the important profit/sales is analysed under the inter-hotel comparison scheme, as in Exhibit 12–1.

Questions and Problems

12–1 Explain what is meant by quartiles when dealing with a large number of recorded items such as the number of days' stock of food relating to 100 similar type hotels.

12–2 From the following recorded data state the median, lower and upper quartiles as well as the 10, 60 and 90 percentiles.

22, 30, 16, 14, 25
16, 40, 45, 30, 38
27, 28, 13, 19, 22
41, 31, 33, 39, 29
27, 24, 41, 21, 20
12, 18, 33, 29, 16
28, 21, 33, 40, 42
41, 19, 22, 15, 39
41, 28, 16, 19, 26
25, 18, 17, 22, 23

12–3 Discuss the benefits likely to accrue to the participator of an Inter-Firm Comparison Scheme.

Further Reading

1. *Reports on the Inter-Hotel and the Inter-Motel Comparison Surveys,* University of Strathclyde.

CHAPTER THIRTEEN

THE RIGHT SOURCE OF FINANCE

EARLY in the life of any business cash is needed to pay for the use of premises and equipment, for the services of personnel and for raw materials such as food in a catering establishment. Assuming good demand exists for the product and the business satisfies that demand, it is the manner in which finances are managed that separates the successful from the unsuccessful business. The successful business man borrows money on a short-term basis and so times his operations as to collect cash from sales in time to settle bills for food, wages, etc. A very profitable product will leave him with sufficient cash to repay fairly quickly his loans and to retain cash in the business so as to increase his resources such as premises and stocks and enabling him to earn more profit. That is the way fortunes have been made. Cash for expansion is provided by the business itself. However, in hotel and catering the very profitable product with the fantastic demand rarely exists, yet the manner in which the finances are managed does provide an example of the importance of 'internal funds'.

The Sole Trader

The decision to expand

If the small business prospers its owner will be faced with the difficult decision to use his profit either to improve his own standard of living or to reinvest it in the business, and it is very largely upon which way this decision goes that the subsequent history of his business will depend.

Reinvestment of profits goes by other terms such as reinvestment of cash or earnings, ploughing back profits, retaining profit or funds, and internal funds; it is essentially a matter of the owner sacrificing cash for personal spending in order to improve the strength and earning power of his business still further.

Seldom does profit generated in a period coincide with extra cash being available at the end of the period, for after the first year's trading food consumed but obtained on credit would mean a higher cash inflow than profit made; on the other hand purchase of any resource paid for but carried forward to the next period such as stocks of food and book value of equipment would result in a smaller increase in cash in the period than profit achieved. This important consideration is explained further in Chapter 14.

If the firm continues to prosper a decision has to be made between turning away customers or providing facilities to cater for their needs. We are concerned with the hotelier/caterer who feels he wants to take advantage of the favourable position of his establishment; not with the man who is content to carry on earning a reasonable living and let chances of an improved standard of living pass him by. To many people and especially more dynamic business men, the attitude of the latter – the anti-expansionist – may seem extraordinarily short-sighted. In the end, however, business goals are an intensely personal matter. There is no law against running a business simply to earn a comfortable living, however deplorable this attitude may be to those who think all businessmen should be go-getting tycoons. Problems of finance and loss of control and contact with customers are a real dis-incentive to expand to many people owning small establishments, so that it is not surprising that they sell out at a good profit to the large company instead of developing the firm themselves.

Retained Profits

Should he decide to expand the business, the owner will consider what cash is available from 'ploughed back' profits, shown in the balance sheet as reserves or capital (liabilities) and as surplus cash or short-term investments (assets), for this is the best and cheapest source of finance for expansion. Otherwise external long term finance must be obtained, or such other sources such as leasing. There is a great temptation to use short-term funds for expansion, such as better credit facilities from suppliers, reduction in stocks and debtors and increased overdraft facilities at the bank. It is right to do these things to make better use of resources, but if the proceeds are used to invest in long term assets such as property and equipment for increasing turnover, there is a grave danger that financial difficulties will arise because with extra funds sunk in long-term assets and the planned additional turnover achieved, more short-term funds will be needed to provide additional stocks. Careful cash planning by using cash forecasts is helpful in this situation. Control of working capital is considered in Chapter 11.

Loans and Overdrafts

The clearing banks can properly claim to be the principal source of external finance available to small firms. Particularly is this the case in the formative and early development stages when much is likely to depend on the support of the branch bank manager who is prepared to back his judgement of the business acumen and vitality of the personalities involved. Bank lending is traditionally recognized to be the provision of short-term assistance for working capital purposes. The bank overdraft is the cheapest and most convenient form of short-term finance. A customer granted an overdraft is permitted to draw cheques up to an agreed figure beyond the amount standing to the credit of his account. The period of the arrangement varies according to individual requirement; the maximum term is usually 12 months, after which the arrangement is reviewed. Interest is assessed only upon the daily cleared debit balance, and rates of interest, tied to bank rate, are significantly lower than rates charged by any other type of lender. This is especially true of the small firm paying a rate which is seldom more than 2% above that charged to the highest class of commercial undertaking, and normally in the region of 1 to 2% above bank rate. The borrower may therefore find the cost rising in times of government restriction, whereas the interest on a loan which has been negotiated for a given term remains fixed in accordance with the terms of the loan. A further disadvantage is that the overdraft may not be renewed.

A loan account with the bank is an alternative facility to an overdraft, by means of which the total amount is advanced by way of lump sum which is credited to the customer's current account balance, to be drawn upon as and when required. Loans may be granted over periods similar to those applicable to overdrafts and subject to periodic review. In agreeing to provide a loan the bank manager will satisfy himself that the money is likely to return sufficient cash to the business to allow repayments to be met. The loan must be self-liquidating, in the sense that the loan is quickly repaid.

Finance available to the small business may be obtained when property is used as security for a loan. Property may be mortgaged to obtain ready cash or may be sold to a property company who would agree to lease the premises back.

Partnerships and Companies

Transition to a Company

Entering into a partnership agreement is a further way of obtaining more funds whereby an agreed sum will be contributed to the business as initial capital. A partnership is in a position to borrow from investment institutions on mortgage and in other ways although it is often difficult to raise substantial amounts of capital without offering a share of the business. A partner investing without taking part in management may limit his liability to the extent of his subscription and this constitutes a limited partnership. The cost of raising funds is relatively low, for others may be persuaded to join the partnership at a nominal charge.

The disadvantages to the sole trader of taking a partner in a business are:

1. He loses control of the management of the business.
2. He must share profits.
3. He is subject to the risk that his partner may involve the firm in exceptional unbearable liabilities.
4. He, as founder partner, puts his private assets at stake.
5. Disposition of his share in the business is restricted.

As a partnership business grows and more cash is required consideration would be given to increasing the number of partners and possibly the formation of a limited company.

One factor limiting the size of a business is the number of members and this is summarized as follows:

	Number of Members	
	Minimum	*Maximum*
Partnerships	2	20
Private limited company	2	50
Public limited company	7	no maximum

When a choice exists, for instance when there are or will be ten members in the business, professional advice of an accountant would be sought and full consideration given to such matters as formation costs, taxation, rights and restrictions of members.

The conversion of a partnership into a private limited company involves ending the partnership which is sold as a going concern to the new company, the partners becoming shareholders and most likely directors.

However, unless expressly forbidden by the memorandum or articles of association, a private limited company may become a public limited company by passing a special resolution, filing the prescribed statement in lieu of prospectus and prescribed statutory declaration with the registrar of companies.

The public company's shares are fully transferable from one person to another and may be quoted on the Stock Exchange although this is not statutory. Of over 400,000 registered public and private companies in 1965, only about 4,600 had Stock Exchange quotations, but profits of these companies were estimated to amount to more than all the other companies put together.

Any further reference made to a company will assume it to be a public limited company with quoted shares, unless otherwise stated.

Ordinary Shares (*called Equity Capital*)

Holders of ordinary shares accept the main risk involved in investing in a limited company but on the other hand stand to gain most when the company makes a high profit. To all intents and purposes ordinary shares are irredeemable and are treated as a permanent investment in the firm. Under conditions of inflation ordinary shareholders tend to keep in step with inflation and more particularly where hotel and restaurant premises are owned because of the significant rise in land and property values.

After all expenses, preference share dividend and taxation payments have been met, any surplus revenue benefits ordinary shareholders in the form of dividend distribution and share value appreciation following the ploughing back into the business of any residual surplus.

At the annual general meeting the board of directors declare a percentage dividend on the nominal value of shares after a consideration of the financial position. In many cases an interim dividend will have been paid in the middle of the financial year, a payment 'on account'.

The ordinary shareholders are entitled to share pro rata in the assets distributed after a forced or voluntary liquidation.

Rights Issue

A company making a definite offer to its own shareholders to take up new shares is said to make a rights issue. The price is usually below market price as an attraction. Although an apparently attractive price may be asked of shareholders, they may benefit more from an alternative source of capital such as a debenture issue. Holders of shares to whom the offer is made may take up their rights or may sell them.

Bonus Issue

Where a company's reserves are considerable and the market price of ordinary shares far above the nominal value, a bonus issue of new shares may be made to shareholders without a charge to them. The issue is in proportion to existing shares held such as an issue of one new share for every one held.

The total market share value, and similarly each shareholder's value of his holdings, will initially remain unchanged although the market price per share will tend to drop proportionately.

A lower declared dividend percentage will provide the shareholder with the same total dividend as before, which may be an advantage from a public relations viewpoint.

A scrip issue is another term for a bonus issue.

Deferred Ordinary Shares

These rank for dividend after other ordinary shares, and usually entitle the holder to the profits then remaining. When profits are high the deferred shareholders take a substantial proportion of them.

Sometimes called founders' shares, they may be issued to managers as a form of incentive to high performance.

They are normally few in number and therefore of no great consequence.

Preference Shares

Although part of the company's share capital, these shares generally attract limited voting rights or no voting rights at all, and since dividends are at a fixed rate, preference shares have much in common with debentures.

These shares, however, are a relatively expensive source of capital compared with debentures because dividends are paid from after tax earnings, whereas debenture interest is an expense which reduces taxable profit. With corporation tax at 45% it costs the company the same to pay interest on 10% debentures as it does to pay dividend on 5½% preference shares.

To illustrate the calculation, suppose company A issued £100,000 of 10% debentures and company B issued £100,000 of 5½% preference shares. All other long-term capital was in ordinary shares, profits for both companies was £1 million, and corporation tax was 45%.

Company	*A*	*B*
	£100,000 in 10% debentures	*£100,000 in 5½% preference shares*
	£	£
Profit	1,000,000	1,000,000
Debenture interest (10%)	10,000	
	990,000	
45% corporation tax	445,500	450,000
	544,500	550,000
Preference dividend (5½%)	—	5,500
Available for equity	544,500	544,500

If market rate of interest for new debentures is 10% then 5½% may be said to be the break-even point for preference shares. Preference shares would clearly not be issued at more than 5½% if 10% debentures are possible, unless some other overriding consideration were taken into account.

The benefit accruing to the company in having debentures rather than preference shares is clearly recognized when companies like Trust Houses Group Ltd. redeem preference shares and issue debentures as replacements.

As with debentures, preference shares may be issued in perpetuity or they may have a specific redemption date.

Debentures

There are two main types of debenture, the mortgage debenture secured by the mortgage of particular property owned by the company, and the debenture with a floating charge. If the company goes into liquidation, mortgage debentures rank ahead of floating debentures up to the value of the secured property, and floating debentures rank ahead of any unsecured creditors. All creditors rank ahead of any shareholder.

The Savoy Hotel Ltd. has £700,000 8% mortgage debenture stock 1991/96 secured against the Savoy Hotel.

Most debenture issues are redeemable, that is repayable at or by a specified date, which may be effected

(*a*) By annual drawings out of profit.

(*b*) By the company purchasing its own debenture in the open market when the price is favourable.

(*c*) In a lump sum at maturity provided by means of a sinking fund. This method is considered in Volume 1. Examples of this method are to be found in the hotel and catering industry, for example:

Myddleton Hotels and Estates Limited. £400,000 7½% mortgage debenture 1991 (year of redemption) in respect of which a sinking fund of £8,000 per annum started in 1971.

Debentures may be issued to named persons or made payable to bearer when they may be quoted on the Stock Exchange.

Convertible Debentures

Loan stock holders who have the right to convert their stock to ordinary shares at a future date or series of dates, hold convertible debentures, the final decision to convert resting with the debenture holder.

An advantage to the company compared with a redeemable debenture is that the debt is self-liquidating in that debentures are exchanged for ordinary shares and no funds are needed with which to redeem them.

Compared with an immediate ordinary share issue the convertible is cheaper in annual outgoings, which is helpful when required for a hotel development likely to take some time to build up to a profit earning stage.

An example is Grand Metropolitan Hotels. 6½% convertible unsecured loan stock 1984/89.

Mortgages

A mortgage loan is one taken out against land or property and is similar in some ways to a secured debenture. However, differences between them include:

1. The interest rate of a mortgage cannot normally be fixed over the life of the agreement as is the interest on a debenture.
2. Regular payments of interest and principal are made to liquidate the loan which are usually for a shorter period of time than a debenture.
3. The mortgage holder has the first call on a company's assets in the event of a default in payment.

International Loans

Borrowing by British hotel groups extends to the international money market, in particular the Euro-dollar market which is the freest sector of this market. The market is so called because most of the banks accepting foreign currency deposits are in Europe, and such deposits are largely in US dollars although they may be for instance pound sterling, the Swiss franc and the German mark.

Examples include Trust Houses Forte, and J. Lyons who in 1970 borrowed £2·5 million in Swiss francs over seven years at 9% for the first three years and subsequent rates to be based on inter-bank borrowing rates. This loan was used to replace short-term borrowings on bank overdraft. A loan of £5 million in Deutschmarks at an initial rate of 9¼% by Lyons in 1969 was said to be used for developments.

Special Finance Institutions

The Industrial and Commercial Finance Corporation Limited (ICFC) was set up in 1945 to assist the smaller concern requiring long-term loan or share capital. At 31st March, 1969, its investments in some 2,000 concerns totalling £102 million were divided as follows:

Loans	68%
Preference shares	15%
Ordinary shares	17%

The Estate Duties Investment Trust Limited (EDITH) was set up in 1952 in order to relieve the immediate problem of finding the finance for meeting estate duties while still allowing the private companies concerned to continue their separate existence. Holders of shares in family businesses and companies whose shares are privately held may be seriously affected by death duties which may lead to loss of control of a business.

Finance Without Initial Ownership

Financial arrangements of obtaining the use of capital facilities without ownership, open to the small and large firm alike, includes leasing, hire purchase, mortgaging and sale and lease back.

There is increasing awareness that two distinct decisions need to be made when obtaining long-term assets, one is to decide whether a particular asset is in fact required – an investment decision – and the other is the most appropriate means of obtaining the asset – a financial decision.

Leasing

This has been common for many years, for example internal telephones, and leasing companies provide virtually every industry with a convenient package deal if required. One lease can embrace complete furnishing of an hotel. The fundamental difference between leasing and other forms of finance is that title in the goods remains permanently vested in the 'lessor'. A lease comprises a primary period and a secondary period. During the primary period a rental commensurate with the cost of the equipment is paid by the lessee; the secondary period rentals are nominal. The total length of the lease is negotiated with the lessee but bears a relationship to the anticipated useful working life of the equipment; the normal primary periods are 3, 4 or 5 years' duration with 2, 6 or 5 year secondary periods respectively. The primary period rentals may be paid monthly, quarterly, half yearly or annually in advance.

Leasing offers a number of advantages to the lessee including:

1. It is the use of equipment, not its ownership, which is vital for profitability.
2. Use of equipment is gained on payment of first rental.
3. Working capital is left free for more profitable employment.
4. Rentals are fully tax-deductible.
5. Budgeting is facilitated.
6. Managers are more easily able to face up to obsolescence of existing plant and equipment because of ease of renewal.

The main reason for buying rather than leasing assets is perhaps that the cost is often higher to lease, although this depends upon the interest cost of raising money to make the purchase, or if money is available, the earnings which would be sacrificed in making the purchase.

Generally speaking the leasing company is content to receive a fair return on their money and to leave the larger share of earnings to the business prepared to use the asset and take the entrepreneurial risks.

Contract Hire
Contract hire is a form of leasing which is generally for shorter periods of time.

Hire Purchase
Hire Purchase may be the only means of acquiring certain assets. The purchaser makes a down payment or deposit and enters into a contract to hire goods for a specific time, say two years, making regular periodic payments for the hire, and at once acquires possession but not ownership of the goods. At the end of the hire period the hirer may purchase the goods outright for a small cash consideration, or the ownership may pass on the last payment. Although the most expensive of all credit facilities hire purchase is particularly useful since no security is needed though the hirer may be required to provide private legal and financial information and offer a guarantee.

Sale and Lease Back
Sale and lease back of property is a popular source of finance for hotel companies. Companies owning freehold properties or long leaseholds and having good profit records may benefit from selling such properties or leases to a finance or life assurance company for full market value and then lease back for a long term frequently, 99–120 years, at a rental directly related to the sale price, including cost of purchase, and would be in the range of $8\frac{1}{2}$–10%. Provision would be made during the course of the lease for upward rental review at intervals now normally of not more than 7 years. During the term of the lease the vendor would normally be responsible for maintaining and insuring the building.

Advantage to the vendor depends upon the use made of the money no longer tied up in the property. Inflation may add considerably to the rental and at the end of the long lease the vendor has no building as an asset. Many companies who have sold and leased back properties believe that with efficient management, monies released will earn a return which, having covered the rental, will provide a satisfactory dividend, allow for inflation, and still leave cash available for ploughing back. In short, many efficient managements consider this method of financing a profitable proposition.

A disadvantage might well be the effect on other sources of finance for instance where property is secured. Too high a proportion of leased properties might inhibit the issue of debentures for lack of security.

Hotels are particularly suitable candidates for sale and lease back transactions because the appreciation in value of the land encourages property and other finance companies to obtain regular revenue and a hedge against inflation, while hotel managements are able to use the funds so freed to take advantage of the tremendous expansion opportunities prevailing in the early 1970s. The

Post Houses are examples of financing by this source. In fact the capital programme of Trust Houses Forte group in 1970 was £20 million of which £10 million was lease-backs and £10 million ownerships.

Long-term Finance – Gearing (Leverage in USA)

The ideal capital structure for an expanding company is difficult to determine since it is largely a matter of opinion. The capital structure is measured by relating the medium- and long-term fixed interest capital to total capital employed. The company is said to be high geared if a large proportion of its capital is in fixed interest securities such as preference shares and debentures. Company gearing may be measured in a number of ways, a common method is

$$\frac{\text{fixed interest securities}}{\text{total capital employed}} \times 100$$

There is no ideal standard percentage, much depending upon the type of industry and whether fixed assets are owned or leased. What is important, however, is the effect on ordinary shareholders' earnings of increasing the gearing as shown in Exhibit 13–1 of two companies with opposite gearings:

Exhibit 13–1	*LG Ltd. at 31/12/75*	*HG Ltd. at 31/12/75*
	£	£
Ordinary shares of £1	1,300,000	750,000
Debentures 10%	200,000	750,000
	1,500,000	1,500,000
Year ended	31/12/75	31/12/75
	£	£
15% return before interest	225,000	225,000
less 10% Debenture interest	20,000	75,000
Equity earnings before tax	205,000	150,000
less Corporation Tax (45%)	92,250	67,500
	112,750	82,500
Earnings per Share	£0·087	£0·110
Gearing	13·3%	50%
	(Low geared)	(High geared)

Because the rate of earnings before interest (15%) is greater than debenture interest rate itself (10%), ordinary shareholders benefit by the residue.

A high-geared company has extreme effects on ordinary shareholders' earnings. If HG Ltd. was successful in 1976 but failed in 1977 to the extent shown in Exhibit 13–2, the fortune of ordinary shareholders can be traced.

Exhibit 13–2

	HG Ltd.	*HG Ltd.*
Year ended	*31/12/76*	*31/12/77*
Return on capital employed before interest	25%	5%
	£	£
Profit before interest	375,000	75,000
Less 10% Debenture interest	75,000	75,000
	300,000	nil
Less Corporation tax (45%)	135,000	
	165,000	
Earnings per share $\frac{£165,000}{750,000}$	=£0·220	nil

It may be seen that with return before interest on capital employed going up from £225,000 to £375,000 in 1976, an increase of 67%, equity earnings have risen by 100% from £0·110 to £0·220 per share because of high gearing. However, when low profits are earned the ordinary shareholders are worse off in a high geared company than a low geared one. HG Shareholders are left with no return when profit before interest drops to £75,000, whereas LG Shareholders

would have received	£75,000
less 10% interest	£20,000
	£55,000
less 45% Cpn. tax	£24,750
	£30,250

If a company is confident of its future prospects it should seek to maximize its gearing subject to limitations to ensure that it does not become over-geared. One guide is that the interest charge should be covered four times.

An efficiently financed industrial company should be able to raise up to 35% of its long-term capital needs in loan form. However, companies with much owned property because of good security are able to raise higher proportions of debt capital. Before their merger in 1970 Trust Houses had long-term debt amounting to 42% of its capital employed whilst Forte at 61·3% was even higher.

Takeovers and Mergers

Managements planning to expand operations can have new facilities built or buy existing facilities. The more usual means of expanding the smaller business, if local demand exists, is the purchase of adjoining premises, a method used by Mario Cassandro and Franco Lagattolla who started in 1959 with a capital of £1,200, earned as waiters. They opened a small trattoria in Soho and a few years later bought two adjoining buildings to start their development, through acquisition of restaurants, into a successful business valued at £1 million when it became a public company in 1968. Reasons for their success are said to be that they found a successful marketing formula and maintained a high standard without losing control of prices; found an understanding bank manager at the beginning; and got on well together and worked extremely hard.

Although a number of hotels have been built by Fortes, Sir Charles Forte prefers buying existing hotels because he reckons that from the turnover record one can better estimate potential turnover and profit, allowing very often for an increase in occupancy rate and catering turnover, and a reduction in wages content.

Expansion is designed to increase earnings per share of a business and buying hotels is a favourite means of achieving this growth. The blending of two or more existing undertakings into one undertaking goes under many names, the popular ones being takeovers and mergers. There is little difference between the two. The city code on takeovers and mergers aimed at protecting shareholders' interests never mentions one without the other.

Generally speaking however when the boards of directors of two companies agree to amalgamate in the interest of both, a merger is the right term. On the other hand a large company wanting to gain control of a smaller business whose board does not recommend the change, is said to be attempting to take over the smaller company.

Differences in corporate structure result from takeovers and mergers.

A takeover bid refers to an offer which may be made either to the whole of a company's shareholders or those owning ordinary shares, to purchase their existing stock holding at a price which is sufficiently over the current Stock Exchange quotation for the shares, so as to induce them to sell out in return for quoted shares in the bidding company, debentures, cash, or some combination of these. If the bid succeeds then the corporate identity of the business taken over may disappear.

A merger between two or more companies often results in a new company being created, and a reorganization of the capital structure takes place, for example Trust Houses and Forte in 1970 merged to become Trust Houses Forte group.

Takeovers

An undertaking which is seen not to be utilizing its resources to the full and whose management does not appear to be of the highest order, tends to be in danger of takeover for the simple reason that there is room for profit improvement under a more effective management. Underutilized resources may be cash, stocks, and fixed assets. The latter, for instance an hotel, may have a low bedroom occupancy rate which might be capable of improvement, and further, it may be owned when a sale and lease back transaction might be more profitable in releasing cash for further expansion.

Mr. Charles Clore was the best known of the financiers who brought to the attention of industry and shareholders alike the importance of under-used assets. His most successful take-over was of J. Sears & Co. (True-Form Boot Co.) owning 900 shops, several hundred of which he sold and leased back thereby gaining control of a good business and property worth more than £8 million for only £3 million. An unsuccessful bid of Mr. Clore's, but one which reminded the brewery industry that they owned valuable property which could raise cash, was for the Watney-Mann group. The bid did the group much good for they carried out a property re-organization themselves.

Mr. Clore developed a takeover technique which became standard practice. Having found a company under-using its assets – a suitable takeover candidate – he spent many months buying shares through a nominee name in the interests of secrecy. If he failed to obtain control by obtaining enough shares he still made a good profit because his action had forced the share prices up, the shares being undervalued in the first instance.

In the hotel world the Savoy Hotel Ltd. has long battled against being taken over, starting with Mr. Clore in 1953, when he obtained 10% of the equity. However Mr. Harold Samual, through his company Land Securities Investment Trust, was also interested and had over 20% of the equity. The plum was said to be the Berkeley Hotel and its site which could be more profitably used as offices and showrooms, although Savoy management, whilst admitting the hotel's unsatisfactory trading results, said to be caused by a decline in restaurant sales, had plans of their own to make the hotel more profitable. Mr. Clore sold his shares to Mr. Samual who now owned 30%. The Savoy directors realizing the threat of being taken over took legal steps to ensure that the target, the Berkeley, be safeguarded,resulting in Mr. Samual admitting defeat by selling his shares.

Seventeen years later the Savoy group was again under attack when Mr. Nigel Broackes, chairman of Trafalgar House Investments, bought over 18 months 10% of their shares, ostensibly to attempt a takeover.

Considerations of takeover situations indicate the separate functions of managing money – financial management – and managing business operations, and this becomes clear in the sale and lease back transaction. From an operational viewpoint it does not matter whether the facilities are owned or leased so long as there are no restrictions in the lease which affect operations. The decision to sell and lease back is essentially a financial one.

Mergers

Three categories can be determined:

1. Horizontal merger where both firms are doing the same kind of work, for instance hotels.
2. Vertical merger linking firms at immediately related stages of operations, for instance restaurants linking with prepackaged food production.
3. Conglomerate merger where activities of the firm are in entirely different spheres such as hotels and copying machine production and hire.

Some advantages of merging are savings in production, administration and selling costs, greater financial strength improving facilities for raising capital, economy in capital expenditure and current assets, greater market share improving and extending corporate image.

The Trust Houses Forte merger in 1970 was said to have benefited both companies in three ways:

1. Management skills and types of activity were complementary specializing between them in the related fields of hotels, catering and entertainment.
2. Geographically the two businesses were complementary.
3. The two companies were each too small to establish their own selling offices in major areas particularly abroad but merging made this possible.

It is probable that the first benefit of the Trust Houses Forte merger is the most important of any advantages through mergers in the industry, and the biggest disadvantage any subsequent loss of personal touch and individualism on the operations side, although modern marketing techniques should cope with this problem.

Company Amalgamations

Various methods of amalgamating are available to limited companies and the chosen method depends on considerations such as taxation, capital structures, share ownership and the marketing policy to be pursued.

The main forms of amalgamation are:

1. The creation of a new company which takes over the assets and liabilities of the merging companies which are wound up.
2. The creation of a new 'holding company' whereby the old companies continue their separate existence.
3. By absorption whereby the purchasing company takes over the whole of the assets and liabilities of the company which goes into liquidation.
4. Amalgamation by company A acquiring a controlling interest in company B whereby sufficient number of shares of company B are purchased.
5. Company A buys less than 51% of the voting shares in company B, both companies having common trade links. Company B is regarded as an associated company by A.

Valuing a Business

The purchase and sale of a business implies that a selling price has been agreed between the parties to the sale, the price normally being a negotiated one.

How will the business be valued to help determine price?

A business with quoted shares has a ready made basis of valuation, namely the quoted price on the Stock Exchange, but all other businesses must rely to some extent on accounting information such as the profit and loss account and balance sheet.

Goodwill

If the latest balance sheet, truly reflecting market values, showed a business to be worth £20,000 consisting of fixed assets £15,000 and net current assets £5,000 and a buyer was prepared to pay £23,000 for it, he would be paying £3,000 for goodwill which had built up over the years. Certainly a business may be worth more than the value of its tangible assets because of good personal service provided or good location although the value representing such benefits does not appear in the balance sheet until the value materializes as the business changes hands.

Goodwill can be seen to be very much tied up with the value placed on a business when it is sold and is the difference between agreed purchase price and balance sheet values taken over.

Lord Macnaughton said of goodwill that it is the attractive force that brings in custom. It is the one thing which distinguishes an old established business from a new business at its first start.

The value of goodwill is what one can get for it. However, there are various methods used to evaluate goodwill so that at least a starting point may be found as a basis for negotiations.

(*a*) Super-profits. This value is based on the excess of a forecast profit on investment for from three to five years over average profit for the same period expected in the industry.

(*b*) Another method first values the business from forecast profit and then derives goodwill by deducting net asset value of the business. If profits were estimated to be £5,000 per annum and a 20% annual return were required, the buyer would be prepared to pay £25,000 $\left(\frac{100 \times £5{,}000}{20}\right)$.

A net asset value of £20,000 would leave £5,000 for goodwill. If a 15% return were required, the price would rise to £33,333 and £13,333 would be paid for goodwill.

(*c*) A method which compares profits from buying the business with profit from alternative use of the purchase money is in line with modern decision making techniques, but its acceptance depends upon the quantification of alternative plans.

Assume that a restaurant was for sale in an area which fitted in with marketing policy and a buying price was required. At the same time a new restaurant could be built for the net asset value of the restaurant for sale.

Profits from the alternative investments are as follows:

End of Year	*Estimated profits from restaurant for sale*	*Estimated profits from new restaurant*
	£	£
1	5,000	2,000
2	5,000	3,000
3	5,000	4,000
4	5,000	5,000
5	5,000	5,000

The amount of goodwill the buyer would be prepared to pay would be the net present value of the difference in the profits, discounting at the cost of capital to the buyer. In other words suppose the buyer had to borrow the purchase price at 10% per annum, what extra would he borrow to pay above the net asset value so as to make both investments of equal value?

The answer is £5,130 which can be proved in Exhibit 13–3, assuming profits and interest payable occur at the year end.

Exhibit 13–3

	Year End	*Restaurant for Sale*	*New restaurant*
		£	£
Amount borrowed		25,130	20,000
Interest at 10%	1	2,513	2,000
		27,643	22,000
Profit reducing loan	1	5,000	2,000
		22,643	20,000
Interest at 10%	2	2,265	2,000
		24,908	22,000
Profit reducing loan	2	5,000	3,000
		19,908	19,000
Interest at 10%	3	1,992	1,900
		21,900	20,900
Profit reducing loan	3	5,000	4,000
		16,900	16,900

No further calculations are needed if profits from each investment are identical after year 3. Further calculations on the same line as the above using an annual profit figure of £5,000 would lead to the conclusion that the loan would be fully repaid about year 8.

If cost of capital is 10% then the restaurant valued at £25,130 with profits as stated is equal to £20,000 investment in a new restaurant with the smaller initial profits.

The actual calculations of the goodwill of £5,130 will be more fully understood after dealing with the topic of discounted cash flow in Chapter 15 where the calculation of £5,130 is made. (Exhibit 15–6.)

For the purpose of valuing a business when net asset value is taken into account, it is important that up-to-date values are used, for example an undervalued freehold property would benefit the purchaser unless the fact were taken into account when negotiating the sale.

Goodwill – Partnerships
Whilst goodwill can only appear in the books of a sole trader if a business has been purchased, the books of a partnership may also show goodwill created to compensate existing partners when a new partner is admitted.

Valuation of the Private Limited Company
The basic principle in share valuations is the determination of a fair price for the shares as between a willing buyer and a willing seller, the business being regarded as a going concern. There would be a close examination of the memorandum and articles, of the asset position as disclosed by the last balance sheet, and of the trading results of the period.

Valuation may be based on:

(*a*) Net tangible assets making allowances for undervalued property and suchlike, also goodwill.

(*b*) Forecast profits, when the value taken is so many years profit according to the industry.

The resulting valuation divided by the number of equity shares will give the share value required. Goodwill is simply the difference between balance sheet valuation and purchase price as described earlier.

Valuation of the Public Limited Company
The price officially quoted on the Stock Exchange forms a ready-made valuation of shares which is the basis of negotiations between potential buyer and seller.

Depreciation of Goodwill
Practice varies on this matter and businessmen may choose to write off goodwill or to maintain it as a permanent asset. Some companies show a nominal £1 goodwill in their accounts. The tendency is to write it down in years when good profits have been made.

Questions and Problems

13–1 Explain what is meant by the term 'gearing' and why certain companies in particular fields tend to be more highly geared than industry as a whole.

13–2 What advantage, if any, accrues to ordinary shareholders when a company issues debentures.

13–3 Why, under the present taxation system, are preference share issues out of favour, but debenture issues popular with company boards of directors? Illustrate with assumed figures.

13–4 A large hotel and catering company is considering raising additional capital for expansion. List the various forms of capital which are available, and give a brief description of each. (HCIMA)

13–5 A successful and expanding but relatively small private company, which owns two hotels and has a profit before tax of £45,000, finds its rate of growth restricted by lack of capital.

You are required to set out the advice which you would give as to how and where the company may obtain both additional working and fixed capital.

Assume such further facts concerning the company as are necessary for your answer. (HCIMA)

13–6 Explain some of the reasons for companies in the hotel and catering industry amalgamating.

13–7 Compare mergers with take-overs by discussing their similarities and differences.

13–8 Calculate goodwill on purchase of Company A, given the following information:

Company A		
Forecast profit – Year	1	15,000
	2	20,000
	3	25,000

Net Assets valued at £100,000
Average return for the industry 15%
You are to use two methods known to you.

13–9 The Golden Restaurant is up for sale. The capital employed amounts to £20,000 and recent profits are:

1972 : £3,000
1973 : £3,200
1974 : £3,500
1975 : £4,000
1976 : £3,700

The profits quoted do not include a figure for proprietor's salary which is reckoned to be about £1,500 p.a.

A close look at the accounts reveals that the 1975 figure included £300 exceptional income but the 1976 profit was determined after £800 had been written off, whereas £1,000 would have been a more reasonable figure.

The proprietor indicates that he wants the goodwill to be valued on the basis of 3 years' purchase of the average net profits for the past five years as shown in his accounts.

Assuming a reasonable return for this type of business is 10%, you should put forward your views as to which method ought to be the basis for negotiations.

Further Reading

1. Clarkson, G. P., and Elliot, B. J., *Managing Money and Finance*, Gower Press; chapters 9 to 13.
2. ACCA, *Sources of Capital.*
3. ACCA, *A Quotation for your Shares.*

CHAPTER FOURTEEN

SOURCE AND APPLICATION OF FUNDS

THE statement of source and application of funds or 'funds statement' is now established as an end of year statement alongside the balance sheet and profit and loss account. It provides a link between the balance sheet at the beginning of the year, the profit and loss account for the year and the balance sheet at the end of the year.

Control of profit performance and liquidity are two of the most important financial aspects of a successful business. Accounting emphasis has always been on profit and the many ways it may be defined and used for various purposes. Indeed the operating statement we have seen helps keep management aware of the profit performance of sections of the business whilst the profit and loss appropriation account shows, inter alia, how profit has been used. The growing importance placed upon the reporting of liquidity and changes in liquidity has led to the funds statement which is designed to show how movements in assets, liabilities and capital in a period have changed the company's net liquid fund position. Net liquid funds are defined as cash at bank and in hand and cash equivalents, e.g. investments held as current assets, less bank overdrafts and other borrowings repayable within one year of the accounting date.

Enterprises with turnover or gross income of £25,000 and over are recommended to include a funds statement as part of their audited accounts for periods beginning on or after 1st January, 1976.[1]

Explanation of Funds

A funds statement is prepared from Balance Sheets at the beginning and end of a period taking account also of further information available in the Profit and Loss Account and elsewhere. First it must be understood what items are regarded as sources of funds and application of funds, secondly a format for presentation is necessary into which each item may be slotted, and thirdly the object of the statement should always be borne in mind, that is to show how net liquid funds (cash and equivalents) have been generated and absorbed by the operations of the business in the period.

To help in the initial understanding, an example follows consisting of:

(*a*) Basic data – being a summary of a first year's operations. (Exhibit 14–1)
(*b*) Notes on the data.
(*c*) The resulting funds statement. (Exhibit 14–2)

[1] Statement of Standard Accounting Practice (SSAP) No. 10.

This approach has been chosen because with no starting balance sheet, the end of period figures given reflect changes in the period, which makes for simplicity.

A further example is used (Exhibit 14–3) to show the more usual situation of preparing a funds statement from balance sheets at two points in time. Here further aspects are developed.

Exhibit 14–1

Summary of first year's operations

Note references	£000	*Source of funds* £000	*Application of funds* £000
(*a*) Cash from share issue		100	
(*b*) Equipment bought for cash			60
(*c*) Sales	600		
Expenses (excluding depreciation)	560		
Cash from operations	40 ⟶	40	
Depreciation	10		
Profit from operations	30		
(*d*) Debtors increase			20
(*e*) Creditors increase		30	
(*f*) Stocks increase			40
(*g*) Tax provision	10		
(*h*) Dividends paid			10
(*i*) Cash balances (increase)			40
		170	170

Notes on first year's operations

(*a*) Cash from debentures is similarly a source. Any premium obtained is an additional source. Cash paid to redeem debentures will be an application.

(*b*) Cash from the sale of fixed assets will be a source. Profit or loss on sale is disregarded.

(*c*) Cash from operations is not strictly correct as a description because £20,000 is still outstanding as Debtors increase. However, it is called in the funds statement funds 'generated from operations'.

Depreciation does not provide cash for replacing fixed assets which lose value. It is not a cash transaction but merely an accounting entry apportioning a part of the historical cost to an accounting period.

(*d*) Debtors increase is an application because cash has been sacrificed. If debtors decreased, cash will have flowed in, the amount of the decrease being a source of funds.

(*e*) Creditors represent a short term source of funds.

(*f*) Stocks increase means that money has been diverted to build up stocks, an application of funds. When stocks are unnecessarily high, their reduction provides cash by avoiding having to purchase so much for operations.

(*g*) Provisions and reserves do not involve movement of cash and are therefore, neither source nor application of funds. Tax paid in a period however, is an application of funds.

(*h*) In the same way as the treatment of Tax, dividends are taken into the statement when they are paid.

(*i*) An increase in the cash balance, like any other asset increase, is an application of funds. A bank overdraft is clearly recognized as a source of funds.

Exhibit 14–2

Statement of Source and Application of Funds[1]
Year 1977

	£000	£000
Source of funds		
Profit before tax		30
Adjustments for items not involving movement of funds:		
Depreciation		10
Total generated from operations		40
Funds from other sources		
Issue of shares for cash		100
		140
Application of funds		
Dividends paid	(10)	
Purchase of fixed assets	(60)	(70)
		70
Increase/decrease in working capital		
Increase in stocks	(40)	
Increase in debtors	(20)	
Increase in creditors – excluding taxation and proposed dividends	30	
Movement in net liquid funds:		
Cash balances	(40)	(70)

[1]Symbols: ( )=application of funds. Other figures are sources.

Funds Statement Preparation

There are two methods of preparing a funds statement from two balance sheets and additional internal information, a short cut method and a longer systematic method. The first method will be demonstrated and the second shown in outline. Information available are the balance sheets and three notes as follows:

Balance Sheets at 31st March

	1978	*1977*
	£000	£000
ASSETS		
Fixed assets at cost	240	220
Depreciation	14	12
	226	208
Current assets:		
Stocks	55	40
Debtors	35	20
Bank and cash balances	10	30
	326	298
LIABILITIES		
Issued share capital	150	150
Revenue reserves	40	30
Retained profits	16	18
Loan capital	60	40
Current liabilities:		
Creditors	36	38
Current taxation	8	7
Proposed dividends	16	15
	326	298

Notes:

1. Equipment was purchased for £60,000.
2. Equipment was sold for £41,000. Depreciation of £5,000 was included in £12,000 charged to 1977. Original cost was £40,000.
3. £10,000 was transferred to revenue reserves in 1978.

Shortcut method

1. Draft the main headings of a funds statement leaving plenty of space under each heading.
2. Any balance sheet differences which need no adjustment are inserted in statement. This will take account of loan capital, creditors, taxation paid,

dividends paid, stocks, debtors, bank and cash balances. Tax and dividends are the 1977 current liabilities assumed to have been paid in 1978.

3. Use the above notes to determine further items such as equipment purchases and sales.
4. Completion of the statement requires the calculation of depreciation for the year if this is not supplied. To insert totals simple deduction is used. Increase in working capital of £12,000 added to other application of funds totalling £82,000 gives £94,000 which is the total source. Total generated from operations is the sum of funds from other sources taken away from total sources giving £33,000. Depreciation deducted from this figure gives profit before tax.

Exhibit 14–3

Statement of Source and Application of Funds
Year 1978

	£000	£000
Source of funds		
Profit before tax		26
Depreciation		7
Total generated from operations		33
Funds from other sources		
Loan capital		20
Sale of equipment		41
		94
Application of funds		
Tax paid	(7)	
Dividend paid	(15)	
Purchase of equipment	(60)	(82)
		12
Increase/decrease in working capital		
Increase in stocks	(15)	
Increase in debtors	(15)	
Decrease in creditors	(2)	
Movement in net liquid funds:		
Bank and cash balances	20	(12)

5. The advantage of speed in preparation must be weighed against the chance of errors creeping in which would make the balancing figure of profit inaccurate. If, however, the profit and loss account is to hand then this creates no problem for the profit before tax figure – the important first item in the

statement – is available. The reconstructed account for this example is as follows:

Appropriation Section of the Profit and Loss Account
for the year to 31st March 1978

	£		£
Tax provision	8,000	Unappropriated profit from 1977	18,000
Proposed dividend	16,000	Profit on equipment sale[2]	6,000
Transfer to Reserve	10,000	Balancing item = Profit before	
Balance c/d	16,000	tax (1978)	26,000
	£50,000		£50,000

Systematic Method

This method ensures a balanced statement by starting with columns for balance sheet differences and applying adjustments which are self-balancing. The adjustments are to take account of sale of fixed assets and of profit and loss account items so that one is left with profit before tax and depreciation.

Exhibit 14–4

Balance sheet items	*Balance sheet differences*		*Adjustments*		*Final figures for statement*	
	Source	*Application*	*Source*	*Application*	*Source*	*Application*
	£000	£000	£000	£000	£000	£000
ASSETS						
Fixed assets at cost		20		+40(b)		60(f)
Depreciation	2		+5(c)		7	
Stocks		15				15
Debtors		15				15
Cash	20				20	
LIABILITIES						
Shares						
Revenue reserves	10		+16(e)	+6(d) }	26	
Retained profit		2	+8(e)			
Loan capital	20				20	
Creditors		2				2
Current tax	1			+8(e)		7
Proposed dividends	1			+16(e)		15
	54	54				
Fixed asset sale			+41(a)		41	
			+70	+70	114	114

[2]Normally profit or loss on sale of assets will feature in the main body of the profit and loss account.

Notes:
(*a*) Cash from equipment sale.
(*b*) Original cost of sale item.
(*c*) Depreciation of sale item.
(*d*) Profit on sale added back.
(*e*) Tax dividends (current liabilities) added back.
(*f*) Resulting figure is cost of purchase.

Review

Only one form of presentation has been used in this chapter to avoid confusion. However, a wide variety of forms are encountered in practice ranging from one which simply lists and totals the sources and applications, to one which may start with the opening net liquid funds and end with the equivalent closing balance. The tendency is to highlight favourable aspects, and the latter form might be used where the improvement in net liquid funds may be negligible whilst the opening and closing balances might each be significantly large. The minimum amount of 'netting off' of say purchase and sale of fixed assets is recommended although some 'netting off' may be inevitable through the lack of information. In published accounts the funds statement should show figures for both the period under review and for the previous period.

Relationships between individual sources and applications can sometimes be recognised such as a long term loan raised in the period providing funds to expand shown as the purchase of fixed assets and increases in stocks and debtors.

Finally a statement of source and application of funds, or funds statement for short, is important as a budget taking its place beside the budgeted balance sheet as an indication of the financial policy of the enterprise.

Questions and Problems

14–1 Describe the meaning of the terms 'cash flow' and 'profit' and explain their differences.

14–2 Indicate by a tick whether each of the following financial changes effect a cash inflow, outflow or no change:

Financial change	*Cash inflow*	*Cash outflow*	*No effect on cash*
Share capital issue			
Decrease in creditors			
Sale of investments			
Annual depreciation charge			
Loan repayment			
Decrease in debtors			
Increase in general reserve			
Increase in stock			
Goodwill written off			
Decrease in cash			
Purchase of fixed assets			

14–3 It is sometimes desirable to ascertain from the balance sheet how changes in the liquid resources of a limited company have arisen.

List the factors which may have caused:

(*a*) A decrease in the liquid position

(*b*) An increase in the liquid position.

14–4 Is it possible for a company to achieve a net profit in a period and yet show a net cash outflow?

14–5 The annual accounts of the Aldo Hotel Co. Ltd. are as follows:

Balance Sheet as at 31st May, 1976

1975 £000		£000	1975 £000		£000
80	Authorized and issued capital	80	170	Fixed assets – at cost	180
5	Reserves	10	10	Additions in year at cost	40
			180		220
10	Unappropriated profits	8	99	Less depreciation	105
–	Loan	12	81		115
			9	Cash	2
15	Current liabilities	30	20	Other current assets	23
110		140	110		140

Profit and Loss Account (including appropriations) for the year ended 31st May, 1976

8	Directors' remuneration	10	14	Profit b/d	20
4	Depreciation	6	8	Unappropriated profits b/f	10
–	Loan interest	1			
–	Transfer to reserves	5			
10	Unappropriated profits c/f	8			
22		30	22		30

You are required to:

(*a*) Prepare a source and application of funds statement reconciling the cash at bank at 1 June, 1975 with the cash at bank at 31st May, 1976;

(*b*) Compare and contrast the information which can be established from the annual accounts above with that in your source and application of funds statement for the Aldo Hotel Co. Ltd. (HCIMA)

14–6 The following is the balance sheet of the Silver Lining Hotel Ltd. for the year ended 30th April 1975:

SILVER LINING HOTEL LTD.
Balance Sheet as at 30th April, 1975

£ 1974	£	£			£ 1975	£
			Fixed assets			
500,000			Freehold hotel at valuation			500,000
	80,000		Equipment at cost		100,000	
	45,000		less depreciation		40,000	
35,000						60,000
535,000						560,000
			less working capital deficit			
			current assets:			
	90,000		stocks		130,000	
	35,000		debtors		50,000	
	8,000		bank		—	
	133,000				180,000	
			Less current liabilities			
		79,000	Creditors	110,000		
		71,000	Corporation tax	60,000		
		—	Overdraft	50,000		
	150,000				220,000	
17,000						40,000
518,000			Net assets			520,000
			Represented by			
			Shareholders' Interest			
400,000			Issued share capital			400,000
60,000			Reserves			60,000
58,000			Unappropriated profit			60,000
518,000						520,000

Movements on the equipment account during the year were:

	1974	*Sold*	*Purchases*	*Depn. charge*	*1975*
Cost	80,000	30,000	50,000	—	100,000
Depn.	45,000	20,000	—	15,000	40,000
	35,000	10,000			60,00
Sale proceeds		4,000			
Loss charged to profit		6,000			

You are required to prepare:

(*i*) a source and application of funds statement reconciling the opening cash at bank with the closing overdraft; and

(*ii*) a critical report on your source and application statement and the balance sheet. (HCIMA)

14–7 The summarized balance sheets of the Alpine Post House at 31st March, 1972 and 1973 are below:

	1972	1973
	£	£
Issued share capital	200,000	230,000
Share premium	20,000	22,000
Capital reserves	35,000	35,000
Retained profits	17,000	28,000
$7\frac{1}{2}$% convertible loan stock	50,000	30,000
$8\frac{1}{2}$% mortgage debentures	40,000	64,000
Trade creditors	8,000	11,000
Overdraft	34,000	—
Corporation tax	3,000	4,000
Proposed dividends	11,000	15,000
	418,000	439,000

	£	£
Freehold land and building at cost	216,000	216,000
Equipment, furniture and fittings (net)	134,000	140,000
Investment at cost	60,000	29,000
Food and beverage stocks	4,000	10,000
Trade debtors	2,000	6,000
Cash at bank and in hand	2,000	38,000
	418,000	439,000

Additional information:

(*a*) Of the £30,000 increase in issued share capital, £20,000 had been in respect of the $7\frac{1}{2}$% convertible loan stock.

(*b*) Corporation tax figures shown are payable early the following year.

(*c*) During the year furniture which had cost £12,000 had been sold for £900. Seven-eighths of its useful life had been written off. New equipment had been purchased for £22,000.

The net closing balances on equipment, furniture and fittings are made up as follows:

	1972	1973
	£	£
Balances at cost	180,000	190,000
Accumulated depreciation	46,000	50,000
	134,000	140,000

(*d*) During the year investments which had cost £31,000 had been sold for £35,000.

You are required to prepare a statement accounting for the cash increase that has occurred during the financial year ended 31st March, 1973.

(HCIMA)

14–8 The summarized balance sheet of Seaton Private Hotel Ltd. as at 31st May 1977, is as follows:

Capital Employed			£
Share capital			20,000
Profit and loss account			20,000
Shareholders funds			40,000
Long term loan			40,000
			80,000
Employment of Capital			£
Fixed Assets at cost			100,000
Less aggregate depreciation			40,000
			60,000
Current assets			
Debtors	20,000		
Stock	15,000		
Cash	5,000	40,000	
Less current liabilities			
Bank overdraft	10,000		
Creditors	10,000	20,000	20,000
			80,000

The company is experiencing trading difficulties and has drawn up a budgeted profit and loss account for the 12 months to 31st May 1978:

Summarized budgeted profit and loss account for the year ending 31st May 1978

		£	£
Contribution from food and beverage operations			19,000
Contribution from sale of accommodation			22,000
Profit on sale of antique furniture			500
			41,500
		£	
Less:	Wages and salaries	17,900	
	Establishment expenses	22,600	
	Advertising expenses	800	
	Depreciation	5,000	
	Loan interest	3,200	
	Amortization of lease	1,200	
	Taxation provision	800	51,500
Net loss after taxation and interest			10,000

Further information:
In the year to 31st May 1978:

(*a*) No dividends will be paid.
(*b*) The antique furniture will be sold for £8,000. (Aggregate depreciation of £2,500 had been provided to 31st May 1977).
(*c*) The directors have undertakings from a group of investors that the proposed issue of £10,000 of loan stock will be fully subscribed at the end of August 1977.
(*d*) The issue of the loan stock is intended to finance new furniture and fittings costing £12,000, to be acquired in September 1977.
(*e*) It is expected that at 31st May 1978 debtors will have reduced to 75% of the previous year's level, stock value will have risen by a third and creditors will have increased by £3,500.
(*f*) The increase in the taxation provision is in respect of Corporation Tax which is payable on 1st July 1978.

You are required to prepare:

(*i*) A budgeted sources and applications of funds statement emphasizing the change in the cash balance assuming the bank overdraft remains at £10,000. The statement should commence with the expected loss after taxation and interest.
(*ii*) The budgeted balance sheet as at 31st May 1978.

(HCIMA)

Further Reading

1. Accounting Standards Committee (ASC), Statement of Standard Accounting Practice (SSAP) No. 10.

CHAPTER FIFTEEN

APPRAISING LONG-TERM INVESTMENTS

A BUSINESS must earn profits over a period of years to be at all successful, short-term gains sometimes having to be sacrificed in the interests of long-term goals. What are these long-term goals? They may be a combination of growth, security, even survival, but profitability is of such importance that where a business is faced with a choice between profit and some other goal, profit is usually preferred because survival depends upon it.

Opportunities for Achieving Long-term Goals

A successful business must recognize opportunities which might lead to a profitable long-term investment and the larger the firm the more important it is to seek out and find opportunities by applying some or all of the following:

(*a*) Forceful management with the persistence and personality to push forward proposals if they are considered viable.
(*b*) Appointment of staff to seek and find opportunities.
(*c*) Contacts with other bodies who could stimulate recognition of opportunities – trade associations, firms, etc.
(*d*) Procedures for producing statistics relating to changes in the activity of customers and competitors.
(*e*) Procedures to show changes in the balance between market demand and facilities available to meet it – leading to long-term forecasts.

Capital Investment

Whether the opportunity involves building a new hotel, modernizing an old one, or extending an hotel, money must be made available and spent on what might be called a 'Capital Investment' – that is expenditure incurred now in order to produce a stream of benefits over a period of years which will, it is hoped, result in the firm being in a more favourable position. Capital investment decisions differ from operating decisions by reason of the nature of the expenditure and the length of time before the full effect of the decision is felt.

Merrett and Sykes open their book[1] on the subject by stating 'the selection and financing of capital projects are indisputably two of the most important and critical business decisions'.

[1] *The Finance and Analysis of Capital Projects.*

Savage and Small in their book[2] state 'probably the most important decision which any management has to take is the decision to invest'.

Wright states in his book[3] 'probably the most significant factor affecting the level of profitability in a business is the quality of the management's decisions relating to the commitment of the company's resources to new investment within the business'.

In order to formalize data associated with a project it is likely that the larger business would produce a 'feasibility study' which involves collecting and assembling information in terms of physical quantities and money. It will become an 'economic feasibility study' when there is included an appraisal of the project in terms of return on capital invested.

The study will include all information bearing on the project such as:

Marketing forecasts	– potential customers of varying categories showing basis of forecast – jumbo jets, etc.,
Additional physical facilities	– numbers of rooms of each kind, style of hotel, site, bar, games room, petrol station, etc.,
Government regulations	– planning permission, access, etc.,
Competition	– existing and forecast
Appraisal of project in financial terms	– taxation, inflation, etc.

Measuring Investment Returns

Bearing in mind the significance of a capital investment decision, care should be used in assessing the worth of proposed projects, and a simple example is here used to compare available evaluation methods.

A company with £1,116 available to invest is considering the following capital project, which after writing off depreciation of £279 per annum over its four-year life, shows forecast profits of:

Proposed project 123

	£
31st December, 1978	121
31st December, 1979	121
31st December, 1980	121
31st December, 1981	121
	484

[2] *Introduction to Managerial Economics.*
[3] *Discounted Cash Flow.*

Average annual profit on investment method

This is simply the average annual profit as a percentage of investment, in this case:

$$\frac{£121}{£1,116} \times 100 = 10{\cdot}8\%$$

For short-term investments of up to two years' duration this method might provide a reasonable basis for assessing their worth to the business, but the longer the period of the investment the less satisfactory the method becomes. The concern in this chapter will be with investments of longer than two years' duration in order to emphasize the importance of using the most appropriate method of assessment. Nevertheless, once the virtues of the appropriate method have been established, it can be seen to apply to all investment projects whether of short or long duration.

There are two serious limitations to the average annual profit on investment method.

(*a*) The resultant percentage is too imperfect to be of real value in assessing whether the investment should be accepted as a profitable one. Where profits are constant per annum, the percentage will always err on the low side and profitable projects may thus be rejected.

(*b*) In comparisons between competing projects the resultant percentage could easily favour the least profitable one because the method takes no account of the timing of profits and cash flows.

Average annual return on average investment

This is a variation of the first method in so far as only half the original investment is related to the average annual profit. Since the investment is worthless after four years, the average investment over the period is opening + closing investment ÷ 2.

$$\frac{£1,116 + £0}{2} = £558$$

The average return on £1,116 is 21·7%, double the first method.

The resultant percentage for a project with constant annual profits is always an optimistic figure.

Discounted cash flow technique

This takes into account the fact that as cash is received it is available for reducing the investment itself or for further investment, in the one case saving interest and in the other, gaining interest for the business. Profit each year must be converted to cash flow, which is a matter of adding back depreciation. Therefore in the example, £121 + £279 = £400 cash flow inwards each year.

Suppose the £1,116 were borrowed at 16% interest, payable on the balance outstanding at the end of each year, and that as cash comes in it is used to repay the loan. The result would be:

			£
1/1/78	Loan		1,116
31/12/78	Interest payable on loan outstanding at 16%	+	179
			1,295
	Repayment	−	400
			895
31/12/79	Interest payable at 16%	+	143
			1,038
	Repayment	−	400
			638
31/12/80	Interest payable at 16%	+	102
			740
	Repayment	−	400
			340
31/12/81	Interest payable at 16%	+	54
			394
	Repayment completing repayment of loan	−	400
	Terminal Value	−	6 (negligible difference)

This indicates that it cost 16% to borrow the cash for the investment which provided the £400 per annum cash inflows and the interest paid had swallowed up all the proceeds, leaving no profit for the firm. But at the other extreme, if the investment cost the company nothing at all, then the cash return equals 16% over the period and the project produces a profit of 16%. More likely, however, the investment might cost anything between 0% and 16%, leaving some profit for the company.

Ignoring cost – which the average annual return does anyway – the project's true return of 16% compares with 10·8% and 21·7% of the first two methods.

To calculate the 16% in the normal way cash flows are discounted as in Exhibit 15–1, which is explained later.

Comparing Competing Projects

It is clearly better to receive £400 in cash now than in three years' time, even in one year's time, because of the opportunity afforded of reinvesting the cash over the interim period. Suppose another project (X47) was available to use up the £1,116 capital, and both projects' cash flows were as follows:

Cash flows

	Project 123		*Project X47*	
	In	*Out*	*In*	*Out*
	£	£	£	£
1/1/78		1,116		1,116
31/12/78	400		NIL	
31/12/79	400		400	
31/12/80	400		400	
31/12/81	400		800	
	1,600	1,116	1,600	1,116
Less investment	1,116		1,116	
Total profit	484		484	
Average annual profit	121		121	

Both projects would give a 10·8% return based on the average annual return method, favouring neither. By merely inspecting the cash flows, Project 123 can be seen to be worth more than X47 because the £400 receivable 31/12/78 on 123 is available for three years until 31/12/81 when the other project's cash flow catches up. If £400 were invested at 16% per annum with interest undrawn (compound interest) the £400 would accumulate to be worth £624 on 31/12/81, the interest being £224. This gives some idea of the difference in value of the projects when interest is considered.

The orthodox way of taking interest into account in investment projects is to eliminate the compound interest from cash flows and bringing them all down to a common value at the present moment in time – when the cash is invested. Therefore by discounting (the opposite of compounding interest) both projects' cash flows at the same rate of interest, they are reduced to a present value for easy comparison. Present value (p.v.) factors are available as tables[4] and they simply eliminate the interest factor. Exhibit 15–1 shows the calculation for each project. It will be noted that the discounted inflows exactly equal the outflow and the net present value @ 16% is nil, indicating that this is the DCF return on the project. With project X47 the discounted inflows are £124 less than the outflow (investment) indicating the return to be less than 16%. But why is the difference in value of the projects only £124 when discounting is used, but £224 when the £400 cash flow difference is invested at 16% compound interest? Discounting has been said to be the reverse of adding compound interest, and this is true because each sum is at a different point in time:

£124 at 1/1/78
£224 at 31/12/81

[4]For present value table, see page 282.

a difference of four years. They must be at the same point in time for proper comparison, so that £124 with compound interest @ 16% = £224, and £224 discounted (multiplied by present value factor for 4 years of 0·55) = £124.

Exhibit 15–1

Statement comparing Project 123 with x47
on a Discounted Cash Flow Basis

		123					*X47*				
Year	*Date*	*Cash flow*		*PV factor*	*Discounted Cash flows*		*Cash flow*		*PV factor*	*Discounted Cash flows*	
		In	*Out*	*16%*	*In*	*Out*	*In*	*Out*	*16%*	*In*	*Out*
		£	£		£	£	£	£		£	£
0	1st Jan., '78		1,116	1·00		1,116		1,116	1·00		1,116
1	31st Dec., '78	400		0·86	344		—		0·86	—	
2	31st Dec., '79	400		0·74	296		400		0·74	296	
3	31st Dec., '80	400		0·64	256		400		0·64	256	
4	31st Dec., '81	400		0·55	220		800		0·55	440	
		1,600	1,116		1,116	1,116	1,600	1,116		992	1,116
					1,116					1,116	
Net Present Value of projects at 16%					Nil					−124	

Discounting: Compound Interest in Reverse

To demonstrate this approach to an understanding of DCF, the compound interest formula is introduced and then the discounting formula is seen to be the reverse of it.

Date	31st Dec. 78	31st Dec. 79	31st Dec. 80	31st Dec. 81
Calculation of interest at 16%	—	$£400\times\frac{16}{100}$	$£464\times\frac{16}{100}$	$£538.24\times\frac{16}{100}$
Interest	—	£64	£74.24	£86.12
Investment value	£400	£464	£538.24	£624.36 (say £624)

It can be said that £400 'accumulates' to £624 which is the 'future worth' of £400 at 16% for three years; also that £624 receivable after three years 'discounts' at 16% to £400 'present value'.

The formula for calculating this 'compound interest' of £224 is:

$$S = P(1+r)^n$$

where S = the future worth
P = the present value
r = the rate of return or interest
n = the number of periods

Substituting, we have $S = £400\ (1 + \cdot16)^3 = £624$
Therefore the compound interest is £224.

Present Value

The present value is seen to be compound interest in reverse and can be derived by reversing the formula for compound interest. The formula for calculating the present value of an amount receivable at some future time is therefore $P = \frac{S}{(1+r)^n}$ and substituting, $P = \frac{£624}{(1\cdot16)^3} = £400$. Alternatively, the present value of £1 can be calculated and multiplied by the amount which is to be reduced to present value. The present value of £1 is known as the present value factor or discount factor.

The present value of £1 at 16% receivable in 1 year's time is	$\frac{£1}{(1\cdot16)^1}$	=	£0·86207
receivable in 2 years' time is	$\frac{£1}{(1\cdot16)^2}$	=	£0·74316
receivable in 3 years' time is	$\frac{£1}{(1\cdot16)^3}$	=	£0·64066
receivable in 4 years' time is	$\frac{£1}{(1\cdot16)^4}$	=	£0·55229

The present value of £624·36 receivable 3 years hence at 16% is therefore £624·36 × 0·64066 = £400.

Present value of an annuity

When constant period cash flows are forecast a short-cut method of discounting is advised. The PV factors are summed and multiplied once by the constant cash flow. Project 123 (Exhibit 15–1) would be discounted by this method:

$$£400\ (0\cdot86 + 0\cdot74 + 0\cdot64 + 0\cdot55)$$
$$= £400 \times 2\cdot79 = £1{,}116$$

The constant cash flow has the same characteristic as an annuity in that a sum of money is paid or received yearly during a specified time. A table is often available which shows the present value of the annuity of £1 for *n* periods, which simply saves the effort of adding PV factors. An extract from the 16% column of an annuity table would read:

1 year	0·86 more precisely	0·86207
2 years	1·60	1·60523
3 years	2·24	2·24589
4 years	2·79	2·79818

DCF Methods

Net Present Value method
This method is used when it is required to determine whether a project is expected to exceed a particular percentage return set by management. If 16% was the minimum return a firm would accept from a new project, the discounting at this rate of proposed projects 123 and X47 in Exhibit 15–1 reveals 123 to be right on 16%, but X47 to be less than 16% because discounted inflows fall short of outflows.

Yield or Internal Rate of Return method
If management required to know the rate a project is expected to achieve, a project's cash flows are discounted at various rates until the rate is found which discounts inflows to equal outflows. A lucky guess might find the right rate straightaway like project 123 at 16%. However, X47 is known to be less than 16%. If a lower discount rate is used, and the inflows and outflows do not coincide, the true rate may be found by the use of ratios.

For example:

Investment £1,116

	Cash inflows £	*16% factors*	£	*10% factors*	£
Year 1	—	0·86	—	0·91	—
2	400	0·74	296	0·83	332
3	400	0·64	256	0·75	300
4	800	0·55	440	0·68	544
			992		1,176
Less outflow (investment)			1,116		1,116
Net present value (NPV)			−124		+60

The position may be shown:

←— — — — — — — — — — — — —→

Range of 6%

Rate	10%	?	16%
N.P.V.	£ +60	£0	£ −124

Range of £184

←— — — — — — — — — — — — —→

The difference in rates used is 6% (16% −10%)
The difference in NPV is the addition of £124 and £60 = £184.
The rate to add to 10% so that NPV = £0 is:

$$\frac{£60}{£184} \times 6\% = 2\%.$$

Therefore the DCF rate of return, the true rate is 12%.

A lucky choice would have been 12% in the first instance, e.g.

	Cash inflows £	*12% factors*	£
Year 1	—	0·89	—
2	400	0·80	320
3	400	0·71	284
4	800	0·64	512
			1,116
Less outflow (investment)			1,116
N.P.V. @ 12%			nil

Basic DCF Considerations

1. Assumptions made in simple appraisal of projects giving adequate results are:
   (*a*) Cash flow inwards is on the last day of the period, although in practice it is a daily process.
   (*b*) Investment is reckoned to be at the beginning of the period, sometimes taken as Year 0 when no discounting is required.
2. Taxation may have a marked effect on the results of an appraisal and should be estimated for each project.
3. Inflationary effects should be considered if income and costs are not expected to rise in step with each other.
4. Most capital projects involve investment in working capital which must be regarded as a cash flow outwards once only when the increased level of working capital is required. Similarly it should be regarded as cash flow inwards when the project is expected to end.
5. Benefits obtained by using Discounted Cash Flow technique in judging proposed projects tend to be twofold. Firstly a more consistent financial appraisal is produced, and secondly the discipline in calculating after tax cash flows on an annual basis means that more care is likely to be exercised, an important consideration when so much is generally at stake.
6. The use of discounting techniques is only an aid to decision making. In the same way that control figures are no substitute for good supervision, so DCF calculations are no substitute for a well prepared forecast of financial matters concerning a proposed project.

DCF Example

Golden Hotels Ltd. are considering purchasing a suitable site and having an hotel built on it. A feasibility study shows the following figures: Cost of site and building £100,000, furniture and fittings £80,000, working capital £1,400, making a total initial investment of £181,400. Ten years has been considered as a reasonable life before drastic alterations require to be made, and after this time the building site is expected to be worth about £80,000 and the working capital will be regarded as no longer required. The net cash flows after tax each year are shown in the working statement. The cost of capital to the company is 6% and the return after tax on capital employed for the business is planned to be not less than 10%. The following is a summarized statement prepared to show whether the project meets the minimum criterion of 6% and the minimum planned rate of 10%. Inflation factors have been ignored. The present value factors are given to 3 decimal places. Tables are available which give 5 decimal places, but for most purposes 2 decimal places are accurate enough.

Payback Method of Appraisal (PB)

Payback period is defined as the number of years it takes for an investment to generate sufficient cash to recover its initial capital outlay in full. Its popularity is mainly due to its simplicity of application. Other reasons for its use are:

(*a*) A business with liquidity problems will be aided in the short term if projects with low PB periods are preferred.

(*b*) Using a low PB period it is said to reflect a dynamic management who want quick returns.

(*c*) It allows for a special type of risk which will bring the cash flow to a halt, such as foreign intervention or sudden competition.

Its chief draw-back is that it takes no account of the project's overall earnings or of the significance of cash flows within the PB period. It is not therefore a measure of profitability because one project might have a rating of two years and be unprofitable with no further net cash inflows whereas another project may have a three year PB period with high net cash inflows for another three years.

The payback period for project 123 is calculated as follows:

Year	*Outflow*	*Inflow*	*Cumulative*
	£	£	£
0	(1,116)	—	(1,116)
1	—	400	(716)
2	—	400	(316) (a)
3	—	400 (b)	84

$$\text{Payback} = 2 \text{ years} + \frac{a}{b} = 2 + \frac{316}{400} = 2{\cdot}79 \text{ years}$$

The period would be stated as 2·8 years or nearly 3 years.

It should be noted that it would be inadvisable to be too precise as the data on which the period is based – the cash flows – are themselves uncertain.

Exhibit 15–2

GOLDEN HOTELS LTD

PROPOSED PROJECT x50

Year		Notes		Cash Flow inwards (profit before depreciation and after tax)	Present value factor at 6%	Discounted at 6%	Present value factor at 10%	Discounted at 10%
				£		£		£
1	1978			5,000	0·943	4,715	0·909	4,545
2	1979			20,000	0·890	17,800	0·826	16,520
3	1980			20,000	0·840	16,800	0·751	15,020
4	1981			20,000	0·792	15,840	0·683	13,660
5	1982	(£22,000 less £1,000 furniture)		21,000	0·747	15,687	0·621	13,041
6	1983			23,000	0·705	16,215	0·564	12,972
7	1984	(£23,000 less £2,000 carpets)		21,000	0·665	13,965	0·513	10,773
8	1985			23,000	0·627	14,421	0·467	10,741
9	1986			23,000	0·592	13,616	0·424	9,752
10	1987			23,000	0·558	12,834	0·386	8,878
			£					
		Residual value	80,000					
		Working capital	1,400					
				81,400	0·558	45,421	0·386	31,420
						187,314		147,322
		Less: Investment in Year 0 (beginning of year 1)				181,400		181,400
		NET PRESENT VALUE at 6%				+5,914		
		NET PRESENT VALUE at 10%						−34,078

Notes: 1. The table indicates that the rate of return is just over 6%, 6·59% by interpolation and falls well short of the rate of 10% that the company is looking for from its future enterprises. On financial grounds the project, as it stands, would be rejected.
2. Using PV factors to two decimal places the rate would be 6·61%, a negligible difference.

Further DCF Considerations

Taxation

After-tax cash flows should be used in DCF calculations because tax payments constitute an outflow of cash, and competing projects may have different tax allowances and charges which might influence the investment decision.

The following procedure is used for converting pre-tax cash flows to post-tax cash flows.

1. Determine the investment incentives available for the purchase. E.g. (*a*) Plant and machinery which includes office furniture, attracts 100% First Year Allowance. (*b*) Motor cars attract a writing down allowance of 25% of cost in year of purchase and then a written down value in subsequent years. There is however, a maximum allowance per year. (*c*) Construction of new hotels, extensions and structural alterations to existing hotels (minimum ten letting bedrooms), qualify for an initial allowance of 20% and a writing down allowance of 4% per annum.
2. The allowances are deducted from the pre-tax cash flow (profit + depreciation) leaving a figure of taxable profit.
3. When the plant is disposed of, any residual revenue is shown as cash inflow, and the writing down allowance in the final year adjusted (called the balancing allowance or balancing charge) so that capital allowances in total equal net cost of the asset (original cost less residual revenue).
4. Corporation tax is chargeable on each year's taxable profit and on average reckoned to be paid 12 months later.
5. Post-tax cash flows which come in for discounting consist of pre-tax cash flows less tax paid.
6. It is usually assumed that there are profits being generated elsewhere in the company against which capital allowances may be offset. Therefore a cash inflow of tax may be recorded in respect of a project where insufficient profit is made on it to absorb tax allowances.
7. If no profits are available in the company to use up capital allowances they may be carried forward until such time as there are profits available against which to set the allowances.

The following is an example of the above procedure.

Exhibit 15–3

The AB Hotel Group are considering the purchase of four new vending machines which will cost £36,000 to buy outright. It is estimated that they will have lives of seven years at the end of which their scrap value will be £1,000. To operate them an average investment in working capital of £3,000 will be required.

After depreciation of £5,000 per annum, the forecast operating profits are:

	£		£
Year 1	3,000	Year 5	3,000
2	4,000	6	2,000
3	5,000	7	1,000
4	5,000		

The company target rate of return on this activity is 10% after tax and discounting. The machines will qualify for 100% first year allowance in respect of tax and the company pays Corporation tax at the rate of 52%.

One manager supports the purchase because he has worked out the rate of return to be 18¾% as follows:

$$\frac{\text{Average annual profit}}{\text{Average investment}} \quad \frac{£3{,}286}{£17{,}500} \times 100$$

However, the after tax discounted rate is barely 10% worked out as follows:

Tax Calculations

Year	*Operating profit* £	*Depre-ciation* £	*Pre-tax cash flows* £	*Capital allowance and charge* £	*Taxable profit* £	*Corporation Tax @ 52%* £
1	3,000	5,000	8,000	36,000	(28,000)	—
2	4,000	5,000	9,000		9,000	(14,560)
3	5,000	5,000	10,000		10,000	4,680
4	5,000	5,000	10,000		10,000	5,200
5	3,000	5,000	8,000		8,000	5,200
6	2,000	5,000	7,000		7,000	4,160
7	1,000	5,000	6,000	(1,000)	7,000	3,640
8	—					3,640
	23,000	35,000	58,000	35,000	23,000	11,960

DCF Calculations ( ) = cash outflows

(*a*) *Operating cash flows*

Year	*Pre-tax cash flows* £	*Tax payable* £	*Post-tax cash flows* £	*10% PV factors* £	*Discounted cash flows* £
1	8,000	—	8,000	0·91	7,280
2	9,000	14,560	23,560	0·83	19,555
3	10,000	(4,680)	5,320	0·75	3,990
4	10,000	(5,200)	4,800	0·68	3,264
5	8,000	(5,200)	2,800	0·62	1,736
6	7,000	(4,160)	2,840	0·56	1,590
7	6,000	(3,640)	2,360	0·51	1,204
8	—	(3,640)	(3,640)	0·47	(1,711)
	58,000	(11,960)	46,040		36,908

(b) Investments Cash Flows		10% PV factors			
0	Machines	(36,000)	1·00	(36,000)	
	Working capital	(3,000)	1·00	(3,000)	
7	Machines – scrap	1,000	0·51	510	
	Working capital recouped	3,000	0·51	1,530	(36,960)
	Net present value @ 10%				– £52

Cost of Capital

One criticism of DCF is that although a percentage rate of return is at the heart of the technique, there is no universal method of calculating a minimum or a target rate for projects in different organizations. DCF tends to get singled out for this criticism but it applies to all percentage appraisal methods. Golden Hotels Project X50 (Exhibit 15–2) mentions a 6% cost of capital and 10% being a minimum planned rate. This second rate is subjective in that the company may set a different rate target for different investments based on various factors, for example risk involved, whether a replacement or an expansion project, and how desirable is the project. The first rate, the cost of capital, can be calculated in different ways giving broadly similar results. One way is to determine the cost of each course of capital and weighting each according to its proportion to total capital. For example 9% cost of capital would result from:

	Amount	*Proportion*	*Source Cost*	*Weighted Cost*
	(1)	(2)	(3)	(4) = (2 × 3)
	£	%	%	%
Ordinary shares – market value	100,000	66·67	11·0	7·33
10% Debentures (52% Tax)	50,000	33·33	4·8	1·60
	150,000	100·00		8·93
				9%

The cost of debentures is straightforward, being the gross amount less the current corporation tax percentage because the interest is allowable for tax purposes.

The cost of capital derived from the issue of ordinary shares and likewise of equity is a difficult concept and one about which little agreement exists in practice. One method which appears to be useful is a variation of the price earnings ratio namely, the best estimate of what average future earnings per share would be if the proposed capital expenditure were not made, relative to the current market price of the shares.

The marginal cost of capital is another concept, but this is not generally recommended. If a debenture issue were made to fund a particular capital project, the cost of the issue and interest payable less tax could be regarded as the marginal cost. The danger is that a project returning only the marginal cost might lower overall company profitability.

It should be borne in mind that as some projects may be for non profit making purposes, the minimum rate for profitable new work must well exceed the average return from all investments.

Uncertainty in investment projects
Because there can be no certainty that forecasts will be achieved, attempts are sometimes made to take uncertainty into account to help the decision maker. Some methods employed are:

1. Adjusting the basic cash flows.
2. Adjusting the rate required. A higher rate of return may be required from projects of higher than average risk.
3. Three level estimates. High, medium and low values of the estimated factors making up the cash flows are taken and rates of return are calculated based on the various combinations, giving optimistic, average and pessimistic estimates. These help the decision maker by showing up the possible extreme results.
4. Applying probabilities to factors. If probabilities are applied to factors such as sales, costs, etc., then the probability of various returns being achieved may be calculated. This is a sophisticated method used mainly in conjunction with a computer.
5. Sensitivity analysis. This term refers to a statement of the likely effects on the return of changes in the factors such as a 10% drop in sales, compared with the average forecast.

Yield or Net Present Value method?
Generally both methods lead one to reach the same accept or reject decision for they are variations of the DCF technique. An advantage of the Yield method is that it is more easy to understand. The assessment of project X47 sounds better

as (*a*) 12% rate of return
than (*b*) NPV of −£124 at 16%

Some companies use both methods although NPV would seem to have the overall advantage if only one method is used.

A project such as Golden Hotels' project X50 which is assumed to be the sole capital project planned, needs to meet certain criteria laid down by the company in the form of cost capital and/or a target rate of return. Either Yield or NPV will achieve this end.

Moving on to other common situations, there are two to consider:
(*a*) capital rationing
(*b*) mutually exclusive projects

Capital Rationing is the term used in capital budgeting to indicate that an overall maximum is being included in a period's budget for capital expenditure and the company selects that combination of a number of investments which will maximize profit. The procedure for selection is to list projects in order of profitability and to accept the first say five projects which will use up the capital budgeted. One way to list them in order is by DCF yield. However, there is a way without requiring the yield by a further simple calculation to the NPV for each project, called the 'Profitability Index'. In respect of each project, this is the present value of future net cash flows divided by the initial cash outlay.

Projects A and B in Exhibit 15–4 (a) are for this purpose assumed to be two of say ten projects to be placed in order of profitability and it can be seen that B would be placed higher than A on the list. If the £15,000 outflow on B happened to use up the last sum in the budget then A would be rejected.

Exhibit 15–4 (a)

Project		*Basic cash flows* £	*NPV @ 25%* £	*Profitability Index*		*Yield*
A	year 0	(35,000)	(35,000)	40,727 / 35,000	= 1·16	35%
	2	63,636	40,727			
			+5,727			
B	year 0	(15,000)	(15,000)	18,824 / 15,000	= 1·25	40%
	2	29,412	18,824			
			+3,824			

Exhibit 15–4 (b)

A–B	year 0	(20,000)	(20,000)	21,903 / 20,000	= 1·09	31%
	2	34,224	21,903			
			+1,903			

Mutually Exclusive Projects. Two mutually exclusive projects are so called if the acceptance of one means the automatic rejection of the other. They may have similar or different outlays.

The choice between mutually exclusive projects is generally based on net present values and of A and B in Exhibit 15–4(a) A would be chosen as it produces the higher NPV If 25% used for discounting is the cost of capital (albeit rather high), then A gives the higher absolute return over the cost of capital. As a further check that A is the better project, the incremental cash flows (Exhibit 15–4(b)) show that 31% will be gained on the extra £20,000, still above the 25% cost of capital.

The Yield may be compared with the NPV method visually to show that at one point two projects will have the same NPV – about 30·5% in the case of A and B. Exhibit 15–5 illustrates the result of sample NPV calculations.

For the Yield and NPV methods to hold good it is assumed that there is the opportunity for cash inflows to be reinvested at the Yield rate and the NPV rate respectively. From the graph it is evident that for rates up to about 31%, project A ranks higher than B. At about 31% the projects have equal ranking, but above 31% B ranks higher than A.

Exhibit 15–5

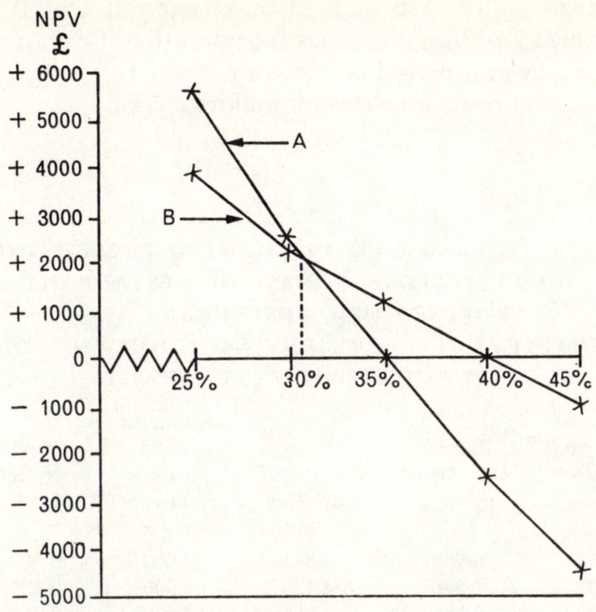

Table of Sample NPV (£)

Project	*Basic cash flows* (0%)	25%	30%	35%	40%	45%
A year 0	(35,000)	(35.000)	(35,000)	(35,000)	(35,000)	(35,000)
2	63,636	40,727	37,545	35,000	32,454	30,545
NPVs	28,636	5,727	2,545	Nil	(2,546)	(4,455)
B year 0	(15,000)	(15,000)	(15,000)	(15,000)	(15,000)	(15,000)
2	29,412	18,824	17,353	16,177	15,000	14,117
NPVs	14,412	3,824	2,353	1,117	Nil	(883)

The graph also illustrates a method of determining the approximate Yield, for example A's Yield of 35% is where the NPV curve cuts the horizontal axis after inserting points for 30% and 40%. It should be noted that curves rather than straight lines represent the changing NPVs although with a narrow range of points about the Yield, 30% and 40% in this case a straight line would be sufficiently accurate.

Goodwill
Finding a value for goodwill by discounting future estimated profits was discussed in Chapter 13, and the method of calculating the discounted cash

flows should now be clear. Exhibit 13–3 showed proof that £5,130 was the calculated goodwill figure. The method of arriving at £5,130 by discounting is shown in Exhibit 15–6. This illustrates the point that if a choice exists between alternatives which cover a period of more than say two years, then DCF can provide a more useful basis for decision making.

Exhibit 15–6

STATEMENT SHOWING DISCOUNTED PROFITS FROM
(*a*) PROPOSED PURCHASE OF RESTAURANT
(*b*) PROPOSED NEW RESTAURANT
DIFFERENCE REPRESENTING GOODWILL ON
PURCHASE OF RESTAURANT

End of year	*Estimated profits from restaurant for sale*	*Present value factor @ 10%*	*Discounted Cash flow*	*Estimated profits from new restaurant*	*Present value factor @ 10%*	*Discounted Cash flow*
	£		£	£		£
1	5,000	0·909	4,545	2,000	0·909	1,818
2	5,000	0·826	4,130	3,000	0·826	2,478
3	5,000	0·751	3,755	4,000	0·751	3,004
4	5,000	0·683	3,415	5,000	0·683	3,415
5	5,000	0·621	3,105	5,000	0·621	3,105
			18,950			13,820
			13,820			
Present value of increased profits from restaurant for sale at 10%			5,130			

Inflation and Investment Projects

The object of appraising projects by using discounted cash flow or any other yardstick is to help management decide whether or not a proposed investment project is likely to be worthwhile. The standard the project should pass, say a minimum of 15% per annum on a DCF basis, is probably based on recent experience of rates achieved by the business on other projects or some calculation of the cost of capital.

Forecasts of cash flows are generally in current money values which ignore expected inflation. These forecasts can be said to be in 'real' terms whilst cash flow forecasts which include an allowance for expected inflation are in money terms.

Most businesses ignore inflation when appraising projects for the simple reason that all factors are in current, that is, in real terms. They expect all costs and selling prices to rise in sympathy with general inflation so that their profit will rise as prices rise.

If forecast annual inflation is to be built into forecast cash flows then it is vital that the minimum rate of return is increased by the inflation rate otherwise projects will be accepted and proved to be unprofitable.

Example: Return required 15%. Inflation 10% p.a. Investment £2,284.

Year	*Forecast cash flows at current prices* £		*Add 10% p.a. for inflation* £
1	1,000	× 1·1	1,100
2	1,000	$\times (1{\cdot}1)^2$	1,210
3	1,000	$\times (1{\cdot}1)^3$	1,331

At this stage two courses are open.

1. Eliminate the inflation element and check resulting 'real' cash flows against the 15% rate required, or
2. Increase the 'real' required rate of 15% by the annual inflation rate, resulting in $1{\cdot}15 \times 1{\cdot}10 = 1{\cdot}265$ or 26·5%.

It can be seen that the first course of eliminating the inflation effect brings the inflated cash flows back to 'real' cash flows of £1,000 per annum. Which, discounted at 15% results in a net present value of nil. The project therefore yields 15%.

The second course is to discount at 26·5%. The PV factors are:

Year 1	$1/1{\cdot}265$	$=0{\cdot}791$
Year 2	$1/(1{\cdot}265)^2$	$=0{\cdot}625$
Year 3	$1/(1{\cdot}265)^3$	$=0{\cdot}494$

Discounting the inflated cash flows gives:

Year	*Cash Flows* £	*PV Factors @ 26·5%*	*Discounted Cash Flow* £
0	(2,284)	1.000	(2,284)
1	1,100	0.791	870
2	1,210	0·625	756
3	1,331	0·494	658
	Net present value		NIL

It can be seen that if all prices in the forecast cash flows are expected to be inflated by 10% per annum, then the project just meets the 'real' 15% return that is required whether or not the forecast cash flows are adjusted for inflation. It is therefore, unnecessary in most cases to make adjustments for inflation.

The exceptions are where inflation rates of significant factors making up the forecast cash flows are expected to differ. If wages, for example, were expected to rise by 10% per annum but food and all other items as well as general inflation were to rise by only 5% per annum, then inflated adjusted cash flows would be calculated and discounted by $1{\cdot}05 \times 1{\cdot}15$ or 20·75% if a 15% rate of return were required. In effect the future cash flows are discounted by the general inflation factor of 5% and the required rate of 15%.

DCF Conclusion

The main work in any investment decision is forecasting the profit and cash flows expected to result from the project. DCF is only a calculation applied to figures which should be in the hands of management anyway. With tables available the time taken to discount cash flows is short.

However, the problem does exist of management gaining sufficient understanding of the technique to have confidence in using it, which is basically a problem of education.

Questions and Problems

15–1 Why are capital investment decisions so important?

15–2 What do you understand by the term 'Net Present Value'?

15–3 Explain the following methods of capital investment appraisal:
(*a*) profit return on investment
(*b*) payback period
(*c*) discounted cash flow.

15–4 A company with £10,000 to invest internally has produced economic feasibility studies in respect of four projects whose life would in each instance be four years. The net annual cash flows are estimated as follows:

	Projects			
	A	*B*	*C*	*D*
Years	£	£	£	£
1	Nil	Nil	5,000	20,000
2	Nil	5,000	5,000	3,000
3	15,000	5,000	5,000	1,000
4	15,000	10,000	5,000	1,000

The company borrows capital at 10% and expects a project to return 20%.

You are required to rank the projects in order of merit under the following methods of appraisal:
(*a*) payback
(*b*) average annual profit on investment
(*c*) average annual profit on average investment
(*d*) net present value at 10%
(*e*) net present value at 20%.

15–5 A catering organization is considering the purchase of a new washing-up machine at a cost of £80,000. It should save £16,000 in cash operating costs per year and has an estimated useful life of 8 years, with a zero disposal value.

You are required to calculate:

(*a*) the payback period;

(*b*) the net present value if the minimum rate of return desired is 10% and state with reasons whether or not the company should buy; and

(*c*) the DCF yield.

15–6 The Brighton Horizon Co. Ltd., has £40,000 to invest. Out of the investment opportunities available, two have been selected for special attention. The immediate initial cash outlay for both is £40,000. It is forecast that for project A the net cash inflows arising from this investment will be:

Year	*net cash inflows*
	£
1	10,000
2	20,000
3	20,000
4	25,000

At the end of the 4th year the investment will be sold for £5,000.

For project B; net cost savings of £18,000 for each of the four years will be achieved.

You are required to:

(*i*) determine which project to recommend according to the

(*a*) pay back period method; and

(*b*) net present value method, assuming a discount factor of 20%

(*ii*) compare the payback period and net present value methods of investment appraisal. (HCIMA)

15–7 AM Co. Ltd. require a DCF return of 15% or more on any capital project it undertakes. Three projects have been presented to the Capital Projects Committee for consideration, supported by the following projections:

			Projects	
		X	*Y*	*Z*
		£	£	£
Expenditure	Year 0	10,000	15,000	20,000
Cash inflow	Year 1	3,000	11,000	10,000
	2	3,000	11,000	10,000
	3	3,000		10,000
	4	3,000		
	5	3,000		
	6	3,000		

Assuming only one project can be chosen, state which project you would choose and give your reasons.

15–8 The Golden Chain Restaurants have been buying Danish pastries from a baker at £0·04 each, but are now considering producing them themselves if this is likely to prove profitable.

Two possible machines are available, A and B, and the costs in respect of each have been forecast as follows:

	Machines A £	B £
Variable costs per pastry	·02	·0125
Fixed costs:		
Annual cash costs	2,500	3,500
Initial machine costs	6,000	15,000
Residual value at end of life	Nil	3,000
Estimated life of machine	4 years	4 years

You are required to:

1. Calculate how many pastries must be sold in order that total average annual costs equal the outside purchase costs in respect of each machine.
2. Calculate the annual number of pastries at which the cost would be the same whether produced on A or B machine.
3. Show which machine should be purchased on financial grounds if the annual sales forecast is 400,000 pastries, and the minimum desired rate of return is 10%.

15–9 The following information is given relating to a proposed capital expenditure project:

	£
Cost of project	350,000
Cash inflow per annum, prior to tax	80,000
Scrap/residual value	Nil
Working capital requirements:	
At commencement of project	10,000
After one year, a further	10,000
All released at end of the seventh year	20,000

Taxation assumptions:

(*i*) corporation tax is at the rate of 50%;

(*ii*) the first year allowance is at the rate of 100% and there are sufficient corporate profits available from other activities to absorb the whole amount of this allowance in the first year;

(*iii*) tax payments are made and allowances are received in the year following that to which they relate.

Grant:

A 20% tax free regional development grant is available and it is expected that this will be received one year after the purchase and installation of capital equipment.

Expected life of equipment	6 years
Company cut-off rate	18% after tax

You are required to:

(*a*) compile a discounted cash flow (DCF) statement to ascertain whether or not the project is acceptable;

(*b*) calculate the approximate DCF rate of return (internal rate of return) for the project. (ICMA)

15–10 The trustees of a museum, which has surplus accommodation, propose to provide for visitors a cafeteria service of light meals and refreshments on a break-even basis. They further propose to use existing funds to meet initial capital costs. These funds now earn an income of 12% per annum. A condition of granting the loan for the capital costs is that the funds should be repaid over a five-year period and provide the same rate of interest as is now being earned.

It is estimated that investment in cooking equipment and furniture with a five-year life will cost £32,000. A supervisor and four other staff will be needed at an annual cost of £12,000. Selling prices of the food and refreshments will be based on a 50% uplift from direct costs. The cafeteria will be charged £2,000 at the end of each operating year to cover heating, lighting and other property expenses.

You are required to:

(*a*) estimate the annual sales necessary to meet the trustees' requirements, assuming a constant value of sales each year;

(*b*) assuming that business will build up gradually and annual sales in year one will be 40% of capacity, in year two 60 % of capacity and in years three, four and five each at full capacity, estimate the annual sales necessary in each of the five years to meet the trustees' requirements;

(*c*) assuming (*b*) is the more realistic forecast, write a report to the trustees commenting on their proposal, mentioning areas you consider need further investigation.

You should ignore taxation and the effects of inflation.

(ICMA adapted)

Further Reading

1. *Profitable Use of Capital in Industry,* ICMA.
2. Lucey, T., *Investment Appraisal: Evaluating Risk and Uncertainty*, ICMA.

3. Merrett, A. J. and Sykes, A., *Capital Budgeting and Company Finance*, Longmans Green & Co.
4. Wright, M. G., *Discounted Cash Flow*, McGraw-Hill.
5. Cox, B. and Hewgill, J. C. R., *Management Accounting in Inflationary Conditions*, ICMA.

CHAPTER SIXTEEN

PUBLISHED ACCOUNTS OF LIMITED COMPANIES

At the end of its financial year a company is required, under the Companies Act, 1948, to submit a profit and loss account and balance sheet, directors' report and an auditor's report. One of each of these three documents must be sent to each shareholder and debenture holder and filed with the Registrar of Companies.

The Companies Acts, 1948 and 1967, require a considerable amount of disclosures to be made in the annual accounts and directors' report. Perhaps the most important provision is contained in Section 149 of the 1948 Act which states that every profit and loss account of a company shall give a true and fair view of the profit or loss of the company for the financial year, and every balance sheet of a company shall give a true and fair view of the state of the affairs of the company as at the end of its financial year.

Published Profit and Loss Account

Disclosures, other than net profit before and after tax and appropriations, may either be compiled within the body of the profit and loss account or in the form of notes within the directors' report.

The more important disclosures required by the Acts are summarized below:

(*a*) Turnover: must be stated if it exceeds £50,000.

(*b*) Investment Income; this must be separated into
- (*i*) quoted investment income, and
- (*ii*) unquoted investment income

(*c*) Directors' Remuneration; the aggregate totals must be shown for each of the following:
- (*i*) directors' emoluments, i.e. fees, salaries, etc.
- (*ii*) directors' or past directors' pensions
- (*iii*) compensation to directors' or past directors' loss of office.

(*d*) Loan Interest; this must be divided into:
- (*i*) bank loans and overdrafts, and other loans (including debentures), repayable (wholly) in five years, and
- (*ii*) other loans having a period of repayment exceeding five years.

(*e*) Hire of Plant and Machinery; this must be stated if material (this does not include hire-purchase payments).

(*f*) Provision for Depreciation; renewal or diminution of fixed assets; this must be shown and is usually divided into particular asset classes.
(*g*) Taxation; the charge for UK Corporation Tax and the basis under which the charge was computed.
(*h*) Amounts provided for the redemption of share capital or loans. Share capital means redeemable preference shares and loans indicate debentures, etc.
(*i*) Dividends; this means aggregate dividends paid and proposed.
(*j*) Provisions; amounts set aside (other than for depreciation, etc.) if material.
(*k*) Auditors' Remuneration; this includes fees and expenses.
(*l*) Reserves; this includes transfers to and from reserves, if material.
(*m*) Unappropriated profit or loss from the previous year; this is the balance, on the previous year's profit and loss account, brought forward.
(*n*) Comparative Figures; that is, the corresponding profit and loss account figures from the previous year must appear.

Published Balance Sheet

The more important disclosures apparent within the Acts are summarized as follows:

(*a*) Balance sheet items must be classified under the following groupings
- (*i*) Authorized share capital
- (*ii*) Issued share capital
- (*iii*) Reserves
- (*iv*) Provisions (except depreciation, etc.)
- (*v*) Liabilities
- (*vi*) Fixed Assets
- (*vii*) Current Assets
- (*viii*) Assets which are neither fixed nor current.

(items (*iii*)–(*v*): Appropriate to the Company's business.)

(*b*) Reserves; the total amount of reserves must be shown and the following reserves must be shown separately:
- (*i*) Share premium account
- (*ii*) Capital redemption reserves fund, i.e. preference shares not debentures.

(*c*) Provisions; any items coming into the definition of provisions. Corporation Tax and amounts set aside for equalizing taxation charges, if material, must be shown separately.
(*d*) Liabilities: include debentures, bank loans and overdrafts, proposed dividends, creditors and accruals, etc.
(*e*) Fixed Assets; the following should be disclosed:
- (*i*) Aggregate cost and/or valuation of the assets
- (*ii*) Aggregate depreciation/amortization written off
- (*iii*) Value of land and buildings distinguishing freehold long lease (50 years or over) and short lease (under 50 years).
- (*vi*) Goodwill, patents and trade-marks, less amounts written off.

(*f*) Current Assets; if the realizable value is lower than the book value this must be stated.

(*g*) Investments; quoted investments must be shown at cost and market value at the date of the balance sheet. Unquoted investments must be shown at cost and directors' estimated valuation at the date of the balance sheet.

(*h*) Capital Expenditure; the total amount of contracts placed for capital expenditure for which no provision in the accounts has been made, plus the estimated capital expenditure authorized by the directors, not yet contracted for, must be stated.

(*i*) Comparative Figures; as in the case of the profit and loss account, the corresponding balance sheet figures from the previous year must appear.

General Legal Points

Share Premium Account:

It has already been mentioned that when shares are issued at a premium, the premium must be transferred to a share premium account.

A share premium balance (if any) may be used in the following circumstances only:

(*a*) the issue of fully paid bonus shares providing the company has not issued all its authorized capital

(*b*) to write off:

  (*i*) preliminary expenses

  (*ii*) discounts, expenses and commissions incurred in the issue of shares or debentures

(*c*) in the case of the redemption of shares or debentures at a premium, then the premium payable on redemption may be provided out of share premium.

Note: Preliminary expenses may also be written off in the profit and loss appropriation account.

Comprehensive Example

Exhibit 16–1

Circle Hotels Limited have an authorized share capital of £800,000, consisting of 600,000 shares of £1 each, and 200,000 8% cumulative preference shares of £1 each.

The balances in the books at 31st December, 1976, are as below:

	£	£
Ordinary shares issued		590,000
Preference shares issued		150,000
Share premium		10,000
Unquoted investments at cost	70,000	
Quoted investments at cost (market value £81,000)	90,000	
Freehold land at cost	400,000	
Freehold buildings at cost	230,000	
Leasehold buildings on long lease	120,000	
Leasehold buildings on short lease	54,600	
Plant and machinery at cost	187,000	
Furniture and fittings at cost	93,000	
Depreciation to 31st December, 1975:		
Freehold buildings		35,000
Plant and machinery		93,000
Furniture and fittings		9,300
Amortization to 31st December, 1975:		
Long lease		10,000
Short lease		4,600
9% debentures 1983/88, secured on freehold buildings		160,000
General reserve		63,000
Unappropriated profits, for year ended 31st December, 1975		16,000
Corporation Tax, year to 31st December, 1975		79,000
Bank Overdraft		64,000
Creditors		105,700
9% debenture redemption sinking fund		15,000
Provision for doubtful debts		3,300
Stock at or under cost, 1st January 1976	75,100	
Hire of equipment	1,300	
Debtors	276,700	
Cash in hand	15,500	
Debenture interest (gross) for year to 31st December, 1976	14,400	
Income from unquoted investments (gross)		8,700
Income from quoted investments (gross)		6,900
Sales (net)		1,823,200
Purchase of food, liquor, etc.	862,600	
Wages and salaries	273,800	
Operating expenses	470,700	
Preference dividend to 31st December, 1976	12,000	
	3,246,700	3,246,700

The following information is relevant:

1. Capital expenditure; the company has entered into contracts worth £142,000 and authorized £40,000. Neither amounts have been provided for in the accounts.
2. Provision for doubtful debts is to be increased to £5,200.
3. Depreciation and amortization for the year to 31st December, 1976, is as follows:

	£
freehold buildings	4,200
leasehold buildings – long lease	10,000
leasehold buildings – short lease	4,600
plant and machinery	16,700
furniture and fittings	3,900

4. Directors' remuneration of £5,000 fees and £12,000 salaries is to be provided for in the accounts.
5. Provide in the accounts for auditors' remuneration of £4,000.
6. A professional valuation of the company's freehold land was carried out on 31st December, 1976, with a resulting valuation of £625,000, and the directors decided to bring the new value into the balance sheet.
7. Corporation Tax liability for the year ended 31st December, 1976, has now been agreed at £86,000. The estimated corporation tax on the current year's profits is £68,000, based on 50% of assessable profits for the year.
8. The directors decided to pay an ordinary dividend for the year of 11p on 27th March, 1977.
9. Stock on 31st December, 1976, at or under cost is £93,700.
10. It has been decided to transfer £10,000 to the general reserve and £15,000 to the 9% debenture redemption sinking fund.
11. Directors' valuation of the unquoted investment is £75,000.

From the above information, the following documents may be prepared, bearing in mind the Companies Act (as far as possible) in a form suitable for publication and presentation to shareholders at the company's annual general meeting:

(*a*) a profit and loss account for the year ended 31st December, 1976, and
(*b*) a balance sheet as at that date.

CIRCLE HOTELS LIMITED

Profit and Loss Account for the year ended 31st December, 1976

Notes		1976 £	£	1975 £	£
	Turnover for the year		1,823,200		*1,560,800*
1.	Net Profit before Taxation		172,300		*162,500*
	Less: U.K. Corporation Tax		68,000		*79,000*
2.	Net profit after Taxation		104,300		*83,500*
	Less: Appropriations				
	Transfer to 9% debenture redemption sinking fund	15,000		*15,000*	
	Transfer to general reserve	10,000		*10,000*	
	8% preference dividend-paid 31.12.76	12,000		*12,000*	
	Proposed ordinary dividend of 11% – payable 27.3.77	64,900	101,900	*31,000*	*68,000*
			2,400		*15,500*
3.	*Add:* Unappropriated profit from previous year brought forward		9,000		*500*
	Unappropriated profits carried forward to next year		11,400		*16,000*

Notes to the profit and loss account:

	1976	1975
1. Net profit before taxation was arrived at (*a*) after charging:	£	*£*
(*i*) Loan interest on 9% debentures	14,400	*14,400*
(*ii*) Amortization and depreciation :		
Freehold buildings	4,200	*4,200*
Leasehold buildings – long lease	10,000	*10,000*
Leasehold buildings – short lease	4,600	*4,600*
Plant and machinery	16,700	*14,000*
Furniture and fittings	3,900	*3,500*
(*iii*) Directors' emoluments	17,000	*12,500*
Auditors' remuneration	4,000	*3,800*
Hire of equipment	1,300	*3,900*

	1976	1975
	£	£
(*b*) after adding income from:		
(*i*) Quoted investments	6,900	*6,800*
(*ii*) Unquoted investments	8,700	*8,400*
2. Corporation tax is based on assessable profits for the year at a rate of 50%		
3. Unappropriated profit brought forward	16,000	*2,000*
Underprovision of taxation (deduct)	7,000	*1,500*

CIRCLE HOTELS LIMITED

Balance Sheet as at 31st December, 1976

	1976		1975	
Notes	£	£	£	£
1. FIXED ASSETS		1,118,300		*934,700*
2. INVESTMENTS		175,000		*160,000*
3. CURRENT ASSETS				
Stocks	93,700		*75,100*	
Debtors, less provision	271,500		*150,400*	
Cash in hand	500	365,700	*11,300*	*236,800*
Less: CURRENT LIABILITIES				
Creditors and accruals	126,700		*160,500*	
Corporation tax – previous year's profits	86,000		*79,000*	
Bank overdrafts	64,000		*118,000*	
Proposed dividends	64,900	(341,600)	*31,000*	*(388,500)*
		1,317,400		*943,000*
FINANCED BY:		£		£
4. SHARE CAPITAL		740,000		*600,000*
5. RESERVES		349,400		*104,000*
Shareholders Interest/Investment		1,089,400		*704,000*
6. LOAN CAPITAL		160,000		*160,000*
Corporation Tax – current year's profits		68,000		*79,000*
		1,317,400		*943,000*

Arthur Wain, *Chairman* Rex Bonnington, *Managing Director*

Notes to the balance sheet:

1. Fixed Assets:

	1976 Cost or Valuation £	1976 Amort or Depn. £	1976 Net Book Value £	1975 Cost or Valuation £	1975 Amort and Depn. £	1975 Net Book Value £
Freehold land	625,000	—	625,000	400,000	—	400,000
Freehold buildings	230,000	39,200	190,800	230,000	35,000	195,000
Leasehold buildings – long lease	120,000	20,000	100,000	120,000	10,000	110,000
Leasehold buildings – short lease	54,600	9,200	45,400	54,600	4,600	50,000
Plant and machinery	187,000	109,700	77,300	189,000	93,000	96,000
Furniture and fittings	93,000	13,200	79,800	93,000	9,300	83,700
	1,309,600	191,300	1,118,300	1,086,600	151,900	934,700

2. Investments:

	1976 £	1975 £
Quoted (Market value £81,000; 1975 £85,000)	105,000	90,000
Unquoted (Directors' valuation £75,000; 1975 £72,000)	70,000	70,000
	175,000	160,000

3. Stocks have been valued at the lower of cost and net realizable value.

4. Share Capital: 1975 and 1976

	Authorized £	Issued £
8% preference shares of £1 each fully paid	200,000	150,000
Ordinary shares of £1 each fully paid	600,000	590,000
	800,000	740,000

5. Reserves:

	1976 £	*1975* £
Share premium account	10,000	*10,000*
Fixed asset revaluation reserve	225,000	—
9% debenture redemption sinking fund	30,000	*15,000*
General reserve	73,000	*63,000*
Unappropriated profits carried forward to next year	11,400	*16,000*
	349,400	*104,000*

6. Loan Capital:

9% debentures 1983/88 (secured on freehold buildings)

1976 £	*1975* £
160,000	*160,000*

7. Capital expenditure:

	1976 £	*1975* £
Authorized	40,000	*55,000*
Committed	142,000	—
	182,000	*55,000*

The points enumerated below are offered to assist the reader in understanding the construction of the above annual published accounts in Exhibit 2–1.

(*a*) The comparative figures used in the example are not detailed in the initial question information but have been included by reason of completing a more practical picture.

(*b*) The net operating profit after charging legal disclosures was calculated as:

	£	£
Sales (net)		1,823,200
Less: Cost of goods sold		
Stocks (1st January, 1976)	75,100	
Add: Purchases of food, liquor, etc.	862,600	
	937,700	
Less: Stocks (31st December, 1976)	93,700	
		844,000
GROSS PROFIT		979,200
Less: Overheads (that are not required to be disclosed)		
Provision for doubtful debts increase	1,900	
Wages and salaries	273,800	
Operating expenses	470,700	
		746,400
PROFIT (before charging the legal disclosures)		232,800
Less: Other Overheads		
9% debenture interest	14,400	
Amortization and depreciation	39,400	
Directors' remuneration	17,000	
Auditors' remuneration	4,000	
Hire of equipment	1,300	
		76,100
PROFIT (after charging legal disclosures)		156,700

(*c*) The under provision of Corporation Tax is calculated by subtracting the agreed tax (£86,000) from the previous year's estimated tax (£79,000), the result, i.e. £7,000, is adjusted on the unappropriated profits brought forward as this is the profit concerned.

(*d*) Notice both the paid and proposed dividends appear in the profit and loss appropriation account but in the balance sheet only the proposed dividend appears (as a current liability). The reason for this difference is that both are appropriations therefore appear in profit and loss but as the preference dividend has been paid only the proposed ordinary dividend remains a liability.

(*e*) The appreciation on valuation of the company's freehold land (£225,000) is effected in the books (and so on the balance sheet) by increasing (debiting) the freehold land and opening a capital reserve account, i.e. fixed asset revaluation reserve, and crediting the amount therein. As this class of reserve is not strictly required to be disclosed the £225,000 and other similar reserves may be grouped together in the balance sheet under the heading of capital reserves.

(*f*) Again, although not within the context of the example information, it will be observed that the difference between the quoted investments of 1975 and 1976 (£15,000) would in effect represent the amount of cash invested in securities thus complementing the annual instalment of profit transferred to the debenture redemption sinking fund.

Finally, it is important to be aware that the Companies Acts do not stipulate a particular style of presenting published accounts, but only lay down requirements concerning disclosure of information. It will be frequently observed in published accounts that a great deal of the information is within the attached notes whilst the accounts themselves merely house the financial framework of a company, the reason being that excessive detail required by the Acts would cause the annual accounts to become unwieldy.

Directors' Report

This document, along with the notes on the published accounts, must be attached to the balance sheet. The report does not form part of the published accounts but in brief contains the following information:

1. Proposed dividends and transfers to or from reserves.
2. The directors' interests in the company, i.e. any shares or debentures they may own.
3. Any political or charitable donations where they total more than £50.
4. Particulars of significant contracts (if at all) in which the directors have or had material interests.
5. The principal activities of the company and any major changes therein.
6. The average number of employees employed each week and the aggregate total of remuneration due to them. This only applies where the average exceeds 100 employees.
7. The market value of freehold and leasehold lands and buildings if they differ materially from the balance sheet values.

Auditors' Report

This report basically informs the shareholders and other interested parties that the profit and loss account and balance sheet, and the notes pertaining to them, give a true and fair view of the company's profit (or loss) for that year ended and the company's affairs as at that date and comply with the Companies Acts, 1948, 1967. In normal circumstances the actual details of an auditors' report is not required to be disclosed to members, etc., but are retained by the directors for any action to be taken thereon.

Standard Statements of Accounting Practice (SSAP)

Most of the statutory accounting requirements for companies are contained in the eighth schedule to the 1948 Companies Act. The 1967 and 1976 Acts made small changes to the 1948 Act. Companies Acts requirements are mandatory although there are many additional matters which are but recommendations, having no legal backing. Recommendations are made occasionally by the Accounting Standards Committee (ASC) which was set up in 1970 and now consists of equal representation of the six Chartered Accountancy bodies.

The ASC produces an Exposure Draft (ED) of matters thought to warrant standardized treatment in annual accounts. Following discussion with interested parties on an exposure draft a Standard Statement of Accounting Practice (SSAP) may be prepared for which the following rules prevail:

1. They apply to all accounts with a 'true and fair view' audit certificate.
2. Significant departures from standards should be disclosed, explained and, where appropriate, quantified.
3. Auditors should refer to departures in the audit certificate.

The Accounting Standards to December 1977 are:

SSAP 1 January 1971 Accounting for the results of associated companies
2 November 1971 Disclosure of accounting policies
3 August 1974 (Revised) Earnings per share
4 April 1974 The accounting treatment of government grants
5 April 1974 Accounting for value added tax
6 April 1975 (Revised) Extraordinary items and prior year adjustments
7 May 1974 Accounting for the changes in the purchasing power of money (CPP)
8 August 1974 Tax under the imputation system
9 May 1975 Stocks and work in progress
10 July 1975 Statements of source and application of funds
11 August 1975 Accounting for deferred taxation
12 December 1977 Accounting for depreciation
13 December 1977 Accounting for research and development

SSAP7 is likely to be succeeded by a new standard based on the Hyde Report.

Leasing and hire purchase transactions are likely to be the subject of an SSAP in the near future.

Accounting Policies (Ref. SSAP2)

A variety of accounting bases have developed which allow consistent and fair ways of dealing with such problems as depreciation of fixed assets and valuation of stocks. In order to provide a better understanding of the annual accounts, a statement of accounting policies followed for dealing with items which are judged material or critical in determining profit or loss for the year and in stating the financial position, should be disclosed by way of a note to the annual accounts.

Four fundamental accounting concepts are defined in SSAP2, viz the 'going concern' concept, the 'accruals' concept, the 'consistency' concept and the concept of 'prudence'. In the absence of a clear statement to the contrary, there is a presumption that these concepts have been observed in preparing annual accounts.

An example of accounting policies is the following statement disclosed as a note to the Annual Accounts 1977 of Trust Houses Forte Limited (Exhibit 16–2).

Exhibit 16–2

TRUST HOUSES FORTE LIMITED AND SUBSIDIARIES

NOTES

Accounting Policies

Basis of consolidation

(*a*) Acquisitions and disposals
The Group balance sheet includes all the assets and liabilities of subsidiary companies including those acquired during the year. The Group profit after taxation includes only that proportion of the results arising since the effective date of control, or in the case of companies or interests disposed of, for the period of ownership.

(*b*) Associated companies
The Group profit for the year before taxation includes the Group's proportion of the profits and losses of associated companies and the taxation charge correspondingly includes taxation on those results.

(*c*) Goodwill
The amount by which the consideration paid differs from the values attributed to net tangible assets of subsidiaries acquired is written off on acquisition.

(*d*) Overseas companies
In certain countries legislation or local practice prevents some subsidiaries from conforming with all these policies and, therefore, appropriate adjustments are made on consolidation in order that the Group accounts are presented on a consistent basis.

Deferred taxation
Provision is made for deferred taxation arising from timing differences between profits as computed for taxation purposes and profits as stated in the accounts except to the extent that the liability will not be payable in the foreseeable future. Timing differences are due primarily to the excess of tax allowances on fixed assets over the corresponding depreciation charged in the accounts and stock appreciation relief. In previous years full provision was made for deferred taxation calculated on the deferral method.

Interest, internal professional fees and pre-opening expenses
Interest on capital employed on land awaiting development and in the construction of new hotels and also internal professional costs incurred until the hotel starts to trade are capitalized as part of the costs of construction. In addition pre-opening and development expenses incurred up to the date of opening are deferred and written off over five years.

Properties and investments in joint ventures
Properties and investments in joint ventures are revalued at intervals of not more than seven years and the resultant valuation is included in the balance sheet unless the surplus or deficit is immaterial.

Depreciation
No depreciation is provided on freehold properties or properties held on leases with fifty years and over to run at the balance sheet date. Properties held on leases of less than fifty years are amortized over the unexpired term. All other fixed assets are depreciated over their estimated useful lives.

Stocks
Stocks are stated at the lower of cost and net realizable value.

Foreign currencies
Overseas trading results and net assets and United Kingdom loans in foreign currencies are expressed in sterling at the average rates of exchange ruling during one week prior and one week subsequent to the balance sheet dates. Currency translation differences are adjusted on the retained profits brought forward from the previous year. In previous years such differences were included as extraordinary items.

Trading receipts
Trading receipts represent the amounts receivable for goods sold and services provided, excluding inter-group sales.

Added Value Statements
An added value statement is included in the annual report and accounts of many large companies. A discussion document called 'The Corporate Report' was published in 1975 by the Accounting Standards Committee. The report concerned the need for and use of financial reports, and one recommendation was the preparation and presentation of an added value statement.

It is likely that there will be a legislative requirement for the inclusion of such a statement in the annual reports, also called corporate reports, of large companies.

Added value is defined as 'sales less bought-in goods and services'. It is a performance measure of the wealth created by a business in a period and emphasizes the return to those creating the wealth (or added value), namely shareholders, lenders, workers and the government.

The term profit has many meanings and communicating financial information to employees and shareholders in profit terms can be confusing. Added value is regarded as a simple concept in that it measures the value added to the cost of purchases and services.

Exhibit 16–3 opposite provides an opportunity to compare a profit statement with an added value statement.

Exhibit 16–3

PROFIT STATEMENT FOR THE YEAR 1978

		£000	£000
Sales			650
Less:	Materials used	260	
	Wages	180	
	Purchased services	50	
	Depreciation	30	
	Interest paid	20	540
Profit before tax			110
Corporation tax			55
			55
Dividend paid			20
Retained profit for the year			35

ADDED VALUE STATEMENT FOR THE YEAR 1978

		£000	£000
Sources of added value			
Sales			650
Less: Bought-in materials & services			310
Value added by manufacturing and trading			340
Disposal of added value			
To employees			180
To providers of capital			
	Interest on borrowings	20	
	Dividends to shareholders	20	40
To Government – corporation tax			55
Re-investment in the business			
	Depreciation	30	
	Retained profit	35	65
			340

Varying interpretations exist of what is meant by bought-in materials and services. Whilst the popular version has been incorporated in Exhibit 16–3, there are arguments in favour of regarding depreciation as a bought-in item and deducted from sales. Depreciation could for this purpose be regarded as no different from stocks of materials which are used up in a period to generate sales.

A potential problem concerns the danger of overemphasis by management on value added, leading to a reduction in profit. Profit would seem to be the more important ultimate objective.

Advantages of Added Value Statements

1. An added value objective instead of a profit objective shows employees the teamwork required in creating wealth from which they benefit. Profit sharing schemes operate which are designed to reward employees with a share of increased added value.
2. The sum of retained profit and depreciation represents funds generated internally to replace and extend fixed assets. This combined figure is not shown in the profit statement.
3. Size of companies may be measured in a number of ways. Measurement by added value has advantages over a turnover measurement as added value ignores variations in material prices which could distort sales figures. It is a better measure than capital employed, for in the hotel and catering industry this may include leased and owned properties which distort comparisons.

Inflation Accounting Principles

Adjusting for Inflation

Businesses with the following characteristics stand to lose from inflationary conditions unless care is taken: those

owning high-cost fixed assets which depreciate,
holding high stock values,
borrowing only a small proportion of capital requirements.

There is a danger that the increased money needed to replace fixed assets and stocks in order to maintain the same volume of business, will have been distributed to shareholders. This would result in erosion of capital.

Clearly, many hotel and catering businesses are not in this position. Freehold land and premises tend to appreciate in value rather than depreciate, and stocks are relatively low in value. Nevertheless inflation does mean that their profit is likely to be overstated if only traditional accounting concepts are used in preparing final accounts.

The term inflation accounting refers to the presentation of final accounts which have been adjusted to take into account the effects of inflation on expenses charged in arriving at profit.

The effects of inflation on internal management matters have been dealt with separately, for example in the budgeting section. The concern here is with the reporting of financial results which may be of limited value unless inflation-adjusted in some way.

Final accounts are always prepared on an historical cost basis, which tends to show a higher profit than really exists. This is because, for instance, stocks used up are charged against revenue at their historic cost although the cost of replacing them may be far higher. Items of stock remain in the books at their original transaction price until used up or disposed of; the objectivity concept in particular applies here in that suggestions of bias and estimation in the valuation of assets are avoided. Stocks are valued at cost or net realization value whichever is the lower in accordance with the prudence concept and SSAP9.

Satisfactory financial statements resulted from this practice until the monetary unit, the pound, became unstable through inflation.

Indices to Measure Inflation

To highlight the significance of inflation in the mid '70s, reference may be made to the Report and Accounts of Trust Houses Forte Limited for 1977. A statement of results covering 1968 – 1977 starts with trading receipts which rose from £212·7 million in 1972 to £531·0 million in 1977.

If £212·7 in 1972 is represented by 100, then £531·0 = 249·6. Trading receipts in 1977 are therefore $2\frac{1}{2}$ times the 1972 receipts. To measure real business growth in volume however, inflation must be taken into account.

The most well known index is the 'Index of Retail Prices' which is compiled by the Statistics Division of the Department of Employment. It measures the average changes month by month in the retail prices of a large and representative selection of goods and services bought by the great majority of householders in the United Kingdom. The prices relate to a date in the middle of the month.[1]

A table of Retail Price indices is included in a half yearly publication of the HMSO entitled *Price index numbers for Current Cost Accounting*. This index would be suitable for measuring the inflation of hotel and catering sales and is here used to measure real sales growth of THF in the following manner:

The THF year end is 31st October so that an average index for the year to 31st October 1972 can be determined by taking the average of November 1971 and October 1972 which is 85·1, $\left(\frac{82{\cdot}2 + 88{\cdot}0}{2}\right)$. Similarly the average for 1977 is 176·2, $\left(\frac{165{\cdot}8 + 186{\cdot}5}{2}\right)$. The index rose 2·071 times from 85·1 to 176·2.

This means that in the five year period when inflation doubled, sales, by rising $2\frac{1}{2}$ times made a small amount of real growth. Details for intermediate years are shown overleaf.

[1]The index is described more fully in *Method of Construction and Calculation of the Index of Retail Prices* published in 1967 by HMSO.

Year ended 31 Oct.	*Reported Sales £millions* (*a*)	*Average Retail Price Index* (*b*)	*Multiplier Factor* (*c*)	*Sales at 1977 Prices £millions* (*d*)=(*a*)×(*c*)
1972	212·7	(82·2+ 88·0)÷2= 85·1	176·2÷ 85·1=2·071	440·5
1973	271·3	(88·3+ 95.9)÷2= 92·1	176·2÷ 92·1=1·913	519·0
1974	304·0	(97·4+113·2)÷2=105·3	176·2÷105·3=1·673	508·6
1975	369·8	(115·2+142·5)÷2=128·9	176·2÷128·9=1·367	505·5
1976	451·7	(144·2+163·5)÷2=153·9	176·2÷153·9=1.145	517·2
1977	531·0	(165·8+186·5)÷2=176·2	176·2÷176·2=1.000	531·0

Whilst the growth from 1972 to 1973 was 17·8%, $\left(\frac{519\cdot0-440\cdot5}{440\cdot5}\times100\right)$ the growth covering the five years was only 20·5%, $\left(\frac{531\cdot0-440\cdot5}{440\cdot5}\times100\right)$.

This procedure is a general approach to the use of published price indices and demonstrates that trading receipts (sales) used to assess real company growth clearly need to be adjusted for inflation. However, when trading receipts are used in the profit to sales ratio, because both items are equally affected by inflation over time, neither needs to be adjusted.

Historical Note

To show the difficulty the accountancy profession has and experienced in agreeing on a method of 'inflation accounting', it is useful to list the reports on the subject concerning the UK.

March 1952	The Institute of Cost and Management Accountants made recommendations.
May 1952	Institute of Chartered Accountants made recommendations.
January 1973	Exposure draft No. 8 recommended a method known as CPP (Current Purchasing Power).
June 1975	Sandilands Report recommended CCA (Current Cost Accounting) method.
November 1977	Hyde Guidelines recommended a simplified CCA method.
April 1979	Exposure draft No. 24 – Extended Hyde.

Current Value Accounting (*CVA*)

This is a general description of methods of 'inflation accounting' which state economic events in market values at the date financial statements are prepared. This compares with the traditional valuation based on historical costs which are related to dates of purchase. The market value of assets considered by UK methods is associated with a replacement cost (so-called entry value) as compared with sales value of assets (exit value).

Valuation of fixed assets using the accepted historical cost convention is recommended in SSAP 9 to be the lower of cost or net realizable value. As cost is generally the lower, some means is necessary to adjust cost to current values. Annual professional valuations being mainly unnecessary and costly, price indices are generally recommended which take account of inflation over time. Alternatives are to use only the Retail Price Index (RPI) or to use a variety of indices to suit different assets. The CPP (Current Purchasing Power) method would use only the RPI whilst CCA (Current Cost Accounting), the favoured method in 1979, would use specific indices.

Inflation Adjusted Presentations

The effect of inflation on profit can be measured in two ways, using the profit or the net asset (balance sheet) approach:

(*a*) Reported profit on an historical basis can be adjusted to take account of such items as extra depreciation and cost of sales to arrive at real profit.

(*b*) Appropriate assets and liabilities can be revalued in current values. Changes in net assets (or equity) over a period will show the increase or decrease in wealth, representing the period's real profit or loss.

The CPP and the CCA methods use both ways in an integrated approach but these were not acceptable to the accountancy profession partly through being unduly complicated. The CPP method required the presentation of a supplementary statement covering the profit and loss account and balance sheet based on RPI adjustments to all appropriate figures. The CCA method required a similar presentation but was based on a variety of indices.

The Hyde Guidelines recommended a presentation of an adjusted profit and loss account only; that is, in addition to the historical balance sheet and profit and loss account.

Hyde Guidelines: Three adjustments to profit

Two adjustments are common to most methods of adjusting for inflation. One is the calculation of extra depreciation to be charged against revenue so that the replacement cost of a fixed asset is depreciated and not the historic cost. The second adjustment is the cost of sales adjustment which relates to the increasing cost of purchases which are held in stock and then used to produce sales.

A third adjustment continues to be the subject of discussion and that concerns monetary items such as cash, debtors, creditors and debentures. Monetary assets and liabilities are fixed by nature or contract and are automatically in current values. A business holding more monetary assets than liabilities will incur a purchasing power loss under inflation and a number of ways are available to measure this loss. On the other hand, many hotel and catering businesses gain through having an excess of monetary liabilities over monetary assets.

Depreciation Adjustment

The purchase price of an asset which will be replaced at a later date, such as kitchen plant, rises each year through inflation. Only the original cost depreciates in the accounts whereas higher depreciation should be charged against revenue each year as the cost of replacement rises. Unless this is done the profit for the period is overstates. A fixed asset may be replaced by a similar item but costing twice as much. Immediately the annual depreciation doubles and it is clear that the most recent depreciation of the old fixed asset was too low and profits therefore overstated. Exhibit 16–4 contains an example of the depreciation adjustment.

Exhibit 16–4

Details of kitchen plant:

Purchased July 1974 for £5,000
Life of 10 years giving depreciation of £500 p.a. (straight line)
Balance sheet of 30th June 1978 shows:

	£
Fixed asset at cost	5,000
Depreciation to date	2,000
Net book value	3,000

Details of inflation:

Extracts from *Price index numbers for CCA* August 1978 HMSO Table 3 Ref. 3845 Catering Equipment.

July 1974	133·7	
July 1977	243·1	average 258·0
June 1978	272·9	

Calculation of extra depreciation:

Original cost		£5,000
Average index for year to 30th June 1978		258·0
Index for month of purchase		133·7
Replacement cost £5,000 × 258·0/133·7 =		£9,650
		£
Current cost depreciation for year	£9,650 × 1/10 =	965
Less: already charged		500
Extra depreciation to be charged		465

Whilst freehold land does not depreciate some companies depreciate freehold properties because they have a limited life. For current value of freehold buildings professional valuations are used every few years and an index 'Cost of New Constructions' may be used for intermediate years.

e.g. Table 4 Ref. 4100

Index	1960	Quarter 1	71·0
	1978	Quarter 1	315·1

Cost of Sales Adjustment

Stocks held for future consumption rise in value because of inflation. The rise is usually related to the amount of inflation over the period the stocks are held, in a similar manner to fixed assets. If a business already uses a method of pricing material issues which reflects fairly recent prices such as LIFO (last in first out), then no further adjustment may be necessary. However, in other cases the method illustrated in Exhibit 16–5 may be used to find the extra cost of ensuring that most recent prices are charged against revenue.

Exhibit 16–5

Details of stock:

		£
Deep frozen meat:	Opening stock 1st July 1977	300
	Closing stock 30th June 1978	500
	Purchases during year	2,000

Details of inflation:

Table 2 Ref. 2870: Retail Distribution, Butchers

Index	July 1977	296·0	average 316·1
	June 1978	336·2	

Calculation of extra cost of sales:

The value of opening stock is converted to average current cost for the period; the total of purchases is left unaltered; and the value of closing stock is converted to the average current cost for the period.

Opening stock £300 × 316·1/296·0 = £320
Closing stock £500 × 316·1/336·2 = £470

	Historic Cost	*Replacement Cost*
	£	£
Opening Stock	300	320
Purchases	2,000	2,000
	2,300	2,320
Closing stock	500	470
Cost of sales	1,800	1,850

Adjustment £1,850 – £1,800 = £50 extra cost.

Monetary Items Adjustment (Gearing Adjustment)

Holding £100 in cash for a period when the Retail Price Index[2] rose from 100 (January 1974) to 200 (September 1978) meant that the goods £100 would buy

[2]Table 5 Ref. 4010 in *Price index numbers for Current Cost Accounting*.

halved. This is because whilst the pound is still legally a pound, the cost of goods had doubled. Goods generally in January 1974 costing £100 would cost £100 × 200/100 = £200 in September 1978.

Assets held in cash or under contract to be exchanged for cash, e.g. debtors, reduce in real value under inflation. These are monetary assets. On the other hand monetary liabilities such as creditors and debentures become more valuable to the business because the money used to settle the liabilities – some months or years later – is the same in pounds but these are worth less than when the liability was incurred. Therefore a business gains when using other people's money but loses if too much of its own money is kept.

The Hyde Guidelines adjustment is done in the following manner and is called the 'gearing adjustment' and reflects the amount by which third parties help to finance the business.

The concept that equity remains after deducting total liabilities from total assets is used to draw up a balance sheet in current values. This is for the purpose of determining what percentage of company capital is being provided by third parties. The cost of extra depreciation and cost of sales already calculated is reduced by the proportion third parties finance the business.

In the following example, Exhibit 16–6, fixed assets, depreciation and stocks are those used in the depreciation and cost of sales adjustment, viz Exhibits 16–4 and 16–5. Other figures are assumed. The equity figure in the adjusted balance sheet is the balancing figure.

Exhibit 16–6

Balance Sheets at 30th June 1978

Stage 1	*Historic*	*Adjusted*
	£	£
Equity share capital and reserves	3,000	5,760 (balance)
Long term liabilities	500	500
Current liabilities	1,000	1,000
	45,000	7,260
	£	£
Fixed assets at cost	5,000	9,650
Depreciation	2,000	3,860 (2,000×258·0/133·7)
	3,000	5,790
Stocks	500	470
Monetary assets:		
Debtors	600	600
Cash	400	400
	4,500	7,260

Stage 2	*Adjusted balance sheet*	*Net monetary liabilities*	*Equity plus net monetary liabilities*	*Gearing percentage*
	£	£	£	
Equity	5,760		5,760	92%
Long term liabilities	500	500		
Current liabilities	1,000	1,000		
	7,260	1,500		
Fixed assets	5,790			
Stocks	470			
Monetary assets	1,000	1,000		
	7,260			
Net monetary liabilities		500	500	8%
Equity plus net monetary liabilities			6,260	100%

Stage 3

The gearing adjustment is calculated:

	£
Extra depreciation	465
Cost of sales adjustment	50
	515
Gearing adjustment 8% of £515	41
Net inflation adjustment to deduct from historic profit	£474

As shareholders contribute 92% of total capital, only 92% of the loss through inflation should be deducted from historic profit, leaving a real profit which is attributable to shareholders. This amount may be distributed to shareholders without depleting the capital of the business. Taking further sums out of the business would represent erosion of capital.

Where monetary assets exceed monetary liabilities the difference must be multiplied by the change in the Retail Price Index for the year to provide a figure to be added to the extra cost of depreciation and cost of sales adjustment. This figure represents the extra cost of holding net monetary assets which lose value under inflation.

Exposure Draft 24: Current Cost Accounting, April 1979
This is based on, but goes further than the Hyde Guidelines in two main respects, in

(*a*) introducing separate from the 'gearing adjustment', an adjustment which in effect extends the cost of sales adjustment to other working capital items.
(*b*) calling for a current cost balance sheet which includes a capital maintenance reserve reflecting revaluation surpluses and deficits.

Questions and Problems

16–1 Describe, as if to a layman, the main differences between 'published' and 'internal' annual accounts as prepared by a limited liability company.

16–2 The following statement was made by an irate shareholder of a limited liability company. 'It is seemingly absurd that directors and management who are only employees have full access to the annual figures of a limited company whereas we, the shareholders, who are the owners receive only certain disclosures, laid down by law.' Discuss.

16–3 Westminster Hotels Ltd., which has an authorized capital of £700,000 divided into 500,000 ordinary shares of £1 each and 200,000 12% preference shares of £1 each, makes up its accounts on 30th June each year. Its trial balance at 30th June, 1976, was as follows:

	£	£
Issued and fully paid-up capital:		
Ordinary shares		350,000
Preference shares		150,000
Profit and loss account balance 1.7.75		40,000
General reserve		90,000
Freehold land and buildings, at cost	720,000	
Unquoted investment, at cost (Directors valuation £70,000)	55,000	
Quoted investment, at cost (Market value £30,000)	33,400	
Equipment at cost	75,000	
Provision for depreciation on equipment 1.7.75		50,000
Stock 30.6.76, at cost or net realizable value whichever lower	30,000	
Debtors and creditors	140,000	110,000
Balance of cash at bank and in hand	48,500	
Profit for year ended 30.6.76 subject to the adjustments noted below		280,000

	£	£
Preference dividend for half year – paid 1.1.76	9,000	
Interim dividend of 5% on ordinary shares – paid 1.3.76	17,500	
Income from investments:		
Unquoted		5,400
Quoted		3,000
Corporation tax payable on previous year's profits		50,000
	1,128,400	1,128,400

Notes and adjustments:

1. The profit for the year ended 30th June, 1976, has been arrived at after charging £1,500 for audit fee, managing director's salary £8,000 but before charging depreciation and directors' fees which should be provided for as follows:
   (*a*) Depreciation of equipment for the year at 20% of cost; and
   (*b*) Directors fees as below:
   — Chairman £2,000
   — Three other directors including the managing director £1,000 each.
2. Corporation Tax based on assessable profits for the year at 50% is estimated at £100,000 and this should be provided for.
3. The directors recommend:
   (*a*) Payment of a preference dividend for six months on 1.7.76
   (*b*) A final dividend of 10% on the ordinary shares
   (*c*) Transfer of £80,000 to general reserve.
4. The turnover of the company for the year was £1,800,000.

You are required to prepare the profit and loss account for the year ended 30th June, 1976, and a balance sheet as at that date in a form suitable for circulation to members and to conform, as far as the information given will permit, with the requirements of the Companies Acts 1948 and 1967.

16–4 The following list of balances were extracted at 31st March 1976 from the books of the Blossom Hotel Co. Ltd.

	£
Ordinary shares, fully paid	195,000
Preference shares, fully paid	30,000
Reserves	10,965
Freehold property at cost	330,000
Leasehold property, cost less amortization	60,432
Furniture and equipment, at cost less depreciation	52,293
Quoted investments, at cost	24,000

	£
6% debenture stock	225,000
Wages and salaries	204,000
Rates and insurance	13,500
Fuel and light	18,690
Repairs and replacements	7,230
Depreciation charge for the year	5,340
Amortization charge for the year	4,000
Gross profit for the year (Sales £521,500)	312,925
Other expenses	21,160
Unappropriated profit at 1st April 1975	17,050
Stock	26,800
Debtors	15,705
Cash and bank balances	13,040
Deposits received in advance	1,500
Trade creditors	18,300
Preference dividend paid	1,050
Debenture interest paid	13,500

Take the following information into account:

(*a*) The authorized capital of the Blossom Hotel Co. Ltd. is 250,000 ordinary shares of £1 each and 50,000 7% preference shares of £1 each.

(*b*) Provide for the outstanding preference dividend, and an ordinary dividend of 8%.

(*c*) Included in wages and salaries is £50,000 directors' remuneration.

(*d*) Provide for the estimated corporation tax liability of £18,000;

(*e*) The aggregate depreciation on kitchen and restaurant plant and equipment at 31st March 1976 is £16,707, and the amortization on the leasehold property is £14,568.

(*f*) Provide for fuel and light charges due at 31st March 1976, of £810.

You are required:

(*i*) to prepare the profit and loss account, the appropriation account for the year ending 31st March 1976, and the balance sheet as at that date.

(*ii*) indicate four other items of information which could be required to be disclosed in the annual accounts by the Companies Act 1948 and 1967.

(Ignore taxation on distributions).

(HCIMA)

16–5 Prepare an Added Value Statement for the Circle Hotels Co. Ltd. for year to 31st December, 1979, Exhibit 16–1, pages 245–253.

16–6 Discuss the ways in which added value can be increased in an hotel company. Which ways would you favour, and why?

16–7 Write an essay explaining *four* of the problems encountered when interpreting conventionally prepared balance sheets and revenue accounts in hotels, which cover a period during which there has been inflation. (The explanation of each problem should have a numerical illustration to support it).

16–8 The Customer's Right Restaurant is unseasonal. It has two main classifications of assets:

(*a*) a leasehold property in which it operates. The original lease was for ten years and cost £250,000. Amortization has been provided on cost on the straightline method. On 26th March 1981 the lease will have to be renewed and the predicted cost of renewal is £400,000.

(*b*) the base stock for resale would cost now £20,000. The company marks up the cost of stock for resale by 300% to establish the selling price. Normally there is a time lag between buying the stock and selling it of two months.

The proprietors of the Customer's Right Restaurant aim to distribute all the profit after taxation.

The price index for the stock for resale stands at 100. However, there are indications that, for the foreseeable future, this index is likely to rise evenly by 2 points per month.

You are required to:

(*i*) comment on the way in which the proprietors are calculating
– the amortization of the lease; and
– selling price of the stock acquired for resale.

(*ii*) state the changes you would make and their effect on the annual accounts of the Customer's Right Restaurant.

Your answer should consist of 400 to 500 words and should be supported, where appropriate, by calculations.

(HCIMA)

Further Reading

1. Recent published accounts of limited companies will prove useful in appreciating legal disclosures and general style of presentation.

CHAPTER SEVENTEEN

CONSOLIDATED ACCOUNTS OF LIMITED COMPANIES

SINCE so many public companies in the hotel and catering industry produce a group balance sheet and profit and loss account in addition to the usual company final accounts, some understanding is required of the reasons why and how group final accounts are prepared.

A company taking over control of another company by the purchase of shares giving majority votes, becomes a holding company of the one bought, which itself becomes a subsidiary.

The Companies Act, 1948, states it officially in Section 154:

'(1) . . . a company shall . . . be deemed to be a subsidiary of another if, but only if –

(*a*) that other either

(*i*) is a member of it and controls the composition of its board of directors; or

(*ii*) holds more than half in nominal value of its equity share capital; or

(*b*) the first mentioned company is a subsidiary of any company which is that other's subsidiary.'

A holding company with its subsidiaries is known as a group of companies, giving rise to the term 'group accounts'.

Group Accounts

Section 150 of the 1948 Companies Act requires the preparation of group accounts where a company has a subsidiary at the end of its financial year and is not a wholly-owned subsidiary of another company incorporated in Great Britain.

Section 151 of the 1948 Companies Act states among other things:

'. . . the group accounts, shall be consolidated accounts comprising:

(*a*) a consolidated balance sheet dealing with the state of affairs of the company and all the subsidiaries to be dealt with in group accounts.

(*b*) a consolidated profit and loss account dealing with the profit or loss of the company and those subsidiaries.'

Some other parts of Section 151 deal with exceptions to the above requirements but are beyond the scope of this book.

Preparation of Consolidated Balance Sheets

Whilst the consolidation of final accounts in practice is likely to be the work of an accountant, and may be complicated when subsidiaries hold control themselves of subsidiaries, a simple approach will suffice to enable published group accounts to be understood.

Certain rules are necessary to consolidate balance sheets, starting with the rule that the balance sheets of the holding company and its subsidiary are added together and any inter-company balances eliminated.

In all four examples which follow the balance sheet of the holding company 'H' remains unchanged, whilst four different subsidiaries are used, S(A), S(B), S(C), S(D).

Exhibit 17–1

When all shares in subsidiary are bought at nominal value and an inter-company loan exists.

Balance Sheet of 'H' Co. Ltd. on 31st December, 1976

	£		£
Issued ordinary share capital	100,000	Fixed assets	55,000
Current liabilities	10,000	Investment in S(A)	40,000
		Loan to S(A)	3,000
		Current assets	12,000
	110,000		110,000

Balance Sheet of S(A) Co. Ltd. on 31st December, 1976

	£		£
Issued ordinary share capital	40,000	Fixed assets	42,000
Loan from 'H'	3,000	Current assets	7,000
Current liabilities	6,000		
	49,000		49,000

The investment of £40,000 and loan of £3,000 are eliminated in the consolidated balance sheet; all other items are added together.

Consolidated Balance Sheet of 'H' Co. Ltd. and its subsidiary S(A) Co. Ltd. on 31st December, 1976

	£		£
Issued ordinary share capital	100,000	Fixed assets	97,000
Current liabilities	16,000	Current assets	19,000
	116,000		116,000

The above consolidated balance sheet is in summary form only for the sake of simplicity, but reference should be made also to the following which illustrates, with sample details, how the balance sheets are combined to form the consolidated balance sheet.

Consolidated Balance Sheet of 'H' Co. Ltd. and its Subsidiary S(A) Co. Ltd. on 31st December, 1976

	H	S(A)	H and	S(A)
	£	£	£	£
FIXED ASSETS				
Property	45,000	35,000		80,000
Equipment	10,000	7,000		17,000
	55,000	42,000		97,000
CURRENT ASSETS				
Stocks	8,000	5,000	13,000	
Debtors	3,000	1,500	4,500	
Cash and bank	1,000	500	1,500	
	12,000	7,000	19,000	
Less: CURRENT LIABILITIES				
Taxation	2,000	1,000	3,000	
Creditors	3,000	2,000	5,000	
Overdraft	5,000	3,000	8,000	
	10,000	6,000	16,000	
NET CURRENT ASSETS (Working Capital) £19,000 – £16,000 =				3,000
NET ASSETS (Capital Employed)				100,000
SHARE CAPITAL				
100,000 ordinary shares of £1 issued and fully paid up				£100,000

Goodwill on Consolidation

Exhibit 17–2

When purchase price is greater than the value of net assets, and all shares in subsidiary are acquired.

If the cost of acquiring control of a subsidiary is in excess of its net asset value then the difference is regarded as goodwill when consolidating. Net asset value is the total assets less liabilities to outsiders.

Instead of S(A) Co. Ltd. let S(B) Co. Ltd. be acquired:

Balance Sheet of S(B) Co. Ltd. on 31st December, 1976

	£		£
Issued ordinary share capital	20,000	Fixed assets	29,000
Revenue reserves	8,000		
Profit and loss account	2,000	Current assets	7,000
(Net asset value)	30,000		
Loan from 'H'	3,000		
Current liabilities	3,000		
	36,000		36,000

'H' Co. Ltd. paid £40,000 for S(B) Co. Ltd.'s net assets worth £30,000 leaving a figure of £10,000 representing goodwill on purchase. Net assets may be calculated as shown in the balance sheet of S(B) Co. Ltd. by the addition of issued share capital and reserves, or by taking total assets (£36,000) less any liabilities to outside interests (£6,000).

The resulting consolidated balance sheet is as follows:

Consolidated Balance Sheet of 'H' Co. Ltd.
with S(B) Co. Ltd. on 31st December, 1976

	£		£
Issued ordinary share capital	100,000	Fixed assets	84,000
Current liabilities	13,000	Goodwill on Consolidation (£40,000 – £30,000)	10,000
		Current assets	19,000
	113,000		113,000

Goodwill is dealt with in more detail in Chapter 13. Should the price paid for a subsidiary be less than its net asset value, then a capital reserve arises on consolidation.

Minority Interests on Consolidation

Exhibit 17–3

When not all shares in the subsidiary are acquired, but enough to gain control, minority interests result.

A controlling interest in a company is achieved when over 50% of the ordinary shares are acquired, assuming each share carries one vote and other shares are non-voting. If between 50% and 100% of the shares in a subsidiary are acquired, those not acquired are called the Minority Interest, and the value of these attributed to shareholders outside the group must be calculated.

The rule in this situation is that the claims of the minority shareholders must be deducted from the net asset value before calculating the value of the holding company's interest and goodwill. Preference shares, because of limited voting rights, need not be acquired and are normally taken at nominal value.

Consolidation is therefore effected by calculating net assets and deducting nominal value of preference shares. The resulting figure represents the value of equity which is then proportioned according to holding company and minority shareholdings. The consolidated balance sheet is prepared as though 100% control had been achieved, as exhibits 1 and 2, but the value of minority interests shown as a liability.

'H' Co. Ltd. bought for £40,000, 30,000 ordinary shares in S(C) Co. Ltd. whose balance sheet is as follows:

Balance Sheet of S(C) Co. Ltd. on 31st December, 1976

	£		£
Issued preference shares	20,000	Fixed assets	79,000
Issued ordinary shares of £1	50,000	Current assets	7,000
Revenue reserves	8,000		
Profit and Loss account	2,000		
	80,000		
Loan from 'H'	3,000		
Current liabilities	3,000		
	86,000		86,000

	£
Net assets: £86,000 – £6,000	80,000
Preference shareholders' claim	20,000
Value of equity	60,000

'H' Co. Ltd. bought 30,000 shares being valued at

$\frac{30,000}{50,000}$ i.e. 60% of £60,000 £36,000

Since payment of £40,000 is £4,000 more than the value of 30,000 shares, goodwill results.

Minority Interest (including preference shareholders) is

£80,000 – £36,000 £44,000

The consolidated balance sheet will appear as follows:

Consolidated Balance Sheet of 'H' Co. Ltd. and S(C) Co. Ltd. on 31st December, 1976

	£		£
Issued ordinary shares	100,000	Fixed assets	134,000
Minority interest	44,000	Goodwill	4,000
Current liabilities	13,000	Current assets	19,000
	157,000		157,000

Pre-acquisition profits

Exhibit 17–4

Consolidating at a date after the purchase of a subsidiary gives rise to pre-acquisition and post-acquisition profits.

It has so far been assumed that the consolidated balance sheet was prepared at the time of the subsidiary's acquisition. Profits made by the subsidiary were taken into account in determining net assets and consequently goodwill or capital reserve on purchase. Pre-acquisition profits (undistributed) of subsidiary have therefore been capitalized and are not available for distribution. If not all shares are purchased, then it has been shown that only the part of the profits belonging to the holding is capitalized, the remainder being part of minority interests.

If consolidated final accounts are prepared at the end of the financial year following acquisition, it is likely that the subsidiary will have made further profits. These profits made subsequent to acquisition are available for distribution.

Clearly, then, consolidating some time after an acquisition the subsidiary's profit and loss account must be separated into

(*a*) pre-acquisition profit

(*b*) post-acquisition profit

On 30th September 1976 'H' Co. Ltd. bought for £40,000 60% (30,000) of the £1 ordinary shares of S(D) Co. Ltd. whose balance sheet on 31st December, 1976, was:

Balance Sheet of S(D) Co. Ltd. on 31st December, 1976

	£	£		£
Issued preference shares		20,000	Fixed assets	79,000
Issued ordinary shares of £1		50,000	Current assets	7,000
Revenue reserve at 1/1/76		8,000		
Profit and loss account:				
at 30/9/76	1,500			
1/10/76 to 31/12/76	500			
		2,000		
Loan from 'H'		3,000		
Current liabilities		3,000		
		86,000		86,000

Calculation of goodwill by an alternative approach to exhibit 3–2 is as follows:

	£	£
Purchase price		40,000
less: Net assets purchased:		
Nominal value of acquired shares	30,000	
Revenue reserve purchased 60% × £8,000	4,800	
Profit purchased 60% × £1,500	900	
		35,700
Goodwill		4,300

Minority interest is therefore:

		£	£
Preference shares			20,000
Ordinary shares	20,000 @ £1	20,000	
Revenue reserve	40% × £8,000	3,200	
Profit:	40% × £1,500	600	
AND	40% × £500	200	
			24,000
	Minority Interest		44,000

Consolidated Balance Sheet of 'H' Co. Ltd. and S(D) Co. Ltd. on 31st December, 1976

	£		£
Issued ordinary shares	100,000	Fixed assets	134,000
Profit and loss account		Goodwill	4,300
S(D) from 1/10/76 – 60% of £500	300[1]	Current assets	19,000
Minority interest	44,000		
Current liabilities	13,000		
	157,300		157,300

When studying published consolidated balance sheets, two items commonly found which refer to the purchase of subsidiary companies, namely minority interests and goodwill on consolidation, should now be clear. What has happened, then, is that all assets and current liabilities of subsidiaries have been added to the holding company's balances, the value of these items belonging to shareholders who have not sold their shares to the holding company, is deducted as a liability to minority interests, and any excess the company has paid for net assets taken over has been added as goodwill.

The shares bought by the holding company will have been paid for in shares, debentures or cash or some combination of these.

The balance sheet of the holding company only shows interests in subsidiary companies as an asset, and therefore presents few problems in preparation.

Consolidated Profit and Loss Accounts

The preparation of these naturally follows a similar pattern to that required for consolidating the balance sheet, in that the group's figures are added together and necessary adjustments made to them. To be more specific:

(*a*) Previous years' undistributed profit of all companies making up the group *is added to*

(*b*) The past years' profit of all the group.

from which is subtracted (c), (d), (e) and (f) below:

(*c*) Pre-acquisition profits of the subsidiary.

(*d*) Profits of the subsidiary belonging to minority interests.

(*e*) Unrealized profit on inter-company transfers.

(*f*) Inter-company dividends.

Exhibit 17–5

Showing the preparation of a consolidated profit and loss account covering the above points.

H(A) Co. Ltd. bought on 1st January, 1976, 12,000 ordinary shares in S(E) Co. Ltd. out of a total of 16,000. Stock of S(E) includes £1,000 for goods

[1] This represents 'H's' share of profit made by S(D) since acquisition.

invoiced by H(A) at cost + 25%. The following profit and loss accounts were extracted before eliminating the inter-company profit in the stock held.

Profit and Loss Accounts for year ended 31st December, 1976

	H(A)	S(E)		H(A)	S(E)
	£	£		£	£
Interim dividends paid	10,000	4,000	Balance b/f	20,000	6,000
Balance c/f	29,000	10,000	Net profit for year	16,000	8,000
			Interim dividend from S(E)	3,000	
	39,000	14,000		39,000	14,000

Notes on accounts above and below:

1. H(A) Co. Ltd. has a 75% interest in S(E) Co. Ltd. leaving a 25% minority interest.
2. Profit included in stock valuation is £200. (Cost of £800 + 25% profit = £1,000). Since the stock is partly owned by minority shareholders, that portion is regarded as being sold to outsiders and the related profit counted as part of group profit. Profit to be eliminated is therefore 75% of £200.

Much of the detailed consolidation work is not shown in published group profit and loss accounts, reference being limited usually to minority interests.

Consolidated Profit and Loss Account of H(A) Co. Ltd. with S(E) Co. Ltd. for year ended 31st December, 1976

	£	£		£	£
			Balance b/f		
Dividend paid by S(E)	4,000		S(E)	6,000 (a)	
Less minority interest	1,000		*Less* minority interest	1,500 (c)	
	3,000 (f)				
Less contra	3,000			4,500	
		—	H(A)	20,000 (a)	
Dividend paid by H(A)		10,000			24,500
Profit on goods sold to S(E)	200		*Net profit for year* S(E)	8,000 (b)	
Less minority interest	50 (e)				
		150	*Less* minority Interest	2,000 (d)	
Balance c/f					
S(E)	10,000				
Less minority Interest	2,500 (c)&(d)			6,000	
			H(A)	16,000 (b)	
	7,500				22,000
Less stock adjustment	150 (e)		Interim dividend from S(E)	3,000 (f)	
	7,350		*Less* contra	3,000	
H(A)	29,000				—
		36,350			
		46,500			46,500

Associated Company

A company holding 50% or less ordinary share capital in another company may be said to have an investment in an associated company.

Questions and Problems

17–1 Show the consolidated balance sheet as at 30th April, 1976.

PARENT COMPANY

Balance Sheet as at 30th April, 1976

	£		£
Capital	6,000	Investment in S. Ltd. at cost	
Profit loss A/c	3,500	1,000 shares	1,600
Creditors	1,500	Fixed assets	5,400
		Current assets	4,000
	11,000		11,000

SUBSIDIARY COMPANY

Balance Sheet as at 30th April, 1976

	£		£
Capital	1,000	Fixed assets	1,800
Profit and loss A/c	350	Current assets	750
Creditors	1,200		
	2,550		2,550

17–2 The following are the balance sheets of A Ltd. and its subsidiary B Ltd. On the date when A Ltd. acquired the shares in B Ltd., the latter company had a credit balance on the profit and loss account of £5,000. Prepare the consolidated balance sheet at 31st March, 1977.

A LTD.

Balance Sheet at 31st March, 1977

	£		£
Capital – 270,000 £1 shares	270,000	Freehold land and buildings at cost	100,000
Creditors	10,000	Investment in B. Ltd. at cost (144,000 shares)	144,000
		Stock	25,000
		Debtors	3,000
		Balance at bank	8,000
	280,000		280,000

B LTD.

Balance Sheet as at 31st March, 1977

	£		£
Capital – 200,000 £1 shares	200,000	Freehold land and	
Profit and loss A/c	1,500	buildings at cost	150,000
Creditors	43,500	Stock	50,000
		Debtors	30,000
		Balance at bank	15,000
	245,000		245,000

17–3 The balance sheet of A Ltd. on 31st December was:

	£		£
Share capital	14,000	Fixed assets	10,000
Debentures	2,500	Investment in B Ltd.	
Profit and loss A/c	2,000	4,000 shares at cost	5,200
Creditors	1,500	Current assets	4,800
	20,000		20,000

The balance sheet of B Ltd. on 31st December was:

	£		£
Ordinary shares capital	5,000	Fixed assets	5,000
6% preference shares	2,500	Current assets	4,200
Profit and loss A/c	1,000		
Creditors	700		
	9,200		9,200

On the date when A Ltd. acquired the shares in B Ltd., the profit and loss account of B Ltd. stood at £500 (Cr). No dividends have been paid during the year but one year's dividend due to the preference shareholders has not yet been provided for. Prepare the consolidated balance sheet.

17–4 The accounts of A Ltd. and its subsidiary B Ltd. are shown opposite. A Ltd. acquired its holding in B Ltd. two years ago when the balance on B Ltd.'s profit and loss account was £800. Prepare consolidated profit and loss account and balance sheet. (Ignore taxation.)

Profit and Loss Accounts
For the year ended 31st December, 1976

	A Ltd. £	*B Ltd.* £		*A Ltd.* £	*B Ltd.* £
Auditors' remuneration	200	100	Trading profit	3,000	1,600
Depreciation	300	200	Dividend – B Ltd.	300	
Directors' fees	1,000	400			
Net profit c/d.	1,800	900			
	3,300	1,600		3,300	1,600
Income tax	800	380	Balance b/fwd.	550	1,700
Proposed div'd (Gross)	550	220	Net profit b/d.	1,800	900
Balance c/d.	1,000	2,000			
	2,350	2,600		2,350	2,600

Balance Sheet as at 31st December, 1976

	A Ltd.	*B Ltd.*		*A Ltd.*	*B Ltd.*
Authorized & issued capital	9,000	3,000	Fixed assets	5,000	3,000
Profit & loss account	1,000	2,000	3,000 shares in B Ltd. at cost	4,000	
B Ltd.	500				
Sundry creditors	950	780	Current assets	3,000	2,500
Proposed dividend	550	220	A Ltd.		500
	12,000	6,000		12,000	6,000

Note: The Stocks of B Ltd. include £600 goods supplied by A Ltd., the cost to the latter company being £500.

PRESENT VALUE TABLE

PRESENT VALUE OF £1 RECEIVED AT THE END OF n YEARS $\left(P = \frac{S}{(1+r)^n}\right)$

n	1%	2%	3%	4%	5%	6%	7%	8%	9%	10%	11%	12%	13%	14%	15%	n
1	0·990	0·980	0·971	0·962	0·952	0·943	0·935	0·926	0·917	0·909	0·901	0·893	0·885	0·877	0·870	1
2	0·980	0·961	0·943	0·925	0·907	0·890	0·873	0·857	0·842	0·826	0·812	0·797	0·783	0·769	0·756	2
3	0·971	0·942	0·915	0·889	0·864	0·840	0·816	0·794	0·772	0·751	0·731	0·712	0·693	0·675	0·658	3
4	0·961	0·924	0·888	0·855	0·823	0·792	0·763	0·735	0·708	0·683	0·659	0·636	0·613	0·592	0·572	4
5	0·951	0·906	0·863	0·822	0·784	0·747	0·713	0·681	0·650	0·621	0·593	0·567	0·543	0·519	0·497	5
6	0·942	0·888	0·837	0·790	0·746	0·705	0·666	0·630	0·596	0·564	0·535	0·507	0·480	0·456	0·432	6
7	0·933	0·871	0·813	0·760	0·711	0·665	0·623	0·583	0·547	0·513	0·482	0·452	0·425	0·400	0·376	7
8	0·923	0·853	0·789	0·731	0·677	0·627	0·582	0·540	0·502	0·467	0·434	0·404	0·376	0·351	0·327	8
9	0·914	0·837	0·766	0·703	0·645	0·592	0·544	0·500	0·460	0·424	0·391	0·361	0·333	0·308	0·284	9
10	0·905	0·820	0·744	0·676	0·614	0·558	0·508	0·463	0·422	0·386	0·352	0·322	0·295	0·270	0·247	10
11	0·896	0·804	0·722	0·650	0·585	0·527	0·475	0·429	0·388	0·350	0·317	0·287	0·261	0·237	0·215	11
12	0·887	0·788	0·701	0·625	0·557	0·497	0·444	0·397	0·356	0·319	0·286	0·257	0·231	0·208	0·187	12
13	0·879	0·773	0·681	0·601	0·530	0·469	0·415	0·368	0·326	0·290	0·258	0·229	0·204	0·182	0·163	13
14	0·870	0·758	0·661	0·577	0·505	0·442	0·388	0·340	0·299	0·263	0·232	0·205	0·181	0·160	0·141	14
15	0·861	0·743	0·642	0·555	0·481	0·417	0·362	0·315	0·275	0·239	0·209	0·183	0·160	0·140	0·123	15

n	16%	17%	18%	19%	20%	21%	22%	23%	24%	25%	26%	27%	28%	29%	30%	n
1	0·862	0·855	0·847	0·840	0·833	0·826	0·820	0·813	0·806	0·800	0·794	0·787	0·781	0·775	0·769	1
2	0·743	0·731	0·718	0·706	0·694	0·683	0·672	0·661	0·650	0·640	0·630	0·620	0·610	0·601	0·592	2
3	0·641	0·624	0·609	0·593	0·579	0·564	0·551	0·537	0·524	0·512	0·500	0·488	0·477	0·466	0·455	3
4	0·552	0·534	0·516	0·499	0·482	0·467	0·451	0·437	0·423	0·410	0·397	0·384	0·373	0·361	0·350	4
5	0·476	0·456	0·437	0·419	0·402	0·386	0·370	0·355	0·341	0·328	0·315	0·303	0·291	0·280	0·269	5
6	0·410	0·390	0·370	0·352	0·335	0·319	0·303	0·289	0·275	0·262	0·250	0·238	0·227	0·217	0·207	6
7	0·354	0·333	0·314	0·296	0·279	0·263	0·249	0·235	0·222	0·210	0·198	0·188	0·178	0·168	0·159	7
8	0·305	0·285	0·266	0·249	0·233	0·218	0·204	0·191	0·179	0·168	0·157	0·148	0·139	0·130	0·123	8
9	0·263	0·243	0·225	0·209	0·194	0·180	0·167	0·155	0·144	0·134	0·125	0·116	0·108	0·101	0·094	9
10	0·227	0·208	0·191	0·176	0·162	0·149	0·137	0·126	0·116	0·107	0·099	0·092	0·085	0·078	0·073	10
11	0·195	0·178	0·162	0·148	0·135	0·123	0·112	0·103	0·094	0·086	0·079	0·072	0·066	0·061	0·056	11
12	0·168	0·152	0·137	0·124	0·112	0·102	0·092	0·083	0·076	0·069	0·062	0·057	0·052			12
13	0·145	0·130	0·116	0·104	0·093	0·084	0·075	0·068	0·061	0·055						13
14	0·125	0·111	0·099	0·088	0·078	0·069	0·062	0·055								14
15	0·108	0·095	0·084	0·074	0·065	0·057	0·051									15

PRESENT VALUE TABLE

PRESENT VALUE OF £1 RECEIVED ANNUALLY AT THE END OF n YEARS $\left(P_n = \frac{1}{r}\left[1 - \frac{1}{(1+r)^n}\right]\right)$

n	1%	2%	3%	4%	5%	6%	7%	8%	9%	10%	11%	12%	13%	14%	15%	n
1	0·990	0·980	0·971	0·962	0·952	0·943	0·935	0·926	0·917	0·909	0·901	0·893	0·885	0·877	0·870	1
2	1·970	1·942	1·913	1·886	1·859	1·833	1·808	1·783	1·759	1·736	1·713	1·690	1·668	1·647	1·626	2
3	2·941	2·884	2·829	2·775	2·723	2·673	2·624	2·577	2·531	2·487	2·444	2·402	2·361	2·322	2·283	3
4	3·902	3·808	3·717	3·630	3·546	3·465	3·387	3·312	3·240	3·170	3·102	3·037	2·974	2·914	2·855	4
5	4·853	4·713	4·580	4·452	4·329	4·212	4·100	3·993	3·890	3·791	3·696	3·605	3·517	3·433	3·352	5
6	5·795	5·601	5·417	5·242	5·076	4·917	4·767	4·623	4·486	4·355	4·231	4·111	3·998	3·889	3·784	6
7	6·728	6·472	6·230	6·002	5·786	5·582	5·389	5·206	5·033	4·868	4·712	4·564	4·423	4·288	4·160	7
8	7·652	7·325	7·020	6·733	6·463	6·210	5·971	5·747	5·535	5·335	5·146	4·968	4·799	4·639	4·487	8
9	8·566	8·162	7·786	7·435	7·108	6·802	6·515	6·247	5·995	5·759	5·537	5·328	5·132	4·946	4·772	9
10	9·471	8·983	8·530	8·111	7·722	7·360	7·024	6·710	6·418	6·145	5·889	5·650	5·426	5·216	5·019	10
11	10·368	9·787	9·253	8·760	8·306	7·887	7·499	7·139	6·805	6·495	6·207	5·938	5·687	5·453	5·234	11
12	11·255	10·575	9·954	9·385	8·863	8·384	7·943	7·536	7·161	6·814	6·492	6·194	5·918	5·660	5·421	12
13	12·134	11·348	10·635	9·986	9·394	8·853	8·358	7·904	7·487	7·103	6·650	6·424	6·122	5·842	5·583	13
14	13·004	12·106	11·296	10·563	9·899	9·295	8·745	8·244	7·786	7·367	6·982	6·628	6·302	6·002	5·724	14
15	13·865	12·849	11·938	11·118	10·380	9·712	9·108	8·559	8·061	7·606	7·191	6·811	6·462	6·142	5·847	15

n	16%	17%	18%	19%	20%	21%	22%	23%	24%	25%	26%	27%	28%	29%	30%	n
1	0·862	0·855	0·847	0·840	0·833	0·826	0·820	0·813	0·806	0·800	0·794	0·787	0·781	0·775	0·769	1
2	1·605	1·585	1·566	1·546	1·528	1·509	1·492	1·474	1·457	1·440	1·424	1·407	1·392	1·376	1·361	2
3	2·246	2·210	2·174	2·140	2·106	2·074	2·042	2·011	1·981	1·952	1·923	1·896	1·868	1·842	1·816	3
4	2·798	2·743	2·690	2·639	2·589	2·540	2·494	2·448	2·404	2·362	2·320	2·280	2·241	2·203	2·166	4
5	3·274	3·199	3·127	3·058	2·991	2·926	2·864	2·803	2·745	2·689	2·635	2·583	2·532	2·483	2·436	5
6	3·685	3·589	3·498	3·410	3·326	3·245	3·167	3·092	3·020	2·951	2·885	2·821	2·759	2·700	2·643	6
7	4·039	3·922	3·812	3·706	3·605	3·508	3·416	3·327	3·242	3·161	3·083	3·009	2·937	2·868	2·802	7
8	4·344	4·207	4·078	3·954	3·837	3·726	3·619	3·518	3·421	3·329	3·241	3·156	3·076	2·999	2·925	8
9	4·607	4·451	4·303	4·163	4·031	3·905	3·786	3·673	3·566	3·463	3·366	3·273	3·184	3·100	3·019	9
10	4·833	4·659	4·494	4·339	4·192	4·054	3·923	3·799	3·682	3·571	3·465	3·364	3·269	3·178	3·092	10
11	5·029	4·836	4·656	4·486	4·327	4·177	4·035	3·902	3·776	3·656	3·544	3·437	3·335	3·239	3·147	11
12	5·197	4·988	4·793	4·610	4·439	4·278	4·127	3·985	3·851	3·725	3·606	3·493	3·387	3·286	3·190	12
13	5·342	5·118	4·910	4·715	4·533	4·362	4·203	4·053	3·912	3·780	3·656	3·538	3·427	3·322	3·223	13
14	5·468	5·229	5·008	4·802	4·611	4·432	4·265	4·108	3·962	3·824	3·695	3·573	3·459	3·351	3·249	14
15	5·575	5·324	5·092	4·876	4·675	4·489	4·315	4·153	4·001	3·859	3·726	3·601	3·483	3·373	3·268	15

INDEX

ACCOUNTING AND FINANCIAL MANAGEMENT IN THE HOTEL AND CATERING INDUSTRY

Volume 1

Contents